Clinical Supervision and Professional Development of the Substance Abuse Counselor

Treatment Improvement Protocol (TIP) Series

52

D1501215

U.S. DEPARTMENT OF HEALTH AND HUMAN SERVICES
Substance Abuse and Mental Health Services Administration
Center for Substance Abuse Treatment

1 Choke Cherry Road
Rockville, MD 20857

Acknowledgments

This publication was produced under the Knowledge Application Program, contract number 270-04-7049, a Joint Venture of The CDM Group, Inc. and JBS International, Inc., for the Center for Substance Abuse Treatment CSAT), Substance Abuse and Mental Health Services Administration SAMHSA), U.S. Department of Health and Human Services (HHS). Christina Currier served as the CSAT Government Project Officer.

Electronic Access and Copies of Publication

This publication may be downloaded or ordered at http://www.samhsa.gov/shin. Or, please call SAMHSA's Health Information Network at 1-877-SAMHSA-7 (1-877-726-4727) (English and Español).

Recommended Citation

Center for Substance Abuse Treatment. *Clinical Supervision and Professional Development of the Substance Abuse Counselor.* Treatment Improvement Protocol (TIP) Series 52. DHHS Publication No. (SMA) 09-4435. Rockville, MD: Substance Abuse and Mental Health Services Administration, 2009.

Originating Office

Quality Improvement and Workforce Development Branch, Division of Services Improvement, Center for Substance Abuse Treatment, Substance Abuse and Mental Health Services Administration, 1 Choke Cherry Road, Rockville, MD 20857.

HHS Publication No. (SMA) 09-4435.
Printed 2009

Contents

Consensus Panel v

What Is a TIP? vii

Foreword ix

How This TIP Is Organized xi

Part 1 1

Overview of Part 1 1

Chapter 1 3

Introduction 3
Central Principles of Clinical Supervision 5
Guidelines for new Supervisors 6
Models of Clinical Supervision 8
Developmental Stages of Counselors 9
Developmental Stages of Supervisors. 10
Cultural and Contextual Factors 11
Ethical and Legal Issues 13
Monitoring Performance 17
Methods of Observation. 20
Practical Issues in Clinical Supervision. 24
Methods and Techniques of Clinical Supervision 30
Administrative Supervision. 33
Resources 34

Chapter 2 35

Introduction 35
Vignette 1—Establishing a New Approach for Clinical Supervision 35
Vignette 2—Defining and Building the Supervisory Alliance 44
Vignette 3—Addressing Ethical Standards 51
Vignette 4—Implementing an Evidence-Based Practice 58
Vignette 5—Maintaining Focus on Job Performance 64
Vignette 6—Promoting a Counselor From Within 69
Vignette 7—Mentoring a Successor 73
Vignette 8—Making the Case for Clinical Supervision to Administrators 78

Part 2 85

Chapter 1 87

Benefits and Rationale 87
Key Issues for Administrators in Clinical Supervision. 88
Administrative and Clinical Supervision. 89

Legal and Ethical Issues for Administrators 90
Diversity and Cultural Competence 91
Developing a Model for Clinical Supervision 92
Implementing a Clinical Supervision Program 92
Professional Development of Supervisors 99

Chapter 2 101

Introduction 101
Assessing Organizational Readiness 101
Legal and Ethical Issues of Supervision 106
Supervision Guidelines 109
The Supervision Contract 111
The Initial Supervision Sessions 113
Evaluation of Counselors and Supervisors 118
Individual Development Plan 122
Outline for Case Presentations 123
Audio- and Videotaping 124

Appendix A—Bibliography 127

**Appendix B—New York State Office of Alcoholism and Substance Abuse
Services Clinical Supervision Vision Statement** 135

Appendix C—Advisory Meeting Panel 139

Appendix D—SAMHSA Stakeholders Meeting Attendees 141

Appendix E—Field Reviewers 143

Appendix F—Acknowledgments 145

Index 147

Consensus Panel

Chair, Part 1 and Part 2 Consensus Panels

David J. Powell, Ph.D. (Chair)
President
International Center for Health Concerns, Inc.
East Granby, Connecticut

Part 1 Consensus Panel Members

Bruce Carruth, Ph.D.
KAP Expert Content Director
The CDM Group, Inc.
Bethesda, Maryland

Bettye Harrison
Opioid Treatment Program Accreditation Director
CARF International
Tucson, Arizona

Sharon Hartman, M.B.A., LSW
Director of Professional Training and Education
Caron Treatment Centers
Wernersville, Pennsylvania

Pamela Mattel, M.S.W., LCSW-R, ACSW, CASAC
Executive Deputy Director
BASICS, Inc.
New York, New York

John Porter, M.S.
Northwest Frontier Addiction Technology Transfer Center
Wilsonville, Oregon

Part 2 Consensus Panel Members

Bruce Carruth, Ph.D.
KAP Expert Content Director
The CDM Group, Inc.
Bethesda, Maryland

Charles F. Gressard, Ph.D., LPC, NCC
Associate Professor, School of Education
College of William & Mary
Williamsburg, Virginia

Pamela Mattel, M.S.W., LCSW-R, ACSW, CASAC
Executive Deputy Director
BASICS, Inc.
New York, New York

What Is a TIP?

Treatment Improvement Protocols (TIPs), developed by the Center for Substance Abuse Treatment (CSAT), part of the Substance Abuse and Mental Health Services Administration (SAMHSA) within the U.S. Department of Health and Human Services (HHS), are best-practices guidelines for the treatment of substance use disorders. CSAT draws on the experience and knowledge of clinical, research, and administrative experts to produce the TIPs, which are distributed to facilities and individuals across the country. As alcohol and drug use disorders are increasingly recognized as a major problem, the audience for the TIPs is expanding beyond public and private treatment facilities to include practitioners in mental health, criminal justice, primary care, and other healthcare and social service settings.

The recommendations contained in each TIP are grounded in scientific research findings and the opinion of the TIP consensus panel of experts that a particular practice will produce a specific clinical outcome (measurable change in client status). In making recommendations, consensus panelists engage in a process of "evidence-based thinking" in which they consider scientific research, clinical practice theory, practice principles, and practice guidelines, as well as their own individual clinical experiences. Based on this thinking, they arrive at recommendations for optimal clinical approaches for given clinical situations. Relevant citations (to research outcome reports, theoretic formulations, and practice principles and guidelines) are provided.

TIP Format

This TIP is organized into three parts:
* *Part 1 for substance abuse clinical supervisors focuses on providing appropriate supervision methods and frameworks.*

* *Part 2 for program administrators focuses on providing administrative support to implement adoption of the counseling recommendations made in Part 1.*

* *Part 3 for clinical supervisors, program administrators, and interested counselors is an online literature review that provides an in-depth look at relevant published resources. Part 3 will be updated every 6 months for 5 years following publication of the TIP.*

Ideally this TIP might be used in a series of six or so meetings in which the materials in the TIP would be reviewed, discussed, and in other ways used as an educational and training vehicle for the improvement of clinical supervision skills (with the particulars of how this training would be done determined by the trainer, based upon her or his unique situation, needs, and preferences). Thus, after a relatively short period of time and with few or no additional resources, this TIP could meet the challenge of fostering improvement in the delivery of substance abuse treatment services.

Development Process

The topic for this TIP was selected following an advisory meeting of experts in substance use disorders (appendix C). Two Consensus Panels of experts on clinical supervision and substance abuse treatment were convened: one for clinical issues, and the other for administrative guidelines (p. v). The TIP then was field reviewed by an external group of subject matter experts, who provided suggestions for further refining the document (see appendix E).

TIPs Online

TIPs can be accessed via the Internet at http://www.kap.samhsa.gov. The online *Clinical Supervision and Professional Development of the Substance Abuse Counselor: Part 3, A Review of the Literature*, which will be updated every 6 months for 5 years, is also available at http://www.kap.samhsa.gov.

Terminology

Throughout the TIP, the term "substance abuse" has been used to refer to both substance abuse and substance dependence (as defined by the *Diagnostic and Statistical Manual of Mental Disorders, 4th edition, Text Revision* [DSM-IV-TR] [American Psychiatric Association 2000]). This term was chosen partly because substance abuse treatment professionals commonly use the term "substance abuse" to describe any excessive use of addictive substances. In this TIP, the term refers to the use of alcohol as well as other substances of abuse. Readers should attend to the context in which the term occurs in order to determine what possible range of meanings it covers; in most cases, however, the term will refer to all varieties of substance use disorders described by DSM-IV.

Foreword

The Treatment Improvement Protocol (TIP) series supports SAMHSA's mission of building resilience and facilitating recovery for people with or at risk for mental or substance use disorders by providing best practices guidance to clinicians, program administrators, and payors to improve the quality and effectiveness of service delivery and, thereby, promote recovery. TIPs are the result of careful consideration of all relevant clinical and health services research findings, demonstration experience, and implementation requirements. Clinical researchers, clinicians, and program administrators meet to debate and discuss their particular areas of expertise until they reach a consensus on best practices. This panel's work is then reviewed and critiqued by field reviewers.

The talent, dedication, and hard work that TIP panelists and reviewers bring to this highly participatory process have helped bridge the gap between the promise of research and the needs of practicing clinicians and administrators to serve, in the most scientifically sound and effective ways, people who abuse substances. We are grateful to all who have joined with us to contribute to advances in the substance abuse treatment field.

Eric Broderick, D.D.S., M.P.H.
Acting Administrator
Substance Abuse and Mental Health Services Administration

H. Westley Clark, M.D., J.D., M.P.H., CAS, FASAM
Director
Center for Substance Abuse Treatment
Substance Abuse and Mental Health Services Administration

How This TIP Is Organized

This TIP is divided into three parts:

- *Clinical Supervision and Professional Development of the Substance Abuse Counselor, Part 1.*

- *Clinical Supervision and Professional Development of the Substance Abuse Counselor: An Implementation Guide for Administrators, Part 2.*

- *Clinical Supervision and Professional Development of the Substance Abuse Counselor: A Review of the Literature, Part 3.*

Parts 1 and 2 are presented in this publication; Part 3 is available only online at http://www.kap.samhsa.gov.

Part 1 of the TIP is for clinical supervisors and consists of two chapters. Chapter 1 presents basic information about clinical supervision in the substance abuse treatment field. It covers:

- Central principles of clinical supervision and guidelines for new supervisors, including the functions of a clinical supervisor.
- The developmental levels of counselors and clinical supervisors.
- Information on cultural competence, ethical and legal issues such as direct and vicarious liability, dual relationships and boundary issues, informed consent, confidentiality, and supervisor ethics.
- Information about monitoring clinical performance of counselors, the various methods commonly used for observing counselors, the methods and techniques of supervision and administrative supervision, and practical issues such as balancing one's clinical and administrative duties, finding the time to do clinical supervision, documentation, and structuring clinical supervision sessions.

Chapter 2 presents the "how to" of clinical supervision. Chapter 2 contains:

- Representative vignettes of clinical supervision scenarios.
- Master supervisor notes and comments that help you understand the thinking behind the supervisor's approach in each vignette.
- "How-to" descriptions of specific techniques.

It is strongly recommended that you read chapter 1 before reading chapter 2.

Part 2 is an implementation guide for program administrators and consists of two chapters. Chapter 1 lays out the rationale for the approach taken in chapter 2 and will help administrators understand the benefits and rationale behind providing clinical supervision for their program's substance abuse counselors. Chapter 2 provides tools for making the tasks associated with implementing a clinical supervision system easier.

The following topics are addressed in Part 2:

- How to develop a model for clinical supervision and implement a clinical supervision program.
- Key issues for administrators to consider, including assessing organizational structure and readiness.
- Legal and ethical issues to consider.
- Cultural competence issues.
- Providing professional development for clinical supervisors.

Part 3 of this TIP is a literature review on the topic of clinical supervision and is available for use by clinical supervisors, interested counselors, and administrators. Part 3 consists of three sections: an analysis of the available literature, an annotated bibliography of the literature most central to the topic, and a bibliography of other available literature. It includes literature that addresses both clinical and administrative concerns. To facilitate ongoing updates (which will be performed every 6 months for up to 5 years from first publication), the literature review will be available only online at http://www.kap.samhsa.gov.

Clinical Supervision and Professional Development of the Substance Abuse Counselor

Part 1

Overview of Part 1

Chapter 1: Information You Need To Know

This chapter presents the basic information about clinical supervision in the substance abuse treatment field and is organized as follows:

- **Introduction** (pp. 3–4)
- **Central Principles of Clinical Supervision** (pp. 5–6)
- **Guidelines for New Supervisors** (pp. 6–8)
- **Models of Clinical Supervision** (pp. 8–9)
- **Developmental Stages of Counselors** (pp. 9–10)
- **Developmental Stages of Supervisors** (pp. 10–11)
- **Cultural and Contextual Factors** (pp. 11–13)
- **Ethical and Legal Issues** (pp. 13–17)
- **Monitoring Performance** (pp. 17–20)
- **Methods of Observation** (pp. 20–24)
- **Practical Issues in Clinical Supervision** (pp. 24–29)
- **Methods and Techniques of Clinical Supervision** (pp. 30–32)
- **Administrative Supervision** (pp. 33–34)
- **Resources** (p. 34)

Chapter 2: Clinical Scenarios Showing How To Apply the Information

This chapter presents several realistic clinical supervision scenarios that could take place in a substance abuse treatment agency to demonstrate the material presented in chapter 1. *Master Supervisor Notes* are provided to explain the thinking behind these actions. *How-to Notes* instruct supervisors on using a specific technique. The scenarios should be useful to both counselors and supervisors.

Chapter 1

Introduction

Clinical supervision is emerging as the crucible in which counselors acquire knowledge and skills for the substance abuse treatment profession, providing a bridge between the classroom and the clinic. Supervision is necessary in the substance abuse treatment field to improve client care, develop the professionalism of clinical personnel, and impart and maintain ethical standards in the field. In recent years, especially in the substance abuse field, clinical supervision has become the cornerstone of quality improvement and assurance.

Your role and skill set as a clinical supervisor are distinct from those of counselor and administrator. Quality clinical supervision is founded on a positive supervisor–supervisee relationship that promotes client welfare and the professional development of the supervisee. You are a teacher, coach, consultant, mentor, evaluator, and administrator; you provide support, encouragement, and education to staff while addressing an array of psychological, interpersonal, physical, and spiritual issues of clients. Ultimately, effective clinical supervision ensures that clients are competently served. Supervision ensures that counselors continue to increase their skills, which in turn increases treatment effectiveness, client retention, and staff satisfaction. The clinical supervisor also serves as liaison between administrative and clinical staff.

This TIP focuses primarily on the teaching, coaching, consulting, and mentoring functions of clinical supervisors. Supervision, like substance abuse counseling, is a profession in its own right, with its own theories, practices, and standards. The profession requires knowledgeable, competent, and skillful individuals who are appropriately credentialed both as counselors and supervisors.

Definitions

This document builds on and makes frequent reference to CSAT's Technical Assistance Publication (TAP), *Competencies for Substance Abuse Treatment Clinical Supervisors* (TAP 21-A; CSAT, 2007). The clinical supervision competencies identify those responsibilities and activities that define the work of the clinical supervisor. This TIP provides guidelines and tools for the effective delivery of clinical supervision in substance abuse treatment settings. TAP 21-A is a companion volume to TAP 21, *Addiction Counseling Competencies* (CSAT, 2006), which is another useful tool in supervision.

The perspective of this TIP is informed by the following definitions of supervision:

- "Supervision is a disciplined, tutorial process wherein principles are transformed into practical skills, with four overlapping foci: administrative, evaluative, clinical, and supportive" (Powell & Brodsky, 2004, p. 11). "Supervision is an intervention provided by a senior member of a profession to a more junior member or members. . . . This relationship is evaluative, extends over time, and has the simultaneous purposes of enhancing the professional functioning of the more junior person(s); monitoring the quality of professional services offered to the clients that she, he, or they see; and serving as a gatekeeper of those who are to enter the particular profession" (Bernard & Goodyear, 2004, p. 8).
- Supervision is "a social influence process that occurs over time, in which the supervisor participates with supervisees to ensure quality of clinical care. Effective supervisors observe, mentor, coach, evaluate, inspire, and create an atmosphere that promotes self-motivation, learning, and professional development. They build teams, create cohesion, resolve conflict, and shape agency culture, while attending to ethical and diversity issues in all aspects of the process. Such supervision is key to both quality improvement and the successful implementation of consensus- and evidence-based practices" (CSAT, 2007, p. 3).

Rationale

For hundreds of years, many professions have relied on more senior colleagues to guide less experienced professionals in their crafts. This is a new development in the substance abuse field, as clinical supervision was only recently acknowledged as a discrete process with its own concepts and approaches.

As a supervisor to the client, counselor, and organization, the significance of your position is apparent in the following statements:

- Organizations have an obligation to ensure quality care and quality improvement of all personnel. The first aim of clinical supervision is to ensure quality services and to protect the welfare of clients.
- Supervision is the right of all employees and has a direct impact on workforce development and staff and client retention.
- You oversee the clinical functions of staff and have a legal and ethical responsibility to ensure quality care to clients, the professional development of counselors, and maintenance of program policies and procedures.
- Clinical supervision is how counselors in the field learn. In concert with classroom education, clinical skills are acquired through practice, observation, feedback, and implementation of the recommendations derived from clinical supervision.

Functions of a Clinical Supervisor

You, the clinical supervisor, wear several important "hats." You facilitate the integration of counselor self-awareness, theoretical grounding, and development of clinical knowledge and skills; and you improve functional skills and professional practices. These roles often overlap and are fluid within the context of the supervisory relationship. Hence, the supervisor is in a unique position as an advocate for the agency, the counselor, and the client. You are the primary link between administration and front line staff, interpreting and monitoring compliance with agency goals, policies, and procedures and communicating staff and client needs to administrators. Central to the supervisor's function is the alliance between the supervisor and supervisee (Rigazio-DiGilio, 1997).

As shown in Figure 1, your roles as a clinical supervisor in the context of the supervisory relationship include:

- **Teacher:** Assist in the development of counseling knowledge and skills by identifying learning needs, determining counselor strengths, promot-

ing self-awareness, and transmitting knowledge for practical use and professional growth. Supervisors are teachers, trainers, and professional role models.
- **Consultant:** Bernard and Goodyear (2004) incorporate the supervisory consulting role of case consultation and review, monitoring performance, counseling the counselor regarding job performance, and assessing counselors. In this role, supervisors also provide alternative case conceptualizations, oversight of counselor work to achieve mutually agreed upon goals, and professional gatekeeping for the organization and discipline (e.g., recognizing and addressing counselor impairment).
- **Coach:** In this supportive role, supervisors provide morale building, assess strengths and needs, suggest varying clinical approaches, model, cheerlead, and prevent burnout. For entry-level counselors, the supportive function is critical.
- **Mentor/Role Model:** The experienced supervisor mentors and teaches the supervisee through role modeling, facilitates the counselor's overall professional development and sense of professional identity, and trains the next generation of supervisors.

Figure 1. Roles of the Clinical Supervisor

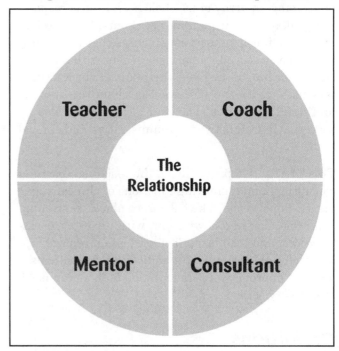

Central Principles of Clinical Supervision

The Consensus Panel for this TIP has identified central principles of clinical supervision. Although the Panel recognizes that clinical supervision can initially be a costly undertaking for many financially strapped programs, the Panel believes that ultimately clinical supervision is a cost-saving process. Clinical supervision enhances the quality of client care; improves efficiency of counselors in direct and indirect services; increases workforce satisfaction, professionalization, and retention (see vignette 8 in chapter 2); and ensures that services provided to the public uphold legal mandates and ethical standards of the profession.

The central principles identified by the Consensus Panel are:

1. **Clinical supervision is an essential part of all clinical programs.** Clinical supervision is a central organizing activity that integrates the program mission, goals, and treatment philosophy with clinical theory and evidence-based practices (EBPs). The primary reasons for clinical supervision are to ensure (1) quality client care, and (2) clinical staff continue professional development in a systematic and planned manner. In substance abuse treatment, clinical supervision is the primary means of determining the quality of care provided.

2. **Clinical supervision enhances staff retention and morale.** Staff turnover and workforce development are major concerns in the substance abuse treatment field. Clinical supervision is a primary means of improving workforce retention and job satisfaction (see, for example, Roche, Todd, & O'Connor, 2007).

3. **Every clinician, regardless of level of skill and experience, needs and has a right to clinical supervision. In addition, supervisors need and have a right to supervision of their supervision.** Supervision needs to be tailored to the knowledge base, skills, experience, and assignment of each counselor. All staff need supervision, but the frequency and intensity of the oversight and training will depend on the role, skill level, and competence of the individual.

The benefits that come with years of experience are enhanced by quality clinical supervision.

4. **Clinical supervision needs the full support of agency administrators.** Just as treatment programs want clients to be in an atmosphere of growth and openness to new ideas, counselors should be in an environment where learning and professional development and opportunities are valued and provided for all staff.

5. **The supervisory relationship is the crucible in which ethical practice is developed and reinforced.** The supervisor needs to model sound ethical and legal practice in the supervisory relationship. This is where issues of ethical practice arise and can be addressed. This is where ethical practice is translated from a concept to a set of behaviors. Through supervision, clinicians can develop a process of ethical decisionmaking and use this process as they encounter new situations.

6. **Clinical supervision is a skill in and of itself that has to be developed.** Good counselors tend to be promoted into supervisory positions with the assumption that they have the requisite skills to provide professional clinical supervision. However, clinical supervisors need a different role orientation toward both program and client goals and a knowledge base to complement a new set of skills. Programs need to increase their capacity to develop good supervisors.

7. **Clinical supervision in substance abuse treatment most often requires balancing administrative and clinical supervision tasks.** Sometimes these roles are complementary and sometimes they conflict. Often the supervisor feels caught between the two roles. Administrators need to support the integration and differentiation of the roles to promote the efficacy of the clinical supervisor. (See Part 2.)

8. **Culture and other contextual variables influence the supervision process; supervisors need to continually strive for cultural competence.** Supervisors require cultural competence at several levels. Cultural competence involves the counselor's response to clients, the supervisor's response to counselors, and the program's response to the cultural needs of the diverse community it serves. Since supervisors are in a position to serve as catalysts for change, they need to develop proficiency in addressing the needs of diverse clients and personnel.

9. **Successful implementation of EBPs requires ongoing supervision.** Supervisors have a role in determining which specific EBPs are relevant for an organization's clients (Lindbloom, Ten Eyck, & Gallon, 2005). Supervisors ensure that EBPs are successfully integrated into ongoing programmatic activities by training, encouraging, and monitoring counselors. Excellence in clinical supervision should provide greater adherence to the EBP model. Because State funding agencies now often require substance abuse treatment organizations to provide EBPs, supervision becomes even more important.

10. **Supervisors have the responsibility to be gatekeepers for the profession.** Supervisors are responsible for maintaining professional standards, recognizing and addressing impairment, and safeguarding the welfare of clients. More than anyone else in an agency, supervisors can observe counselor behavior and respond promptly to potential problems, including counseling some individuals out of the field because they are ill-suited to the profession. This "gatekeeping" function is especially important for supervisors who act as field evaluators for practicum students prior to their entering the profession. Finally, supervisors also fulfill a gatekeeper role in performance evaluation and in providing formal recommendations to training institutions and credentialing bodies.

11. **Clinical supervision should involve direct observation methods.** Direct observation should be the standard in the field because it is one of the most effective ways of building skills, monitoring counselor performance, and ensuring quality care. Supervisors require training in methods of direct observation, and administrators need to provide resources for implementing direct observation. Although small substance abuse agencies might not have the resources for one-way mirrors or videotaping equipment, other direct observation methods can be employed (see the section on methods of observation, pp. 20–24).

Guidelines for New Supervisors

Congratulations on your appointment as a supervisor! By now you might be asking yourself a few questions: What have I done? Was this a good career decision?

There are many changes ahead. If you have been promoted from within, you'll encounter even more hurdles and issues. First, it is important to face that your life has changed. You might experience the loss of friendship of peers. You might feel that you knew what to do as a counselor, but feel totally lost with your new responsibilities (see vignette 6 in chapter 2). You might feel less effective in your new role. Supervision can be an emotionally draining experience, as you now have to work with more staff-related interpersonal and human resources issues.

Before your promotion to clinical supervisor, you might have felt confidence in your clinical skills. Now you might feel unprepared and wonder if you need a training course for your new role. If you feel this way, you're right. Although you are a good counselor, you do not necessarily possess all the skills needed to be a good supervisor. Your new role requires a new body of knowledge and different skills, along with the ability to use your clinical skills in a different way. Be confident that you will acquire these skills over time (see the Resources section, p. 34) and that you made the right decision to accept your new position.

Suggestions for new supervisors:

- Quickly learn the organization's policies and procedures and human resources procedures (e.g., hiring and firing, affirmative action requirements, format for conducting meetings, giving feedback, and making evaluations). Seek out this information as soon as possible through the human resources department or other resources within the organization.
- Ask for a period of 3 months to allow you to learn about your new role. During this period, do not make any changes in policies and procedures but use this time to find your managerial voice and decisionmaking style.
- Take time to learn about your supervisees, their career goals, interests, developmental objectives, and perceived strengths.
- Work to establish a contractual relationship with supervisees, with clear goals and methods of supervision.
- Learn methods to help staff reduce stress, address competing priorities, resolve staff conflict, and other interpersonal issues in the workplace.
- Obtain training in supervisory procedures and methods.

- Find a mentor, either internal or external to the organization.
- Shadow a supervisor you respect who can help you learn the ropes of your new job.
- Ask often and as many people as possible, "How am I doing?" and "How can I improve my performance as a clinical supervisor?"
- Ask for regular, weekly meetings with your administrator for training and instruction.
- Seek supervision of your supervision.

Problems and Resources

As a supervisor, you may encounter a broad array of issues and concerns, ranging from working within a system that does not fully support clinical supervision to working with resistant staff. A comment often heard in supervision training sessions is "My boss should be here to learn what is expected in supervision," or "This will never work in my agency's bureaucracy. They only support billable activities." The work setting is where you apply the principles and practices of supervision and where organizations are driven by demands, such as financial solvency, profit, census, accreditation, and concerns over litigation. Therefore, you will need to be practical when beginning your new role as a supervisor: determine how you can make this work within your unique work environment.

Working With Staff Who Are Resistant to Supervision

Some of your supervisees may have been in the field longer than you have and see no need for supervision. Other counselors, having completed their graduate training, do not believe they need further supervision, especially not from a supervisor who might have less formal academic education than they have. Other resistance might come from ageism, sexism, racism, or classism. Particular to the field of substance abuse treatment may be the tension between those who believe that recovery from substance abuse is necessary for this counseling work and those who do not believe this to be true.

In addressing resistance, you must be clear regarding what your supervision program entails and must consistently communicate your goals and expectations to staff. To resolve defensiveness and engage your supervisees, you must also honor the resistance and acknowledge their concerns. Abandon trying to push the supervisee too far, too fast. Resistance is an expression of ambivalence about change and not a personality defect of the counselor. Instead of arguing with or exhorting staff, sympathize with their concerns, saying, "I understand this is difficult. How are we going to resolve these issues?"

When counselors respond defensively or reject directions from you, try to understand the origins of their defensiveness and to address their resistance. Self-disclosure by the supervisor about experiences as a supervisee, when appropriately used, may be helpful in dealing with defensive, anxious, fearful, or resistant staff. Work to establish a healthy, positive supervisory alliance with staff. Because many substance abuse counselors have not been exposed to clinical supervision, you may need to train and orient the staff to the concept and why it is important for your agency.

Things a New Supervisor Should Know

Eight truths a beginning supervisor should commit to memory are listed below:

1. The reason for supervision is to ensure quality client care. As stated throughout this TIP, the primary goal of clinical supervision is to protect the welfare of the client and ensure the integrity of clinical services.
2. Supervision is all about the relationship. As in counseling, developing the alliance between the counselor and the supervisor is the key to good supervision.
3. Culture and ethics influence all supervisory interactions. Contextual factors, culture, race, and ethnicity all affect the nature of the supervisory relationship. Some models of supervision (e.g., Holloway, 1995) have been built primarily around the role of context and culture in shaping supervision.
4. Be human and have a sense of humor. As role models, you need to show that everyone makes mistakes and can admit to and learn from these mistakes.

5. Rely first on direct observation of your counselors and give specific feedback. The best way to determine a counselor's skills is to observe him or her and to receive input from the clients about their perceptions of the counseling relationship.
6. Have and practice a model of counseling and of supervision; have a sense of purpose. Before you can teach a supervisee knowledge and skills, you must first know the philosophical and theoretical foundations on which you, as a supervisor, stand. Counselors need to know what they are going to learn from you, based on your model of counseling and supervision.
7. Make time to take care of yourself spiritually, emotionally, mentally, and physically. Again, as role models, counselors are watching your behavior. Do you "walk the talk" of self-care?
8. You have a unique position as an advocate for the agency, the counselor, and the client. As a supervisor, you have a wonderful opportunity to assist in the skill and professional development of your staff, advocating for the best interests of the supervisee, the client, and your organization.

Models of Clinical Supervision

You may never have thought about your model of supervision. However, it is a fundamental premise of this TIP that you need to work from a defined model of supervision and have a sense of purpose in your oversight role. Four supervisory orientations seem particularly relevant. They include:

• Competency-based models.
• Treatment-based models.
• Developmental approaches.
• Integrated models.

Competency-based models (e.g., microtraining, the Discrimination Model [Bernard & Goodyear, 2004], and the Task-Oriented Model [Mead, 1990], focus primarily on the skills and learning needs of the supervisee and on setting goals that are specific, measurable, attainable, realistic, and timely (SMART). They construct and implement strategies to accomplish these goals. The key strategies of competency-based models include applying social learning principles (e.g., modeling role reversal, role playing, and practice), using demonstrations, and using

various supervisory functions (teaching, consulting, and counseling).

Treatment-based supervision models train to a particular theoretical approach to counseling, incorporating EBPs into supervision and seeking fidelity and adaptation to the theoretical model. Motivational interviewing, cognitive–behavioral therapy, and psychodynamic psychotherapy are three examples. These models emphasize the counselor's strengths, seek the supervisee's understanding of the theory and model taught, and incorporate the approaches and techniques of the model. The majority of these models begin with articulating their treatment approach and describing their supervision model, based upon that approach.

Developmental models, such as Stoltenberg and Delworth (1987), understand that each counselor goes through different stages of development and recognize that movement through these stages is not always linear and can be affected by changes in assignment, setting, and population served. (The developmental stages of counselors and supervisors are described in detail below).

Integrated models, including the Blended Model, begin with the style of leadership and articulate a model of treatment, incorporate descriptive dimensions of supervision (see below), and address contextual and developmental dimensions into supervision. They address both skill and competency development and affective issues, based on the unique needs of the supervisee and supervisor. Finally, integrated models seek to incorporate EBPs into counseling and supervision.

In all models of supervision, it is helpful to identify culturally or contextually centered models or approaches and find ways of tailoring the models to specific cultural and diversity factors. Issues to consider are:

• Explicitly addressing diversity of supervisees (e.g., race, ethnicity, gender, age, sexual orientation) and the specific factors associated with these types of diversity;
• Explicitly involving supervisees' concerns related to particular client diversity (e.g., those whose culture, gender, sexual orientation, and other attributes differ from those of the supervisee) and addressing specific factors associated with these types of diversity; and

- Explicitly addressing supervisees' issues related to effectively navigating services in intercultural communities and effectively networking with agencies and institutions.

It is important to identify your model of counseling and your beliefs about change, and to articulate a workable approach to supervision that fits the model of counseling you use. Theories are conceptual frameworks that enable you to make sense of and organize your counseling and supervision and to focus on the most salient aspects of a counselor's practice. You may find some of the questions below to be relevant to both supervision and counseling. The answers to these questions influence both how you supervise and how the counselors you supervise work:

- What are your beliefs about how people change in both treatment and clinical supervision?
- What factors are important in treatment and clinical supervision?
- What universal principles apply in supervision and counseling and which are unique to clinical supervision?
- What conceptual frameworks of counseling do you use (for instance, cognitive–behavioral therapy, 12-Step facilitation, psychodynamic, behavioral)?
- What are the key variables that affect outcomes? (Campbell, 2000)

According to Bernard and Goodyear (2004) and Powell and Brodsky (2004),the qualities of a good model of clinical supervision are:

- Rooted in the individual, beginning with the supervisor's self, style, and approach to leadership.
- Precise, clear, and consistent.
- Comprehensive, using current scientific and evidence-based practices.
- Operational and practical, providing specific concepts and practices in clear, useful, and measurable terms.
- Outcome-oriented to improve counselor competence; make work manageable; create a sense of mastery and growth for the counselor; and address the needs of the organization, the supervisor, the supervisee, and the client.

Finally, it is imperative to recognize that, whatever model you adopt, it needs to be rooted in the learning and developmental needs of the supervisee, the spe-

cific needs of the clients they serve, the goals of the agency in which you work, and in the ethical and legal boundaries of practice. These four variables define the context in which effective supervision can take place.

Developmental Stages of Counselors

Counselors are at different stages of professional development. Thus, regardless of the model of supervision you choose, you must take into account the supervisee's level of training, experience, and proficiency. Different supervisory approaches are appropriate for counselors at different stages of development. An understanding of the supervisee's (and supervisor's) developmental needs is an essential ingredient for any model of supervision.

Various paradigms or classifications of developmental stages of clinicians have been developed (Ivey, 1997; Rigazio-DiGilio, 1997; Skolvolt & Ronnestrand, 1992; Todd and Storn, 1997). This TIP has adopted the Integrated Developmental Model (IDM) of Stoltenberg, McNeill, and Delworth (1998) (see figure 2, p. 10). This schema uses a three-stage approach. The three stages of development have different characteristics and appropriate supervisory methods. Further application of the IDM to the substance abuse field is needed. (For additional information, see Anderson, 2001.)

It is important to keep in mind several general cautions and principles about counselor development, including:

- There is a beginning but not an end point for learning clinical skills; be careful of counselors who think they "know it all."
- Take into account the individual learning styles and personalities of your supervisees and fit the supervisory approach to the developmental stage of each counselor.
- There is a logical sequence to development, although it is not always predictable or rigid; some counselors may have been in the field for years but remain at an early stage of professional development, whereas others may progress quickly through the stages.

Figure 2. Counselor Developmental Model			
Developmental Level	**Characteristics**	**Supervision Skills Development Needs**	**Techniques**
Level 1	• Focuses on self • Anxious, uncertain • Preoccupied with performing the right way • Overconfident of skills • Overgeneralizes • Overuses a skill • Gap between conceptualization, goals, and interventions • Ethics underdeveloped	• Provide structure and minimize anxiety • Supportive, address strengths first, then weaknesses • Suggest approaches • Start connecting theory to treatment	• Observation • Skills training • Role playing • Readings • Group supervision • Closely monitor clients
Level 2	• Focuses less on self and more on client • Confused, frustrated with complexity of counseling • Overidentifies with client • Challenges authority • Lacks integration with theoretical base • Overburdened • Ethics better understood	• Less structure provided, more autonomy encouraged • Supportive • Periodic suggestion of approaches • Confront discrepancies • Introduce more alternative views • Process comments, highlight countertransference • Affective reactions to client and/or supervisor	• Observation • Role playing • Interpret dynamics • Group supervision • Reading
Level 3	• Focuses intently on client • High degree of empathic skill • Objective third person perspective • Integrative thinking and approach • Highly responsible and ethical counselor	• Supervisee directed • Focus on personal-professional integration and career • Supportive • Change agent	• Peer supervision • Group supervision • Reading
Source: Stoltenberg, Delworth, & McNeil, 1998			

- Counselors at an advanced developmental level have different learning needs and require different supervisory approaches from those at Level 1; and
- The developmental level can be applied for different aspects of a counselor's overall competence (e.g., Level 2 mastery for individual counseling and Level 1 for couples counseling).

Developmental Stages of Supervisors

Just as counselors go through stages of development, so do supervisors. The developmental model presented in figure 3 provides a framework to explain why supervisors act as they do, depending on their developmental stage. It would be expected that someone new to supervision would be at a Level 1 as a supervisor. However, supervisors should be at least at the second or third stage of counselor development. If a newly appointed supervisor is still at Level 1 as a

Figure 3. Supervisor Developmental Model		
Developmental Level	Characteristics	To Increase Supervision Competence
Level 1	• Is anxious regarding role • Is naïve about assuming the role of supervisor • Is focused on doing the "right" thing • May overly respond as an "expert" • Is uncomfortable providing direct feedback	• Follow structure and formats • Design systems to increase organization of supervision • Assign Level I counselors
Level 2	• Shows confusion and conflict • Sees supervision as complex and multidimensional • Needs support to maintain motivation • Overfocused on counselor's deficits and perceived resistance • May fall back to being a therapist with the counselor	• Provide active supervision of the supervision • Assign Level 1 counselors
Level 3	• Is highly motivated • Can provide an honest self-appraisal of strengths and weaknesses as supervisor • Is comfortable with evaluation process • Provides thorough, objective feedback	• Comfortable with all levels
Source: Stoltenberg, Delworth, & McNeil, 1998		

counselor, he or she will have little to offer to more seasoned supervisees.

Cultural and Contextual Factors

Culture is one of the major contextual factors that influence supervisory interactions. Other contextual variables include race, ethnicity, age, gender, discipline, academic background, religious and spiritual practices, sexual orientation, disability, and recovery versus non-recovery status. The relevant variables in the supervisory relationship occur in the context of the supervisor, supervisee, client, and the setting in which supervision occurs. More care should be taken to:

• Identify the competencies necessary for substance abuse counselors to work with diverse individuals and navigate intercultural communities.
• Identify methods for supervisors to assist counselors in developing these competencies.
• Provide evaluation criteria for supervisors to determine whether their supervisees have met

minimal competency standards for effective and relevant practice.

Models of supervision have been strongly influenced by contextual variables and their influence on the supervisory relationship and process, such as Holloway's Systems Model (1995) and Constantine's Multicultural Model (2003).

The competencies listed in TAP 21-A reflect the importance of culture in supervision (CSAT, 2007). The Counselor Development domain encourages self-examination of attitudes toward culture and other contextual variables. The Supervisory Alliance domain promotes attention to these variables in the supervisory relationship. (See also the planned TIP, *Improving Cultural Competence in Substance Abuse Counseling* [CSAT, in development b].)

Cultural competence "refers to the ability to honor and respect the beliefs, language, interpersonal styles, and behaviors of individuals and families receiving services, as well as staff who are providing such services. Cultural competence is a dynamic, ongoing, developmental process that requires a commitment and is achieved over time" (U.S. Department of Health and Human Services, 2003, p. 12). Culture shapes belief systems, particularly concerning issues related to mental health and substance abuse, as well as the manifestation of symptoms, relational styles, and coping patterns.

There are three levels of cultural consideration for the supervisory process: the issue of the culture of the client being served and the culture of the counselor in supervision. Holloway (1995) emphasizes the cultural issues of the agency, the geographic environment of the organization, and many other contextual factors. Specifically, there are three important areas in which cultural and contextual factors play a key role in supervision: in building the supervisory relationship or working alliance, in addressing the specific needs of the client, and in building supervisee competence and ability. It is your responsibility to address your supervisees' beliefs, attitudes, and biases about cultural and contextual variables to advance their professional development and promote quality client care.

Becoming culturally competent and able to integrate other contextual variables into supervision is a complex, long-term process. Cross (1989) has identified several stages on a continuum of becoming culturally competent (see figure 4).

Although you may never have had specialized training in multicultural counseling, some of your super-visees may have (see Constantine, 2003). Regardless, it is your responsibility to help supervisees build on the cultural competence skills they possess as well as to focus on their cultural competence deficits. It is important to initiate discussion of issues of culture, race, gender, sexual orientation, and the like in supervision to model the kinds of discussion you would like counselors to have with their clients. If these issues are not addressed in supervision, counselors may come to believe that it is inappropriate to discuss them with clients and have no idea how such dialog might proceed. These discussions prevent misunderstandings with supervisees based on cultural or other factors. Another benefit from these discussions is that counselors will eventually achieve some level of comfort in talking about culture, race, ethnicity, and diversity issues.

If you haven't done it as a counselor, early in your tenure as a supervisor you will want to examine your culturally influenced values, attitudes, experiences, and practices and to consider what effects they have on your dealings with supervisees and clients. Counselors should undergo a similar review as preparation for when they have clients of a culture different from their own. Some questions to keep in mind are:

- What did you think when you saw the supervisee's last name?

Figure 4. Continuum of Cultural Competence

Cultural Destructiveness
Superiority of dominant culture and inferiority of other cultures; active discrimination

Cultural Incapacity
Separate but equal treatment; passive discrimination

Cultural Blindness
Sees all cultures and people as alike and equal; discrimination by ignoring culture

Cultural Openness (Sensitivity)
Basic understanding and appreciation of importance of sociocultural factors in work with minority populations

Cultural Competence
Capacity to work with more complex issues and cultural nuances

Cultural Proficiency
Highest capacity for work with minority populations; a commitment to excellence and proactive effort

Source: Cross, 1989.

- What did you think when the supervisee said his or her culture is X, when yours is Y?
- How did you feel about this difference?
- What did you do in response to this difference?

Constantine (2003) suggests that supervisors can use the following questions with supervisees:

- What demographic variables do you use to identify yourself?
- What worldviews (e.g., values, assumptions, and biases) do you bring to supervision based on your cultural identities?
- What struggles and challenges have you faced working with clients who were from different cultures than your own?

Beyond self-examination, supervisors will want continuing education classes, workshops, and conferences that address cultural competence and other contextual factors. Community resources, such as community leaders, elders, and healers can contribute to your understanding of the culture your organization serves. Finally, supervisors (and counselors) should participate in multicultural activities, such as community events, discussion groups, religious festivals, and other ceremonies.

The supervisory relationship includes an inherent power differential, and it is important to pay attention to this disparity, particularly when the supervisee and the supervisor are from different cultural groups. A potential for the misuse of that power exists at all times but especially when working with supervisees and clients within multicultural contexts. When the supervisee is from a minority population and the supervisor is from a majority population, the differential can be exaggerated. You will want to prevent institutional discrimination from affecting the quality of supervision. The same is true when the supervisee is gay and the supervisor is heterosexual, or the counselor is non-degreed and the supervisor has an advanced degree, or a female supervisee with a male supervisor, and so on. In the reverse situations, where the supervisor is from the minority group and the supervisee from the majority group, the difference should be discussed as well.

Ethical and Legal Issues

You are the organization's gatekeeper for ethical and legal issues. First, you are responsible for upholding the highest standards of ethical, legal, and moral practices and for serving as a model of practice to staff. Further, you should be aware of and respond to ethical concerns. Part of your job is to help integrate solutions to everyday legal and ethical issues into clinical practice.

Some of the underlying assumptions of incorporating ethical issues into clinical supervision include:

- Ethical decisionmaking is a continuous, active process.
- Ethical standards are not a cookbook. They tell you what to do, not always how.
- Each situation is unique. Therefore, it is imperative that all personnel learn how to "think ethically" and how to make sound legal and ethical decisions.
- The most complex ethical issues arise in the context of two ethical behaviors that conflict; for instance, when a counselor wants to respect the privacy and confidentiality of a client, but it is in the client's best interest for the counselor to contact someone else about his or her care.
- Therapy is conducted by fallible beings; people make mistakes—hopefully, minor ones.
- Sometimes the answers to ethical and legal questions are elusive. Ask a dozen people, and you'll likely get twelve different points of view.

Helpful resources on legal and ethical issues for supervisors include Beauchamp and Childress (2001); Falvey (2002b); Gutheil and Brodsky (2008); Pope, Sonne, and Greene (2006); and Reamer (2006).

Legal and ethical issues that are critical to clinical supervisors include (1) vicarious liability (or respondeat superior), (2) dual relationships and boundary concerns, (4) informed consent, (5) confidentiality, and (6) supervisor ethics.

Direct Versus Vicarious Liability

An important distinction needs to be made between direct and vicarious liability. Direct liability of the supervisor might include dereliction of supervisory responsibility, such as "not making a reasonable effort to supervise" (defined below).

In vicarious liability, a supervisor can be held liable for damages incurred as a result of negligence in the supervision process. Examples of negligence include providing inappropriate advice to a counselor about a client (for instance, discouraging a counselor from conducting a suicide screen on a depressed client), failure to listen carefully to a supervisee's comments about a client, and the assignment of clinical tasks to inadequately trained counselors. The key legal question is: "Did the supervisor conduct him- or herself in a way that would be reasonable for someone in his position?" or "Did the supervisor make a reasonable effort to supervise?" A generally accepted time standard for a "reasonable effort to supervise" in the behavioral health field is 1 hour of supervision for every 20–40 hours of clinical services. Of course, other variables (such as the quality and content of clinical supervision sessions) also play a role in a reasonable effort to supervise.

Supervisory vulnerability increases when the counselor has been assigned too many clients, when there is no direct observation of a counselor's clinical work, when staff are inexperienced or poorly trained for assigned tasks, and when a supervisor is not involved or not available to aid the clinical staff. In legal texts, vicarious liability is referred to as "respondeat superior."

Dual Relationships and Boundary Issues

Dual relationships can occur at two levels: between supervisors and supervisees and between counselors and clients. You have a mandate to help your supervisees recognize and manage boundary issues. A dual relationship occurs in supervision when a supervisor has a primary professional role with a supervisee and, at an earlier time, simultaneously or later, engages in another relationship with the supervisee that transcends the professional relationship. Examples of dual relationships in supervision include providing therapy for a current or former supervisee, developing an emotional relationship with a supervisee or former supervisee, and becoming an Alcoholics Anonymous sponsor for a former supervisee. Obviously, there are varying degrees of harm or potential harm that might occur as a result of dual relationships, and some negative effects of dual relationships might not be apparent until later.

Therefore, firm, always-or-never rules aren't applicable. You have the responsibility of weighing with the counselor the anticipated and unanticipated effects of dual relationships, helping the supervisee's self-reflective awareness when boundaries become blurred, when he or she is getting close to a dual relationship, or when he or she is crossing the line in the clinical relationship.

Exploring dual relationship issues with counselors in clinical supervision can raise its own professional dilemmas. For instance, clinical supervision involves unequal status, power, and expertise between a supervisor and supervisee. Being the evaluator of a counselor's performance and gatekeeper for training programs or credentialing bodies also might involve a dual relationship. Further, supervision can have therapy-like qualities as you explore countertransferential issues with supervisees, and there is an expectation of professional growth and self-exploration. What makes a dual relationship unethical in supervision is the abusive use of power by either party, the likelihood that the relationship will impair or injure the supervisor's or supervisee's judgment, and the risk of exploitation (see vignette 3 in chapter 2).

The most common basis for legal action against counselors (20 percent of claims) and the most frequently heard complaint by certification boards against counselors (35 percent) is some form of boundary violation or sexual impropriety (Falvey, 2002b). (See the discussion of transference and countertransference on pp. 25–26.)

Codes of ethics for most professions clearly advise that dual relationships between counselors and clients should be avoided. Dual relationships between counselors and supervisors are also a concern and are addressed in the substance abuse counselor codes and those of other professions as well. Problematic dual relationships between supervisees and supervisors might include intimate relationships (sexual and nonsexual) and therapeutic relationships, wherein the supervisor becomes the counselor's therapist. Sexual involvement between the supervisor and supervisee can include sexual attraction, harassment, consensual (but hidden) sexual relationships, or intimate romantic relationships. Other common boundary issues include asking the supervisee to do favors, providing preferential treatment, socializing outside the work setting, and using emotional abuse to enforce power.

It is imperative that all parties understand what constitutes a dual relationship between supervisor and supervisee and avoid these dual relationships. Sexual relationships between supervisors and supervisees and counselors and clients occur far more frequently than one might realize (Falvey, 2002b). In many States, they constitute a legal transgression as well as an ethical violation.

The decision tree presented in figure 5 (p. 16) indicates how a supervisor might manage a situation where he or she is concerned about a possible ethical or legal violation by a counselor.

Informed Consent

Informed consent is key to protecting the counselor and/or supervisor from legal concerns, requiring the recipient of any service or intervention to be sufficiently aware of what is to happen, and of the potential risks and alternative approaches, so that the person can make an informed and intelligent decision about participating in that service. The supervisor must inform the supervisee about the process of supervision, the feedback and evaluation criteria, and other expectations of supervision. The supervision contract should clearly spell out these issues. Supervisors must ensure that the supervisee has informed the client about the parameters of counseling and supervision (such as the use of live observation, video- or audiotaping). A sample template for informed consent is provided in Part 2, chapter 2 (p. 106).

Confidentiality

In supervision, regardless of whether there is a written or verbal contract between the supervisor and supervisee, there is an implied contract and duty of care because of the supervisor's vicarious liability. Informed consent and concerns for confidentiality should occur at three levels: client consent to treatment, client consent to supervision of the case, and supervisee consent to supervision (Bernard & Goodyear, 2004). In addition, there is an implied consent and commitment to confidentiality by supervisors to assume their supervisory responsibilities and institutional consent to comply with legal and ethical parameters of supervision. (See also the Code of Ethics of the Association for Counselor Education and Supervision [ACES], available online at http://www.acesonline.net/ethical_guidelines.asp).

With informed consent and confidentiality comes a duty not to disclose certain relational communication. Limits of confidentiality of supervision session content should be stated in all organizational contracts with training institutions and credentialing bodies. Criteria for waiving client and supervisee privilege should be stated in institutional policies and discipline-specific codes of ethics and clarified by advice of legal counsel and the courts. Because standards of confidentiality are determined by State legal and legislative systems, it is prudent for supervisors to consult with an attorney to determine the State codes of confidentiality and clinical privileging.

In the substance abuse treatment field, confidentiality for clients is clearly defined by Federal law: 42 CFR, Part 2 and the Health Insurance Portability and Accountability Act (HIPAA). Key information is available at http://www.hipaa.samhsa.gov. Supervisors need to train counselors in confidentiality regulations and to adequately document their supervision, including discussions and directives, especially relating to duty-to-warn situations. Supervisors need to ensure that counselors provide clients with appropriate duty-to-warn information early in the counseling process and inform clients of the limits of confidentiality as part of the agency's informed consent procedures.

Under duty-to-warn requirements (e.g., child abuse, suicidal or homicidal ideation), supervisors need to be aware of and take action as soon as possible in situations in which confidentiality may need to be waived. Organizations should have a policy stating how clinical crises will be handled (Falvey, 2002b). What mechanisms are in place for responding to crises? In what timeframe will a supervisor be notified of a crisis situation? Supervisors must document all discussions with counselors concerning duty-to-warn and crises. At the onset of supervision, supervisors should ask counselors if there are any duty-to-warn issues of which the supervisor should be informed.

New technology brings new confidentiality concerns. Websites now dispense information about substance abuse treatment and provide counseling services. With the growth in online counseling and supervision, the following concerns emerge: (a) how to main-

Figure 5: Deciding How To Address Potential Legal or Ethical Violations

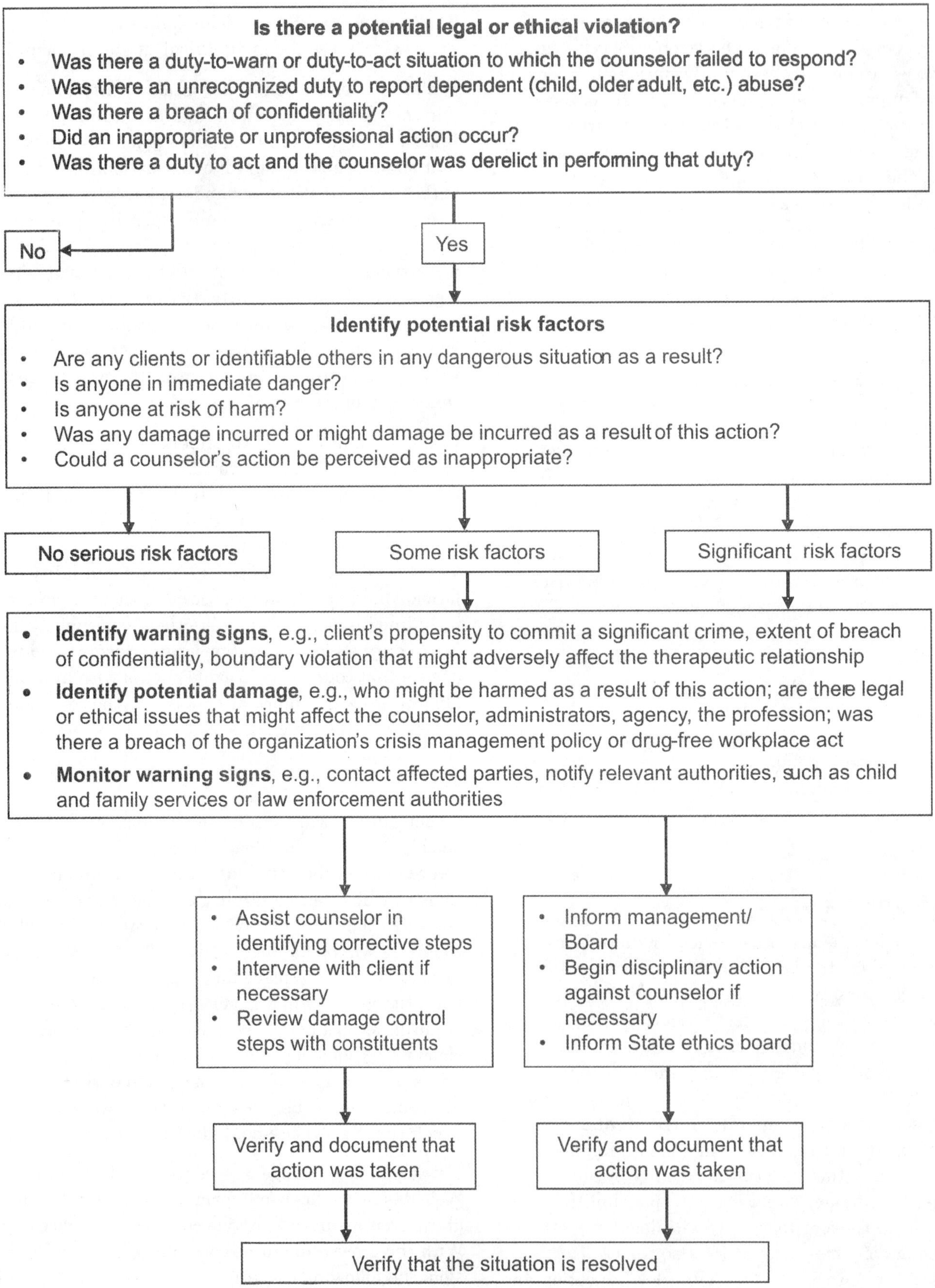

Is there a potential legal or ethical violation?
- Was there a duty-to-warn or duty-to-act situation to which the counselor failed to respond?
- Was there an unrecognized duty to report dependent (child, older adult, etc.) abuse?
- Was there a breach of confidentiality?
- Did an inappropriate or unprofessional action occur?
- Was there a duty to act and the counselor was derelict in performing that duty?

No

Yes

Identify potential risk factors
- Are any clients or identifiable others in any dangerous situation as a result?
- Is anyone in immediate danger?
- Is anyone at risk of harm?
- Was any damage incurred or might damage be incurred as a result of this action?
- Could a counselor's action be perceived as inappropriate?

No serious risk factors

Some risk factors

Significant risk factors

- **Identify warning signs**, e.g., client's propensity to commit a significant crime, extent of breach of confidentiality, boundary violation that might adversely affect the therapeutic relationship
- **Identify potential damage**, e.g., who might be harmed as a result of this action; are there legal or ethical issues that might affect the counselor, administrators, agency, the profession; was there a breach of the organization's crisis management policy or drug-free workplace act
- **Monitor warning signs**, e.g., contact affected parties, notify relevant authorities, such as child and family services or law enforcement authorities

- Assist counselor in identifying corrective steps
- Intervene with client if necessary
- Review damage control steps with constituents

- Inform management/ Board
- Begin disciplinary action against counselor if necessary
- Inform State ethics board

Verify and document that action was taken

Verify and document that action was taken

Verify that the situation is resolved

tain confidentiality of information, (b) how to ensure the competence and qualifications of counselors providing online services, and (c) how to establish reporting requirements and duty to warn when services are conducted across State and international boundaries. New standards will need to be written to address these issues. (The National Board for Certified Counselors has guidelines for counseling by Internet at http://www.nbcc.org/AssetManagerFiles/ethics/internetcounseling.pdf.)

Supervisor Ethics

In general, supervisors adhere to the same standards and ethics as substance abuse counselors with regard to dual relationship and other boundary violations. Supervisors will:

* Uphold the highest professional standards of the field.
* Seek professional help (outside the work setting) when personal issues interfere with their clinical and/or supervisory functioning.
* Conduct themselves in a manner that models and sets an example for agency mission, vision, philosophy, wellness, recovery, and consumer satisfaction.
* Reinforce zero tolerance for interactions that are not professional, courteous, and compassionate.
* Treat supervisees, colleagues, peers, and clients with dignity, respect, and honesty.
* Adhere to the standards and regulations of confidentiality as dictated by the field. This applies to the supervisory as well as the counseling relationship.

Monitoring Performance

The goal of supervision is to ensure quality care for the client, which entails monitoring the clinical performance of staff. Your first step is to educate supervisees in what to expect from clinical supervision. Once the functions of supervision are clear, you should regularly evaluate the counselor's progress in meeting organizational and clinical goals as set forth in an Individual Development Plan (IDP) (see the section on IDPs below). As clients have an individual treatment plan, counselors also need a plan to promote skill development.

Behavioral Contracting in Supervision

Among the first tasks in supervision is to establish a contract for supervision that outlines realistic accountability for both yourself and your supervisee. The contract should be in writing and should include the purpose, goals, and objectives of supervision; the context in which supervision is provided; ethical and institutional policies that guide supervision and clinical practices; the criteria and methods of evaluation and outcome measures; the duties and responsibilities of the supervisor and supervisee; procedural considerations (including the format for taping and opportunities for live observation); and the supervisee's scope of practice and competence. The contract for supervision should state the rewards for fulfillment of the contract (such as clinical privileges or increased compensation), the length of supervision sessions, and sanctions for noncompliance by either the supervisee or supervisor. The agreement should be compatible with the developmental needs of the supervisee and address the obstacles to progress (lack of time, performance anxiety, resource limitations). Once a behavioral contract has been established, the next step is to develop an IDP.

Individual Development Plan

The IDP is a detailed plan for supervision that includes the goals that you and the counselor wish to address over a certain time period (perhaps 3 months). Each of you should sign and keep a copy of the IDP for your records. The goals are normally stated in terms of skills the counselor wishes to build or professional resources the counselor wishes to develop. These skills and resources are generally oriented to the counselor's job in the program or activities that would help the counselor develop professionally. The IDP should specify the timelines for change, the observation methods that will be employed, expectations for the supervisee and the supervisor, the evaluation procedures that will be employed, and the activities that will be expected to improve knowledge and skills. An example of an IDP is provided in Part 2, chapter 2 (p. 122).

As a supervisor, you should have your own IDP, based on the supervisory competencies listed in TAP 21-A (CSAT, 2007), that addresses your training goals. This IDP can be developed in cooperation with your supervisor, or in external supervision, peer input, academic advisement, or mentorship.

Evaluation of Counselors

Supervision inherently involves evaluation, building on a collaborative relationship between you and the counselor. Evaluation may not be easy for some supervisors. Although everyone wants to know how they are doing, counselors are not always comfortable asking for feedback. And, as most supervisors prefer to be liked, you may have difficulty giving clear, concise, and accurate evaluations to staff.

The two types of evaluation are formative and summative. A formative evaluation is an ongoing status report of the counselor's skill development, exploring the questions "Are we addressing the skills or competencies you want to focus on?" and "How do we assess your current knowledge and skills and areas for growth and development?"

Summative evaluation is a more formal rating of the counselor's overall job performance, fitness for the job, and job rating. It answers the question, "How does the counselor measure up?" Typically, summative evaluations are done annually and focus on the counselor's overall strengths, limitations, and areas for future improvement.

It should be acknowledged that supervision is inherently an unequal relationship. In most cases, the supervisor has positional power over the counselor. Therefore, it is important to establish clarity of purpose and a positive context for evaluation. Procedures should be spelled out in advance, and the evaluation process should be mutual, flexible, and continuous. The evaluation process inevitably brings up supervisee anxiety and defensiveness that need to be addressed openly. It is also important to note that each individual counselor will react differently to feedback; some will be more open to the process than others.

There has been considerable research on supervisory evaluation, with these findings:

- The supervisee's confidence and efficacy are correlated with the quality and quantity of feedback the supervisor gives to the supervisee (Bernard & Goodyear, 2004).

- Ratings of skills are highly variable between supervisors, and often the supervisor's and supervisee's ratings differ or conflict (Eby, 2007).
- Good feedback is provided frequently, clearly, and consistently and is SMART (specific, measurable, attainable, realistic, and timely) (Powell & Brodsky, 2004).

Direct observation of the counselor's work is the desired form of input for the supervisor. Although direct observation has historically been the exception in substance abuse counseling, ethical and legal considerations and evidence support that direct observation as preferable. The least desirable feedback is unannounced observation by supervisors followed by vague, perfunctory, indirect, or hurtful delivery (Powell & Brodsky, 2004).

Clients are often the best assessors of the skills of the counselor. Supervisors should routinely seek input from the clients as to the outcome of treatment. The method of seeking input should be discussed in the initial supervisory sessions and be part of the supervision contract. In a residential substance abuse treatment program, you might regularly meet with clients after sessions to discuss how they are doing, how effective the counseling is, and the quality of the therapeutic alliance with the counselor. (For examples of client satisfaction or input forms, search for Client-Directed Outcome-Informed Treatment and Training Materials at http://www.talkingcure.com.)

Before formative evaluations begin, methods of evaluating performance should be discussed, clarified in the initial sessions, and included in the initial contract so that there will be no surprises. Formative evaluations should focus on changeable behavior and, whenever possible, be separate from the overall annual performance appraisal process. To determine the counselor's skill development, you should use written competency tools, direct observation, counselor self-assessments, client evaluations, work samples (files and charts), and peer assessments. Examples of work samples and peer assessments can be found in Bernard and Goodyear (2004), Powell and Brodsky (2004), and Campbell (2000). It is important to acknowledge that counselor evaluation is essentially a subjective process involving supervisors' opinions of the counselors' competence.

Addressing Burnout and Compassion Fatigue

Did you ever hear a counselor say, "I came into counseling for the right reasons. At first I loved seeing clients. But the longer I stay in the field, the harder it is to care. The joy seems to have gone out of my job. Should I get out of counseling as many of my colleagues are doing?" Most substance abuse counselors come into the field with a strong sense of calling and the desire to be of service to others, with a strong pull to use their gifts and make themselves instruments of service and healing. The substance abuse treatment field risks losing many skilled and compassionate healers when the life goes out of their work. Some counselors simply withdraw, care less, or get out of the field entirely. Most just complain or suffer in silence. Given the caring and dedication that brings counselors into the field, it is important for you to help them address their questions and doubts. (See Lambie, 2006, and Shoptaw, Stein, & Rawson, 2000.)

You can help counselors with self-care; help them look within; become resilient again; and rediscover what gives them joy, meaning, and hope in their work. Counselors need time for reflection, to listen again deeply and authentically. You can help them redevelop their innate capacity for compassion, to be an openhearted presence for others.

You can help counselors develop a life that does not revolve around work. This has to be supported by the organization's culture and policies that allow for appropriate use of time off and self-care without punishment. Aid them by encouraging them to take earned leave and to take "mental health" days when they are feeling tired and burned out. Remind staff to spend time with family and friends, exercise, relax, read, or pursue other life-giving interests.

It is important for the clinical supervisor to normalize the counselor's reactions to stress and compassion fatigue in the workplace as a natural part of being an empathic and compassionate person and not an individual failing or pathology. (See Burke, Carruth, & Prichard, 2006.)

Rest is good; self-care is important. Everyone needs times of relaxation and recreation. Often, a month after a refreshing vacation you lose whatever gain you made. Instead, longer term gain comes from finding what brings you peace and joy. It is not enough

for you to help counselors understand "how" to counsel, you can also help them with the "why." Why are they in this field? What gives them meaning and purpose at work? When all is said and done, when counselors have seen their last client, how do they want to be remembered? What do they want said about them as counselors? Usually, counselors' responses to this question are fairly simple: "I want to be thought of as a caring, compassionate person, a skilled helper." These are important spiritual questions that you can discuss with your supervisees.

Other suggestions include:

- Help staff identify what is happening within the organization that might be contributing to their stress and learn how to address the situation in a way that is productive to the client, the counselor, and the organization.
- Get training in identifying the signs of primary stress reactions, secondary trauma, compassion fatigue, vicarious traumatization, and burnout. Help staff match up self-care tools to specifically address each of these experiences.
- Support staff in advocating for organizational change when appropriate and feasible as part of your role as liaison between administration and clinical staff.
- Assist staff in adopting lifestyle changes to increase their emotional resilience by reconnecting to their world (family, friends, sponsors, mentors), spending time alone for self-reflection, and forming habits that re-energize them.
- Help them eliminate the "what ifs" and negative self-talk. Help them let go of their idealism that they can save the world.
- If possible in the current work environment, set parameters on their work by helping them adhere to scheduled time off, keep lunch time personal, set reasonable deadlines for work completion, and keep work away from personal time.
- Teach and support generally positive work habits. Some counselors lack basic organizational, teamwork, phone, and time management skills (ending sessions on time and scheduling to allow for documentation). The development of these skills helps to reduce the daily wear that erodes well-being and contributes to burnout.
- Ask them "When was the last time you had fun?" "When was the last time you felt fully alive?" Suggest they write a list of things about their job

about which they are grateful. List five people they care about and love. List five accomplishments in their professional life. Ask "Where do you want to be in your professional life in 5 years?"

You have a fiduciary responsibility given you by clients to ensure counselors are healthy and whole. It is your responsibility to aid counselors in addressing their fatigue and burnout.

Gatekeeping Functions

In monitoring counselor performance, an important and often difficult supervisory task is managing problem staff or those individuals who should not be counselors. This is the gatekeeping function. Part of the dilemma is that most likely you were first trained as a counselor, and your values lie within that domain. You were taught to acknowledge and work with individual limitations, always respecting the individual's goals and needs. However, you also carry a responsibility to maintain the quality of the profession and to protect the welfare of clients. Thus, you are charged with the task of assessing the counselor for fitness for duty and have an obligation to uphold the standards of the profession.

Experience, credentials, and academic performance are not the same as clinical competence. In addition to technical counseling skills, many important therapeutic qualities affect the outcome of counseling, including insight, respect, genuineness, concreteness, and empathy. Research consistently demonstrates that personal characteristics of counselors are highly predictive of client outcome (Herman, 1993, Hubble, Duncan & Miller, 1999). The essential questions are: Who should or should not be a counselor? What behaviors or attitudes are unacceptable? How would a clinical supervisor address these issues in supervision?

Unacceptable behavior might include actions hurtful to the client, boundary violations with clients or program standards, illegal behavior, significant psychiatric impairment, consistent lack of self-awareness, inability to adhere to professional codes of ethics, or consistent demonstration of attitudes that are not conducive to work with clients in substance abuse treatment. You will want to have a model and policies and procedures in place when disciplinary action is undertaken with an impaired counselor. For example, progressive disciplinary policies clearly state the pro-

cedures to follow when impairment is identified. Consultation with the organization's attorney and familiarity with State case law are important. It is advisable for the agency to be familiar with and have contact with your State impaired counselor organization, if it exists.

How impaired must a counselor be before disciplinary action is needed? Clear job descriptions and statements of scope of practice and competence are important when facing an impaired counselor. How tired or distressed can a counselor be before a supervisor takes the counselor off-line for these or similar reasons? You need administrative support with such interventions and to identify approaches to managing worn-out counselors. The Consensus Panel recommends that your organization have an employee assistance program (EAP) in place so you can refer staff outside the agency. It is also important for you to learn the distinction between a supervisory referral and a self-referral. Self-referral may include a recommendation by the supervisor, whereas a supervisory referral usually occurs with a job performance problem.

You will need to provide verbal and written evaluations of the counselor's performance and actions to ensure that the staff member is aware of the behaviors that need to be addressed. Treat all supervisees the same, following agency procedures and timelines. Follow the organization's progressive disciplinary steps and document carefully what is said, how the person responds, and what actions are recommended. You can discuss organizational issues or barriers to action with the supervisee (such as personnel policies that might be exacerbating the employee's issues). Finally, it may be necessary for you to take the action that is in the best interest of the clients and the profession, which might involve counseling your supervisee out of the field.

Remember that the number one goal of a clinical supervisor is to protect the welfare of the client, which, at times, can mean enforcing the gatekeeping function of supervision.

Methods of Observation

It is important to observe counselors frequently over an extended period of time. Supervisors in the substance abuse treatment field have traditionally relied on indirect methods of supervision (process recordings, case notes, verbal reports by the supervisees, and verbatims). However, the Consensus Panel recommends that supervisors use direct observation of counselors through recording devices (such as video and audio taping) and live observation of counseling sessions, including one-way mirrors. Indirect methods have significant drawbacks, including:

- A counselor will recall a session as he or she experienced it. If a counselor experiences a session positively or negatively, the report to the supervisor will reflect that. The report is also affected by the counselor's level of skill and experience.
- The counselor's report is affected by his or her biases and distortions (both conscious and unconscious). The report does not provide a thorough sense of what really happened in the session because it relies too heavily on the counselor's recall.
- Indirect methods include a time delay in reporting.
- The supervisee may withhold clinical information due to evaluation anxiety or naiveté.

Your understanding of the session will be improved by direct observation of the counselor. Direct observation is much easier today, as a variety of technological tools are available, including audio and videotaping, remote audio devices, interactive videos, live feeds, and even supervision through web-based cameras.

Guidelines that apply to all methods of direct observation in supervision include:

- Simply by observing a counseling session, the dynamics will change. You may change how both the client and counselor act. You get a snapshot of the sessions. Counselors will say, "it was not a representative session." Typically, if you observe the counselor frequently, you will get a fairly accurate picture of the counselor's competencies.
- You and your supervisee must agree on procedures for observation to determine why, when, and how direct methods of observation will be used.
- The counselor should provide a context for the session.
- The client should give written consent for observation and/or taping at intake, before beginning counseling. Clients must know all the conditions of

their treatment before they consent to counseling. Additionally, clients need to be notified of an upcoming observation by a supervisor before the observation occurs.

- Observations should be selected for review (including a variety of sessions and clients, challenges, and successes) because they provide teaching moments. You should ask the supervisee to select what cases he or she wishes you to observe and explain why those cases were chosen. Direct observation should not be a weapon for criticism but a constructive tool for learning: an opportunity for the counselor to do things right and well, so that positive feedback follows.
- When observing a session, you gain a wealth of information about the counselor. Use this information wisely, and provide gradual feedback, not a litany of judgments and directives. Ask the salient question, "What is the most important issue here for us to address in supervision?"
- A supervisee might claim client resistance to direct observation, saying, "It will make the client nervous. The client does not want to be taped." However, "client resistance" is more likely to be reported when the counselor is anxious about being taped. It is important for you to gently and respectfully address the supervisee's resistance while maintaining the position that direct observation is an integral component of his or her supervision.
- Given the nature of the issues in drug and alcohol counseling, you and your supervisee need to be sensitive to increased client anxiety about direct observation because of the client's fears about job or legal repercussions, legal actions, criminal behaviors, violence and abuse situations, and the like.
- Ideally, the supervisee should know at the outset of employment that observation and/or taping will be required as part of informed consent to supervision.

In instances where there is overwhelming anxiety regarding observation, you should pace the observation to reduce the anxiety, giving the counselor adequate time for preparation. Often enough, counselors will feel more comfortable with observation equipment (such as a video camera or recording device) rather than direct observation with the supervisor in the room.

The choice of observation methods in a particular situation will depend on the need for an accurate sense of counseling, the availability of equipment, the context in which the supervision is provided, and the counselor's and your skill levels. A key factor in the choice of methods might be the resistance of the counselor to being observed. For some supervisors, direct observation also puts the supervisor's skills on the line too, as they might be required to demonstrate or model their clinical competencies.

Recorded Observation

Audiotaped supervision has traditionally been a primary medium for supervisors and remains a vital resource for therapy models such as motivational interviewing. On the other hand, videotape supervision (VTS) is the primary method of direct observation in both the marriage and family therapy and social work fields (Munson, 1993; Nichols, Nichols, & Hardy, 1990). Video cameras are increasingly commonplace in professional settings. VTS is easy, accessible, and inexpensive. However, it is also a complex, powerful and dynamic tool, and one that can be challenging, threatening, anxiety-provoking, and humbling. Several issues related to VTS are unique to the substance abuse field:

- Many substance abuse counselors "grew up" in the field without taping and may be resistant to the medium;
- Many agencies operate on limited budgets and administrators may see the expensive equipment as prohibitive and unnecessary; and
- Many substance abuse supervisors have not been trained in the use of videotape equipment or in VTS.

Yet, VTS offers nearly unlimited potential for creative use in staff development. To that end, you need training in how to use VTS effectively. The following are guidelines for VTS:

- Clients must sign releases before taping. Most programs have a release form that the client signs on admission (see Tool 19 in Part 2, chapter 2). The supervisee informs the client that videotaping will occur and reminds the client about the signed release form. The release should specify that the taping will be done exclusively for training purposes and will be reviewed only by the counselor, the supervisor, and other supervisees in group supervision. Permission will most likely be granted if the request is made in a sensitive and appropriate manner. It is critical to note that even if permission is initially given by the client, this permission can be withdrawn. You cannot force compliance.
- The use and rationale for taping needs to be clearly explained to clients. This will forestall a client's questioning as to why a particular session is being taped.
- Risk-management considerations in today's litigious climate necessitate that tapes be erased after the supervision session. Tapes can be admissible as evidence in court as part of the clinical record. Since all tapes should be erased after supervision, this must be stated in agency policies. If there are exceptions, those need to be described.
- Too often, supervisors watch long, uninterrupted segments of tape with little direction or purpose. To avoid this, you may want to ask your supervisee to cue the tape to the segment he or she wishes to address in supervision, focusing on the goals established in the IDP. Having said this, listening only to segments selected by the counselor can create some of the same disadvantages as self-report: the counselor chooses selectively, even if not consciously. The supervisor may occasionally choose to watch entire sessions.
- You need to evaluate session flow, pacing, and how counselors begin and end sessions.

Some clients may not be comfortable being videotaped but may be more comfortable with audio taping. Videotaping is not permitted in most prison settings and EAP services. Videotaping may not be advisable when treating patients with some diagnoses, such as paranoia or some schizophrenic illnesses. In such cases, either live observation or less intrusive measures, such as audio taping, may be preferred.

Live Observation

With live observation you actually sit in on a counseling session with the supervisee and observe the session first hand. The client will need to provide informed consent before being observed. Although one-way mirrors are not readily available at most agencies, they are an alternative to actually sitting in on the session. A videotape may also be used either from behind the one-way mirror (with someone else operating the videotaping equipment) or physically located in the counseling room, with the supervisor sitting in the session. This combination of mirror, videotaping, and live observation may be the best of all worlds, allowing for unobtrusive observation of a session, immediate feedback to the supervisee, modeling by the supervisor (if appropriate), and a record of the session for subsequent review in supervision. Live supervision may involve some intervention by the supervisor during the session.

Live observation is effective for the following reasons:

- It allows you to get a true picture of the counselor in action.
- It gives you an opportunity to model techniques during an actual session, thus serving as a role model for both the counselor and the client.
- Should a session become countertherapeutic, you can intervene for the well-being of the client.
- Counselors often say they feel supported when a supervisor joins the session, and clients periodically say, "This is great! I got two for the price of one."
- It allows for specific and focused feedback.
- It is more efficient for understanding the counseling process.
- It helps connect the IDP to supervision.

To maximize the effectiveness of live observation, supervisors must stay primarily in an observer role so as to not usurp the leadership or undercut the credibility and authority of the counselor.

Live observation has some disadvantages:

- It is time consuming.
- It can be intrusive and alter the dynamics of the counseling session.
- It can be anxiety-provoking for all involved.

Some mandated clients may be particularly sensitive to live observation. This becomes essentially a clinical issue to be addressed by the counselor with the client. Where is this anxiety coming from, how does it relate to other anxieties and concerns, and how can it best be addressed in counseling?

Supervisors differ on where they should sit in a live observation session. Some suggest that the supervisor sit so as to not interrupt or be involved in the session. Others suggest that the supervisor sit in a position that allows for inclusion in the counseling process.

Here are some guidelines for conducting live observation:

- The counselor should always begin with informed consent to remind the client about confidentiality. Periodically, the counselor should begin the session with a statement of confidentiality, reiterating the limits of confidentiality and the duty to warn, to ensure that the client is reminded of what is reportable by the supervisor and/or counselor.
- While sitting outside the group (or an individual session between counselor and client) may undermine the group process, it is a method selected by some. Position yourself in a way that doesn't interrupt the counseling process. Sitting outside the group undermines the human connection between you, the counselor, and the client(s) and makes it more awkward for you to make a comment, if you have not been part of the process until then. For individual or family sessions, it is also recommended that the supervisor sit beside the counselor to fully observe what is occurring in the counseling session.
- The client should be informed about the process of supervision and the supervisor's role and goals, essentially that the supervisor is there to observe the counselor's skills and not necessarily the client.
- As preparation, the supervisor and supervisee should briefly discuss the background of the session, the salient issues the supervisee wishes to focus on, and the plans for the session. The role of the supervisor should be clearly stated and agreed on before the session.
- You and the counselor may create criteria for observation, so that specific feedback is provided for specific areas of the session.
- Your comments during the session should be limited to lessen the risk of disrupting the flow or taking control of the session. Intervene only to protect the welfare of the client (should something adverse occur in the session) or if a moment critical to client welfare arises. In deciding to inter-

vene or not, consider these questions: What are the consequences if I don't intervene? What is the probability that the supervisee will make the intervention on his or her own or that my comments will be successful? Will I create an undue dependence on the part of clients or supervisee?

- Provide feedback to the counselor as soon as possible after the session. Ideally, the supervisor and supervisee(s) should meet privately immediately afterward, outlining the key points for discussion and the agenda for the next supervision session, based on the observation. Specific feedback is essential; "You did a fine job" is not sufficient. Instead, the supervisor might respond by saying, "I particularly liked your comment about . . ." or "What I observed about your behavior was . . ." or "Keep doing more of . . . ."

Practical Issues in Clinical Supervision

Distinguishing Between Supervision and Therapy

In facilitating professional development, one of the critical issues is understanding and differentiating between counseling the counselor and providing supervision. In ensuring quality client care and facilitating professional counselor development, the process of clinical supervision sometimes encroaches on personal issues. The dividing line between therapy and supervision is how the supervisee's personal issues and problems affect their work. The goal of clinical supervision must always be to assist counselors in becoming better clinicians, not seeking to resolve their personal issues. Some of the major differences between supervision and counseling are summarized in figure 6.

Figure 6. Differences Between Supervision and Counseling			
	Clinical Supervision	**Administrative Supervision**	**Counseling**
Purpose	• Improved client care • Improved job performance	• Ensure compliance with agency and regulatory body's policies and procedures	• Personal growth • Behavior changes • Better self-understanding
Outcome	• Enhanced proficiency in knowledge, skills, and attitudes essential to effective job performance	• Consistent use of approved formats, policies, and procedures	• Open-ended, based on client needs
Timeframe	• Short-term and ongoing	• Short-term and ongoing	• Based on client needs
Agenda	• Based on agency mission and counselor needs	• Based on agency needs	• Based on client needs
Basic Process	• Teaching/learning specific skills, evaluating job performance, negotiating learning objectives	• Clarifying agency expectations, policies and procedures, ensuring compliance	• Behavioral, cognitive, and affective process including listening, exploring, teaching
Source: Adapted from Dixon, 2004			

The boundary between counseling and clinical supervision may not always be clearly marked, for it is necessary, at times, to explore supervisees' limitations as they deliver services to their clients. Address counselors' personal issues only in so far as they create barriers or affect their performance. When personal issues emerge, the key question you should ask the supervisee is how does this affect the delivery of quality client care? What is the impact of this issue on the client? What resources are you using to resolve this issue outside of the counseling dyad? When personal issues emerge that might interfere with quality care, your role may be to transfer the case to a different counselor. Most important, you should make a strong case that the supervisee should seek outside counseling or therapy.

Problems related to countertransference (projecting unresolved personal issues onto a client or supervisee) often make for difficult therapeutic relationships. The following are signs of countertransference to look for:

- A feeling of loathing, anxiety, or dread at the prospect of seeing a specific client or supervisee.
- Unexplained anger or rage at a particular client.
- Distaste for a particular client.
- Mistakes in scheduling clients, missed appointments.
- Forgetting client's name, history.
- Drowsiness during a session or sessions ending abruptly.
- Billing mistakes.
- Excessive socializing.

When countertransferential issues between counselor and client arise, some of the important questions you, as a supervisor, might explore with the counselor include:

- How is this client affecting you? What feelings does this client bring out in you? What is your behavior toward the client in response to these feelings? What is it about the substance abuse behavior of this client that brings out a response in you?
- What is happening now in your life, but more particularly between you and the client that might be contributing to these feelings, and how does this affect your counseling?

- In what ways can you address these issues in your counseling?
- What strategies and coping skills can assist you in your work with this client?

Transference and countertransference also occur in the relationship between supervisee and supervisor. Examples of supervisee transference include:

- The supervisee's idealization of the supervisor.
- Distorted reactions to the supervisor based on the supervisee's reaction to the power dynamics of the relationship.
- The supervisee's need for acceptance by or approval from an authority figure.
- The supervisee's reaction to the supervisor's establishing professional and social boundaries with the supervisee.

Supervisor countertransference with supervisees is another issue that needs to be considered. Categories of supervisor countertransference include:

- The need for approval and acceptance as a knowledgeable and competent supervisor.
- Unresolved personal conflicts of the supervisor activated by the supervisory relationship.
- Reactions to individual supervisees, such as dislike or even disdain, whether the negative response is "legitimate" or not. In a similar vein, aggrandizing and idealizing some supervisees (again, whether or not warranted) in comparison to other supervisees.
- Sexual or romantic attraction to certain supervisees.
- Cultural countertransference, such as catering to or withdrawing from individuals of a specific cultural background in a way that hinders the professional development of the counselor.

To understand these countertransference reactions means recognizing clues (such as dislike of a supervisee or romantic attraction), doing careful self-examination, personal counseling, and receiving supervision of your supervision. In some cases, it may be necessary for you to request a transfer of supervisees with whom you are experiencing countertransference, if that countertransference hinders the counselor's professional development.

Finally, counselors will be more open to addressing difficulties such as countertransference and compassion fatigue with you if you communicate understanding and awareness that these experiences are a normal part of being a counselor. Counselors should be rewarded in performance evaluations for raising these issues in supervision and demonstrating a willingness to work on them as part of their professional development.

Balancing Clinical and Administrative Functions

In the typical substance abuse treatment agency, the clinical supervisor may also be the administrative supervisor, responsible for overseeing managerial functions of the organization. Many organizations cannot afford to hire two individuals for these tasks. Hence, it is essential that you are aware of what role you are playing and how to exercise the authority given you by the administration. Texts on supervision sometimes overlook the supervisor's administrative tasks, but supervisors structure staff work; evaluate personnel for pay and promotions; define the scope of clinical competence; perform tasks involving planning, organizing, coordinating, and delegating work; select, hire, and fire personnel; and manage the organization. Clinical supervisors are often responsible for overseeing the quality assurance and improvement aspects of the agency and may also carry a caseload. For most of you, juggling administrative and clinical functions is a significant balancing act. Tips for juggling these functions include:

- Try to be clear about the "hat you are wearing." Are you speaking from an administrative or clinical perspective?
- Be aware of your own biases and values that may be affecting your administrative opinions.
- Delegate the administrative functions that you need not necessarily perform, such as human resources, financial, or legal functions.
- Get input from others to be sure of your objectivity and your perspective.

There may be some inherent problems with performing both functions, such as dual relationships. Counselors may be cautious about acknowledging difficulties they face in counseling because these may affect their performance evaluation or salary raises.

On the other hand, having separate clinical and administrative supervisors can lead to inconsistent messages about priorities, and the clinical supervisor is not in the chain of command for disciplinary purposes.

Finding the Time To Do Clinical Supervision

Having read this far, you may be wondering, "Where do I find the time to conduct clinical supervision as described here? How can I do direct observation of counselors within my limited time schedule?" Or, "I work in an underfunded program with substance abuse clients. I have way too many tasks to also observe staff in counseling."

One suggestion is to begin an implementation process that involves adding components of a supervision model one at a time. For example, scheduling supervisory meetings with each counselor is a beginning step. It is important to meet with each counselor on a regular, scheduled basis to develop learning plans and review professional development. Observations of counselors in their work might be added next. Another component might involve group supervision. In group supervision, time can be maximized by teaching and training counselors who have common skill development needs.

As you develop a positive relationship with supervisees based on cooperation and collaboration, the anxiety associated with observation will decrease. Counselors frequently enjoy the feedback and support so much that they request observation of their work. Observation can be brief. Rather than sitting in on a full hour of group, spend 20 minutes in the observation and an additional 20 providing feedback to the counselor.

Your choice of modality (individual, group, peer, etc.) is influenced by several factors: supervisees' learning goals, their experience and developmental levels, their learning styles, your goals for supervisees, your theoretical orientation, and your own learning goals for the supervisory process. To select a modality of supervision (within your time constraints and those of your supervisee), first pinpoint the immediate function of supervision, as different modalities fit different functions. For example, a supervisor might wish to conduct group supervision when the team is intact and functioning well, and individual supervision when specific skill development or countertransferential issues need additional attention. Given the variety of treatment environments in substance abuse treatment (e.g., therapeutic communities, intensive outpatient services, transitional living settings, correctional facilities) and varying time constraints on supervisors, several alternatives to structure supervision are available.

Peer supervision is not hierarchical and does not include a formal evaluation procedure, but offers a means of accountability for counselors that they might not have in other forms of supervision. Peer supervision may be particularly significant among well-trained, highly educated, and competent counselors. Peer supervision is a growing medium, given the clinical supervisors' duties. Although peer supervision has received limited attention in literature, the Consensus Panel believes it is a particularly effective method, especially for small group practices and agencies with limited funding for supervision. Peer supervision groups can evolve from supervisor-led groups or individual sessions to peer groups or can begin as peer supervision. For peer supervision groups offered within an agency, there may be some history to overcome among the group members, such as political entanglements, competitiveness, or personality concerns. (Bernard and Goodyear [2004] has an extensive review of the process and the advantages and disadvantages of peer supervision.)

Triadic supervision is a tutorial and mentoring relationship among three counselors. This model of supervision involves three counselors who, on a rotating basis, assume the roles of the supervisee, the commentator, and the supervision session facilitator. Spice and Spice (1976) describe peer supervision with three supervisees getting together. In current counseling literature, triadic supervision involves two counselors with one supervisor. There is very little empirical or conceptual literature on this arrangement.

Individual supervision, where a supervisor works with the supervisee in a one-to-one relationship, is considered the cornerstone of professional skill development. Individual supervision is the most labor-intensive and time-consuming method for supervision. Credentialing requirements in a particular discipline or graduate studies may mandate individual supervision with a supervisor from the same discipline.

Intensive supervision with selected counselors is helpful in working with a difficult client (such as one with a history of violence), a client using substances unfamiliar to the counselor, or a highly resistant client. Because of a variety of factors (credentialing requirements, skill deficits of some counselors, the need for close clinical supervision), you may opt to focus, for concentrated periods of time, on the needs of one or two counselors as others participate in peer supervision. Although this is not necessarily a long-term solution to the time constraints of a supervisor, intensive supervision provides an opportunity to address specific staffing needs while still providing a "reasonable effort to supervise" all personnel.

Group clinical supervision is a frequently used and efficient format for supervision, team building, and staff growth. One supervisor assists counselor development in a group of supervisee peers. The recommended group size is four to six persons to allow for frequent case presentations by each group member. With this number of counselors, each person can present a case every other month—an ideal situation, especially when combined with individual and/or peer supervision. The benefits of group supervision are that it is cost-effective, members can test their perceptions through peer validation, learning is enhanced by the diversity of the group, it creates a working alliance and improves teamwork, and it provides a microcosm of group process for participants. Group supervision gives counselors a sense of commonality with others in the same situation. Because the formats and goals differ, it is helpful to think through why you are using a particular format. (Examples of group formats with different goals can be found in Borders and Brown, 2005, and Bernard & Goodyear, 2004.)

Given the realities of the substance abuse treatment field (limited funding, priorities competing for time, counselors and supervisors without advanced academic training, and clients with pressing needs in a brief-treatment environment), the plan described below may be a useful structure for supervision. It is based on a scenario where a supervisor oversees one to five counselors. This plan is based on several principles:

- All counselors, regardless of years of experience or academic training, will receive at least 1 hour of supervision for every 20 to 40 hours of clinical practice.

- Direct observation is the backbone of a solid clinical supervision model.
- Group supervision is a viable means of engaging all staff in dialog, sharing ideas, and promoting team cohesion.

With the formula diagramed below, each counselor receives a minimum of 1 hour of group clinical supervision per week. Each week you will have 1 hour of observation, 1 hour of individual supervision with one of your supervisees, and 1 hour of group supervision with five supervisees. Each week, one counselor will be observed in an actual counseling session, followed by an individual supervision session with you. If the session is videotaped, the supervisee can be asked to cue the tape to the segment of the session he or she wishes to discuss with you. Afterwards, the observed counselor presents this session in group clinical supervision.

When it is a counselor's week to be observed or taped and meet for individual supervision, he or she will receive 3 hours of supervision: 1 hour of direct observation, 1 hour of individual/one-on-one supervision, and 1 hour of group supervision when he or she presents a case to the group. Over the course of months, with vacation, holiday, and sick time, it should average out to approximately 1 hour of supervision per counselor per week. Figure 7 shows this schedule.

When you are working with a counselor who needs special attention or who is functioning under specific requirements for training or credentialing, 1 additional hour per week can be allocated for this counselor,

increasing the total hours for clinical supervision to 4, still a manageable amount of time.

Documenting Clinical Supervision

Correct documentation and recordkeeping are essential aspects of supervision. Mechanisms must be in place to demonstrate the accountability of your role. (See Tools 10–12 in Part 2, chapter 2.) These systems should document:

- Informal and formal evaluation procedures.
- Frequency of supervision, issues discussed, and the content and outcome of sessions.
- Due process rights of supervisees (such as the right to confidentiality and privacy, to informed consent).
- Risk management issues (how to handle crises, duty-to-warn situations, breaches of confidentiality).

One comprehensive documentation system is Falvey's (2002a) Focused Risk Management Supervision System (FoRMSS), which provides templates to record emergency contact information, supervisee profiles, a logging sheet for supervision, an initial case review, supervision records, and a client termination form.

Supervisory documents and notes are open to management, administration, and human resources (HR) personnel for performance appraisal and merit pay increases and are admissible in court proceedings. Supervision notes, especially those related to work

Figure 7. Sample Clinical Supervision Schedule					
Counselor	**Week 1**	**Week 2**	**Week 3**	**Week 4**	**Week 5**
A	1 hour direct observation 1 hour individual supervision 1 hour group supervision of A's case (3 hours)	1 hour group	1 hour group	1 hour group	1 hour group
B	1 hour group	3 hour group	1 hour group	1 hour group	1 hour group
C	1 hour group	1 hour group	3 hour group	1 hour group	1 hour group
D	1 hour group	1 hour group	1 hour group	3 hour group	1 hour group
E	1 hour group	1 hour group	1 hour group	1 hour group	3 hour group

with clients, are kept separately and are intended for the supervisor's use in helping the counselor improve clinical skills and monitor client care. It is imperative to maintain accurate and complete notes on the supervision. However, as discussed above, documentation procedures for formative versus summative evaluation of staff may vary. Typically, HR accesses summative evaluations, and supervisory notes are maintained as formative evaluations.

An example of a formative note by a supervisor might be "The counselor responsibly discussed countertransferential issues occurring with a particular client and was willing to take supervisory direction," or "We worked out an action plan, and I will follow this closely." This wording avoids concerns by the supervisor and supervisee as to the confidentiality of supervisory notes. From a legal perspective, the supervisor needs to be specific about what was agreed on and a timeframe for following up.

Structuring the Initial Supervision Sessions

As discussed earlier, your first tasks in clinical supervision are to establish a behavioral contract, get to know your supervisees, and outline the requirements of supervision. Before the initial session, you should send a supportive letter to the supervisee expressing the agency's desire to provide him or her with a quality clinical supervision experience. You might request that the counselor give some thought to what he or she would like to accomplish in supervision, what skills to work on, and which core functions used in the addiction counselor certification process he or she feels most comfortable performing.

In the first few sessions, helpful practices include:

- Briefly describe your role as both administrative and clinical supervisor (if appropriate) and discuss these distinctions with the counselor.
- Briefly describe your model of counseling and learn about the counselor's frameworks and models for her or his counseling practice. For beginning counselors this may mean helping them define their model.
- Describe your model of supervision.
- State that disclosure of one's supervisory training, experience, and model is an ethical duty of clinical supervisors.

- Discuss methods of supervision, the techniques to be used, and the resources available to the supervisee (e.g., agency inservice seminar, community workshops, professional association memberships, and professional development funds or training opportunities).
- Explore the counselor's goals for supervision and his or her particular interests (and perhaps some fears) in clinical supervision.
- Explain the differences between supervision and therapy, establishing clear boundaries in this relationship.
- Work to establish a climate of cooperation, collaboration, trust, and safety.
- Create an opportunity for rating the counselor's knowledge and skills based on the competencies in TAP 21 (CSAT, 2007).
- Explain the methods by which formative and summative evaluations will occur.
- Discuss the legal and ethical expectations and responsibilities of supervision.
- Take time to decrease the anxiety associated with being supervised and build a positive working relationship.

It is important to determine the knowledge and skills, learning style, and conceptual skills of your supervisees, along with their suitability for the work setting, motivation, self-awareness, and ability to function autonomously. A basic IDP for each supervisee should emerge from the initial supervision sessions. You and your supervisee need to assess the learning environment of supervision by determining:

- Is there sufficient challenge to keep the supervisee motivated?
- Are the theoretical differences between you and the supervisee manageable?
- Are there limitations in the supervisee's knowledge and skills, personal development, self-efficacy, self-esteem, and investment in the job that would limit the gains from supervision?
- Does the supervisee possess the affective qualities (empathy, respect, genuineness, concreteness, warmth) needed for the counseling profession?
- Are the goals, means of supervision, evaluation criteria, and feedback process clearly understood by the supervisee?
- Does the supervisory environment encourage and allow risk taking?

Methods and Techniques of Clinical Supervision

A number of methods and techniques are available for clinical supervision, regardless of the modality used. Methods include (as discussed previously) case consultation, written activities such as verbatims and process recordings, audio and videotaping, and live observation. Techniques include modeling, skill demonstrations, and role playing. (See descriptions of these and other methods and techniques in Bernard & Goodyear, 2004; Borders & Brown, 2005; Campbell, 2000; and Powell & Brodsky, 2004.) Figure 8 outlines some of the methods and techniques of supervision, as well as the advantages and disadvantages of each method.

The context in which supervision is provided affects how it is carried out. A critical issue is how to manage your supervisory workload and make a reasonable effort to supervise. The contextual issues that shape the techniques and methods of supervision include:

- The allocation of time for supervision. If the 20:1 rule of client hours to supervision time is followed, you will want to allocate sufficient time for supervision each week so that it is a high priority, regularly scheduled activity.
- The unique conditions, limitations, and requirements of the agency. Some organizations may lack the physical facilities or hardware to use videotaping or to observe sessions. Some organizations may be limited by confidentiality requirements,

	Figure 8. Methods and Techniques in Clinical Supervision		
	Description	**Advantages**	**Disadvantages**
Verbal Reports	Verbal reports of clinical situations Group discussion of clinical situations	• Informal • Time efficient • Often spontaneous in response to clinical situation • Can hear counselor's report, what he or she includes, thus learn of the counselor's awareness and perspective, what he or she wishes to report, contrasted with supervisory observations	• Sessions seen through eyes of beholder • Nonverbal cues missed • Can drift into case management, hence it is important to focus on the clinical nature of chart reviews, reports, etc., linking to the treatment plan and EBPs
Verbatim Reports	Process recordings Verbatim written record of a session or part of session Declining method in the behavioral health field	• Helps track coordination and use of treatment plan with ongoing session • Enhances conceptualization and writing skills • Enhances recall and reflection skills • Provides written documentation of sessions	• Nonverbal cues missed • Self-report bias • Can be very tedious to write and to read
Written/File Review	Review of the progress notes, charts, documentation	• An important task of a supervisor to ensure compliance with accreditation standards for documentation • Provides a method of quality control • Ensures consistency of records and files	• Time consuming • Notes often miss the overall quality and essence of the session • Can drift into case management rather than clinical skills development

	Description	Advantages	Disadvantages
Figure 8. Methods and Techniques in Clinical Supervision (continued)			
Case Consultation/ Case Management	Discussion of cases Brief case reviews	• Helps organize information, conceptualize problems, and decide on clinical interventions • Examines issues (e.g., cross-cultural issues), integrates theory and technique, and promotes greater self-awareness • An essential component of treatment planning	• The validity of self-report is dependent on counselor developmental level and the supervisor's insightfulness • Does not reflect broad range of clinical skills of the counselor
Direct Observation	The supervisor watches the session and may provide periodic but limited comments and/or suggestions to the clinician	• Allows teaching of basic skills while protecting quality of care • Counselor can see and experience positive change in session direction in the moment • Allows supervisor to intervene when needed to protect the welfare of the client, if the session is not effective or is destructive to the client	• May create anxiety • Requires supervisor caution in intervening so as to not take over the session or to create undue dependence for the counselor or client • Can be seen as intrusive to the clinical process • Time consuming
Audiotaping	Audiotaping and review of a counseling session	• Technically easy and inexpensive • Can explore general rapport, pace, and interventions • Examines important relationship issues • Unobtrusive medium • Can be listened to in clinical or team meetings	• Counselor may feel anxious • Misses nonverbal cues • Poor sound quality often occurs due to limits of technology
Videotaping	Videotaping and review of a counseling session	• A rich medium to review verbal and nonverbal information • Provides documentation of clinical skills • Can be viewed by the treatment team during group clinical supervision session • Uses time efficiently • Can be used in conjunction with direct observation • Can be used to suggest different interventions • Allows for review of content, affective and cognitive aspects, process relationship issues in the present	• Can be seen as intrusive to the clinical process • Counselor may feel anxious and self-conscious, although this subsides with experience • Technically more complicated • Requires training before using • Can become part of the clinical record and can be subpoenaed (should be destroyed after review)

Figure 8. Methods and Techniques in Clinical Supervision (continued)			
	Description	**Advantages**	**Disadvantages**
Webcam	Internet supervision, synchronistic and asynchronistic Teleconferencing	• Can be accessed from any computer • Especially useful for remote and satellite facilities and locations • Uses time efficiently • Modest installation and operation costs • Can be stored or downloaded on a variety of media, watched in any office, then erased	• Concerns about anonymity and confidentiality • Can be viewed as invasive to the clinical process • May increase client or counselor anxiety or self-consciousness • Technically more complicated • Requires assurance that downloads will be erased and unavailable to unauthorized staff
Cofacilitation and Modeling	Supervisor and counselor jointly run a counseling session Supervisor demonstrates a specific technique while the counselor observes This may be followed by roleplay with the counselor practicing the skill with time to process learning and application	• Allows the supervisor to model techniques while observing the counselor • Can be useful to the client ("two counselors for the price of one") • Supervisor must demonstrate proficiency in the skill and help the counselor incrementally integrate the learning • Counselor sees how the supervisor might respond • Supervisor incrementally shapes the counselor's skill acquisition and monitors skill mastery • Allows supervisor to aid counselor with difficult clients	• Supervisor must demonstrate proficiency in the skill and help the counselor incrementally integrate the learning • The client may perceive counselor as less skilled than the supervisor • Time consuming
Role Playing	Role play a clinical situation	• Enlivens the learning process • Provides the supervisor with direct observation of skills • Helps counselor gain a different perspective • Creates a safe environment for the counselor to try new skills	• Counselor can be anxious • Supervisor must be mindful of not overwhelming the counselor with information

Source: Adapted from Mattel, 2007.

such as working within a criminal justice system where taping may be prohibited.

• The number of supervisees reporting to a supervisor. It is difficult to provide the scope of supervision discussed in this TIP if a supervisor has more than ten supervisees. In such a case, another supervisor could be named or peer supervision could be used for advanced staff.

• Clinical and management responsibilities of a supervisor. Supervisors have varied responsibilities, including administrative tasks, limiting the amount of time available for clinical supervision.

Administrative Supervision

As noted above, clinical and administrative supervision overlap in the real world. Most clinical supervisors also have administrative responsibilities, including team building, time management, addressing agency policies and procedures, recordkeeping, human resources management (hiring, firing, disciplining), performance appraisal, meeting management, oversight of accreditation, maintenance of legal and ethical standards, compliance with State and Federal regulations, communications, overseeing staff cultural competence issues, quality control and improvement, budgetary and financial issues, problem solving, and documentation. Keeping up with these duties is not an easy task!

This TIP addresses two of the most frequently voiced concerns of supervisors: documentation and time management. Supervisors say, "We are drowning in paperwork. I don't have the time to adequately document my supervision as well," and "How do I manage my time so I can provide quality clinical supervision?"

Documentation for Administrative Purposes

One of the most important administrative tasks of a supervisor is that of documentation and recordkeeping, especially of clinical supervision sessions. Unquestionably, documentation is a crucial risk-management tool. Supervisory documentation can help promote the growth and professional development of the counselor (Munson, 1993). However, adequate documentation is not a high priority in some organizations. For example, when disciplinary action is needed with an employee, your organization's attorney or human resources department will ask for the paper trail, or documentation of prior performance issues. If appropriate documentation to justify disciplinary action is missing from the employee's record, it may prove more difficult to conduct the appropriate disciplinary action (See Falvey, 2002; Powell & Brodsky, 2004.)

Documentation is no longer an option for supervisors. It is a critical link between work performance and service delivery. You have a legal and ethical requirement to evaluate and document counselor performance. A complete record is a useful and necessary part of supervision. Records of supervision sessions should include:

- The supervisor–supervisee contract, signed by both parties.
- A brief summary of the supervisee's experience, training, and learning needs.
- The current IDP.
- A summary of all performance evaluations.
- Notations of all supervision sessions, including cases discussed and significant decisions made.
- Notation of cancelled or missed supervision sessions.
- Progressive discipline steps taken.
- Significant problems encountered in supervision and how they were resolved.
- Supervisor's clinical recommendations provided to supervisees.
- Relevant case notes and impressions.

The following should not be included in a supervision record:

- Disparaging remarks about staff or clients.
- Extraneous or sensitive supervisee information.
- Alterations in the record after the fact or premature destruction of supervision records.
- Illegible information and nonstandard abbreviations.

Several authors have proposed a standardized format for documentation of supervision, including Falvey (2002b), Glenn and Serovich (1994), and Williams (1994).

Time Management

By some estimates, people waste about two hours every day doing tasks that are not of high priority. In your busy job, you may find yourself at the end of the week with unfinished tasks or matters that have not been tended to. Your choices? Stop performing some tasks (often training or supervision) or take work home and work longer days. In the long run, neither of these choices is healthy or effective for your organization. Yet, being successful does not make you manage your time well. Managing your time well makes you successful. Ask yourself these questions about your priorities:

- Why am I doing this? What is the goal of this activity?
- How can I best accomplish this task in the least amount of time?
- What will happen if I choose not to do this?

It is wise to develop systems for managing time-wasters such as endless meetings held without notes or minutes, playing telephone or email tag, junk mail, and so on. Effective supervisors find their times in the day when they are most productive. Time management is essential if you are to set time aside and dedicate it to supervisory tasks.

Resources

The following are resources for supervision:

- Code of Ethics from the Association of Addictions Professionals (NAADAC; http://naadac.org).
- International Certification & Reciprocity Consortium's Code of Ethics (http://www.icrcaoda.org).
- Codes of ethics from professional groups such as the American Association for Marriage and Family Therapy (http://www.aamft.org), the American Counseling Association (http://www.counseling.org), the Association for Counselor Education and Supervision (http://www.acesonline.net), the American Psychological Association (http://www.apa.org), the National Association of Social Workers (http://www.socialworkers.org), and the National Board for Certified Counselors (NBCC; http://www.nbcc.org).
- ACES Standards for Counseling Supervisors; ACES Ethical Guidelines for Counseling Supervisors (http://www.acesonline.net/ethical_guidelines.asp); and NBCC Standards for the Ethical Practice of Clinical Supervision.

TAP 21-A provides detailed appendices of suggested reading and other resources (CSAT, 2007). Additionally, Part 3 of this document provides a literature review and bibliographies (available online only at http://www.kap.samhsa.gov). The following are examples of online classroom training programs in clinical supervision in the substance abuse field:

- http://www.attcnetwork.org/midatlantic, *Clinical Supervision for Substance Abuse Treatment Practitioners Series.*
- http://www.attcnetwork.org/midatlantic, *Motivational Interviewing Assessment: Supervisory Tools for Enhancing Proficiency.*
- http://www.attcnetwork.org/northeast, *Clinical Supervision to Support the Implementation, Fidelity and Sustaining Evidence-Based Practices.*
- http://www.attcnetwork.org/northwestfrontier, *Clinical Supervision, Part 2: What Happens in Good Supervision.*

Other training programs are given in professional graduate schools, such as New York University School of Social Work; Smith College School for Social Work; University of Nevada, Reno, Human and Community Sciences; and Portland State University Graduate School of Education.

For information about tools to measure counselor competencies and supervisor self-assessment tools, along with samples, see the following:

- David J. Powell and Archie Brodsky, *Clinical Supervision in Alcohol and Drug Abuse Counseling,* 2004.
- L. DiAnne Borders and Lori L. Brown, *The New Handbook of Counseling Supervision,* 2005
- Jane M. Campbell, *Becoming an Effective Supervisor,* 2000.
- Janet Elizabeth Falvey, *Managing Clinical Supervision: Ethical Practice and Legal Risk Management,* 2002.
- Carol A. Falender and Edward P. Shafranske, *Clinical Supervision: A Competency-Based Approach,* 2004.
- Cal D. Stoltenberg, Brian McNeill, and Ursula Delworth, *IDM Supervision: An Integrated Developmental Model for Supervising Counselors and Therapists,* 1998.

Chapter 2

Introduction

In this chapter, through vignettes, you will meet eight clinical supervisors with a variety of skill levels, a number of their supervisees, and an administrator. The supervisors face counselors with a variety of issues. One is unfamiliar with supervision, one has ethical issues, one is resistant to change, and another is a problem employee. The supervisors also have issues of their own. One grapples with the challenges of a new position, and another works to create a legacy. The vignettes, which incorporate these issues along with the principles outlined in Part 1, chapter 1, are designed to show how clinical supervisors might manage some fairly typical situations.

Each vignette provides an overview of the agency and of the backgrounds of the supervisor and other individuals in the dialog. A list of the learning objectives for each vignette is also included. Embedded in the dialog are additional features:

Master Supervisor Notes are comments from an experienced clinical supervisor about the strategies used, what the supervisor may be thinking, how supervisors with different levels of experience and competence might have managed the situation, and information supervisors should have.

"How-to" Notes contain information on how to implement a specific method or strategy.

The master supervisor represents the combined experience and wisdom of the TIP Consensus Panel and provides insights into the counselor's relationships with clients and suggests possible approaches. The notes provide some indication of the breadth of the master supervisor's clinical skills as well as the extent to which the supervisor moves effortlessly among clinical, supportive, evaluative, and administrative roles.

"How-to" notes reflect the collected experience of the TIP Consensus Panel along with information gleaned from a variety of textbooks, manuals, and workbooks on clinical supervision. Not all "how-tos" will apply in every situation, but this information can be adapted to meet the specific needs of your case.

This format was chosen to assist clinical supervisors at all levels of mastery, including those who are new in the position, those who have some experience but need more diversity and depth, and those with years of experience and training who are true master supervisors. The Consensus Panel has made significant efforts to present realistic scenes in supervision using clinical approaches that include motivational interviewing (MI), cognitive–behavioral therapy (CBT), supportive psychotherapy, crisis intervention methods, and a variety of supervisory methodologies including live observation, education, and ethical decisionmaking. In all of these efforts, basic dynamics of supervision, such as relationship building, managing rapport in stressful situations, giving feedback, assessing, and understanding and responding to the needs expressed by the counselor are demonstrated. The Panel does not intend to imply that the approach used by the supervisor is the "gold standard," although the approach shown does represent competent supervision that can be performed in real settings.

Vignette 1—Establishing a New Approach for Clinical Supervision

Overview

This vignette illustrates the tasks of a clinical supervisor in describing a range of supervision methods to clinical staff, including establishing a consistent model of direct observation. The vignette begins with the supervisor describing to staff how he will implement a new method of supervision.

Background

Walt has been assigned to redesign the supervision program for a community-based substance abuse treatment program, which includes an inpatient program, intensive outpatient program, family therapy, impaired driver treatment, drug court program, halfway house, and educational services. The decision was made to establish an integrated system of supervision. The agency's staff, with ten full-time-equivalent counseling positions, has a broad range of professional training and experience, from entry-level certified addiction counselors to licensed social workers and licensed professional counselors. All staff, regardless of degrees and training, basically have the same duties.

Until now, staff received primarily administrative supervision with an emphasis on meeting job performance standards. Walt wants to make the supervision more clinical in nature, using direct methods of observation (videotape and live observation). He anticipates program growth in the next few years and wants to mentor key staff who can assume supervisory responsibilities in the future.

Walt has been meeting with clinical staff in small groups organized along work teams into dyads and triads to describe the changes and new opportunities. The vignette begins with Walt meeting with two staff members to discuss their learning needs and to present the new clinical supervision system. Al is in recovery, with 5 years of sobriety and 3 years of experience as a counselor. Carrie has an M.S.W. degree with 6 years of work experience.

Learning Goals

1. To demonstrate a range of supervision methods, with an emphasis on direct observation through videotaping and live observation.

2. To illustrate the mentoring, coaching, and educational functions of supervision.

3. To demonstrate how these functions can be integrated into a consistent model of clinical supervision with fidelity to the methods and adaptability to the unique needs of each organization.

[*After greetings, Walt begins the discussion about the new supervision approach.*]

WALT : As you know, our CEO and senior staff have agreed that we need to establish a program of staff training and supervision that will help achieve the goals of the agency and, at the same time, help counselors improve their skills. We've done a good job developing other administrative systems, and the next step is to implement clinical supervision to address both agency goals and your individual goals for professional development. People are moving into new roles, so new skills will be required of us.

AL: I'm not sure what I need. How will supervision enhance my skills?

WALT: Al, I think that is a great place to start. We've had administrative supervision so far. As we continue to grow individually and together, we'll need new skills. Perhaps a place for us to start is to discuss what will be asked of us in the future, what skills we'll need. How would it be if we had that discussion now?

AL: That sounds a little frightening. We need to know and do more? How much more blood can they get out of us?

Master Supervisor Note: A new supervisor might respond differently to Al's comment, in a more mechanical or authoritarian manner, asserting authority, wanting to be the expert, creating an "us vs. them" scenario. Such an approach might discourage staff from embracing the new supervision system. An experienced supervisor would be less confrontive and authoritarian and would adopt a more consultative posture. He would be direct but not necessarily confrontational.

CARRIE: I remember the good supervision I had in my M.S.W. program. This sort of reminds me of that—that you're suggesting we have more clinical supervision. Not to sound selfish, but what's in it for me, to get more supervision?

WALT: That's a great question, Carrie. We all want to know what's in it for us. I'd like to hear about your experiences in supervision. How did you learn from that process? What direct observation did you have?

How To Provide a Rationale for Clinical Supervision
Clinical supervision has several benefits, which Walt can offer Carrie at this point:

1. Administrative benefits: ensuring quality care, providing a tool to evaluate the staff's strengths and learning needs

2. Clinical benefits: improving counselors' knowledge and skills and offering a forum to implement evidence-based practices within an organization

3. Professional and workforce development: enhancing staff retention, improving morale, providing a benefit to enhance staff recruitment, and upgrading the qualifications and credentials of personnel

4. Program evaluation and research: providing valuable information to determine program outcome and patient success

CARRIE: In school I found observation both frightening and helpful. At first I hated being observed and taped. Very quickly, though, I really saw the benefits of observation and learned a lot from the experience.

WALT: It's been my experience that almost everybody has some initial reservations about direct observation, but at the same time nearly everyone finds it beneficial, too. I think one thing to keep in mind is that good direct observation doesn't focus on the negative—on what somebody did wrong. The objective is to help us look at what we do well, give us new options, build a bigger tool box of skills, and help us to look at the larger process of our counseling, rather than just getting stuck in applying techniques with people. As we look at our goals and what we need to learn, I hope we can see how supervision, and particularly direct observation, will help all of us.

CARRIE: I'm told I'll be doing more group counseling. I certainly need further training and feedback on my group skills. This is something we didn't focus on much in grad school. There are other areas that I'd also like to be more proficient in, such as doing marriage and family counseling.

WALT: Okay. That would be one place for us to begin, Carrie. How about you, Al?

AL: I'm excited. I've wanted to do more counseling, moving out of running DWI groups and doing assessments. I need more training but I have concerns about being videotaped or observed. I'm going to make mistakes. I'll be self-conscious about that. I think videotaping a session or having a supervisor sit in will make the clients nervous, too.

How To Help Counselors and Clients Become Comfortable With Live Observation

The following steps are recommended:

1. Acknowledge and understand the clients' and/or counselors' anxiety about observation or taping.

2. Listen reflectively to these concerns without being dismissive or ignoring the anxiety; noting that these feelings are common may help normalize the counselor's concerns.

3. Clearly state the value of direct observation and reinforce the idea that such methods are "part of how we do business at this agency. We want to be respectful of your concerns. And we believe strongly that it is important for us to do so for quality assurance and improved client service."

4. Keep the door open with the clients and counselors to continue to address their concerns and feelings as part of their normal clinical or supervisory process.

5. Help the counselor to allay clients' anxiety or concerns by coaching the counselor through methods for presenting the direct observation methods to the client.

WALT: I can sure understand your sense of feeling self-conscious and your concerns that clients will, too. You've never been either videotaped or observed before?

AL: No, I haven't. In the DWI program, my supervisor sat in a few times when I first started, but it was more a question of whether I was following the curriculum.

WALT: So, although you did have some observation before, this seems like it will be different for you. Perhaps we could look at your goals and how supervision with observation can assist us in meeting your goals.

[*A discussion follows where Al and Carrie present their ideas for supervision needs. They then discuss what skills they need to develop in the next year.*]

WALT: Perhaps we can discuss what the new supervision system will look like, how it will work, and what's in it for you. First, we're going to have regular observation of all clinical staff, through either one-way mirror (if we can get the audio working in the room), videotaping (my preferred method), or one of the supervisors will sit in and observe counselors with clients. We hope to observe each counselor at least once a month. We'll meet as a group for supervision for an hour a week, and we'll discuss the session that was videotaped or observed that week, with one of you leading the discussion. Each person will get a turn at bat over the course of 1 or 2 months.

[*Walt explains the "how-tos" of live observation and videotaping, including the concept of saliency, bringing to supervision the one issue the counselor wishes to address. Walt presents a step-by-step process to begin doing direct observation.*]

How To Implement Direct Observation or Videotaping

1. Obtain written and verbal agreement from the clients and all concerned parties to be videotaped. Clients should be informed on admission that:

    • Counselor–client contact may be observed by supervisors, and/or audio or videotaped.

    • The conditions under which the tape will be used for training.

    • How the taped material will be stored and destroyed after use.

2. Counselors should briefly explore client concerns about taping and observation, and respect their right not to be observed. If the client objects after the initial exploration, the counselor must respect that choice and ask another client.

3. On the visit before the observation occurs, remind the client that on their next visit, their session will be taped for quality assurance purposes. Ask them if they have any questions about that. If the client strongly objects to the taping, discuss those concerns. If the client repeatedly objects to any form of observation, the counselor should explore the client's resistance, and attempt to understand the client's concerns and point of view. Even though a client has signed an informed consent that discusses the possibility of direct observation by supervisors, a client always has the right to decline any aspect of treatment. Remember, no method of observation should ever exceed the client's level of comfort so as to be detrimental to the therapeutic process.

4. At the beginning of the taping or observation, restate to the client the limits of confidentiality and how the videotape or observation notes will be used by the clinical supervisor and/or the counseling team. Clarify whether or how the supervisor will observe and/or cofacilitate the session or simply observe and intervene only as needed.

5. Be attentive to the counselor's concerns about direct observation. It may be helpful to begin with the idea that "observation gives us a chance to learn from each other." Then you can move into a discussion about the benefits and cost-effectiveness of certain observation methods.

6. Ask the counselor to cue the tape to the most salient points of the session and bring that section to their next supervisory session. In the beginning, counselors might be encouraged to choose the section of a session in which they thought they did well.

CARRIE: I'd like to hear more about why you prefer videotaping.

WALT: I prefer videotaping for several reasons: First, it is the most cost-effective way for us to observe a session. Second, videotaping helps us allocate staff time better; we don't have to sit in on an entire session but can just look at the most salient points in the tape. It gives us all a chance to observe and learn from each other. Sometimes we get a tape where a counselor has done something really special, and we can use that tape again before destroying it, teaching a particularly powerful and effective technique. We can all learn from each other's experiences.

[Walt describes how direct observation works, including the legal requirements such as signed releases by clients, preparation and procedures for observation, and procedures for using tapes and observations and maintaining confidentiality.]

Master Supervisor Note: It is important for you to prepare the counselor for what will happen during the session. If you are sitting in the session to observe, you should explain if and/or when you might intervene in the session, seating arrangements for the session, nonverbal ways of communicating during the session, and how other interruptions, should they occur, might be handled.

AL: As I said before, I've never been observed or taped, and that makes me nervous.

CARRIE: Well Al, I think you'll get comfortable with it, and you'll find it to be very helpful when it comes to areas that you have concerns about. You said that you were concerned about mistakes, but it really won't be about mistakes. My supervisor in grad school had a motto I liked; she always tried to "catch counselors doing something right." I liked that. So, hopefully this is not about making mistakes but learning from each other. When you see yourself on the videotape and you have someone go over it with you, they can give you pointers about what worked and how you might have done other things differently. Over time you become comfortable with it. Observation was very helpful to me. I think your misgivings will go away after a couple of sessions with Walt. You'll be surprised.

Master Supervisor Note: It may be helpful for you, as a supervisor, to find a "champion"—someone who's experienced direct observation and found it helpful. Hearing positive statements about supervision from a colleague is often more acceptable than hearing it from superiors.

WALT: That's been my experience, too, with videotaping and direct observation. Al, you said it would make the client nervous. Actually, we're the ones who're most nervous. We all want to know how we're doing, but often we're afraid to ask, to get feedback and be observed.

AL: Maybe it would be better if I saw tapes of others doing counseling first.

WALT: That's a great idea. I can present a videotape of a session I conduct. Then we can all sit and discuss what I did. How would that work for you if we were to look at a videotape of one of my sessions for our next supervisory meeting? I'd benefit from your reflections. It might be a good place for us to start the process.

How To Encourage Acceptance of Direct Observation

Since you should never ask a staff member to do something you are unwilling to do, it might be helpful for you to:

1. Be the first to be taped or observed.

2. Be open to feedback from staff, setting the tone of acceptance and vulnerability to feedback.

3. Solicit comments and suggestions from the counselors concerning what they might have done differently and why.

4. Model acceptance by committing to trying out these suggestions in future counseling sessions.

AL: Yeah, I like that idea.

CARRIE: That would be fine with me. I'll volunteer to be second. It's been a while since I was observed, but I don't have any problem with it.

WALT: Thanks, Carrie. So, since I'm up to bat first, let's talk about some of the processes of observation.

[*A discussion follows about what will happen in supervision when Walt presents his case.*]

Master Supervisor Note: You will want to state clearly what is expected from counselors in supervision. A supervision contract forms the basis of this statement, and explains the ramifications of missing supervision sessions and what they can expect from you and each other. For example, if a supervisee repeatedly misses supervision sessions, this might be considered an administrative or disciplinary issue, much as if an employee was repeatedly late filling out paperwork or getting to work. Also, if the supervisee does not provide the required videotape of a counseling session for review by the supervisor, the supervisor might need to take action, following the organization's policies for progressive discipline.

WALT: There are different methods that we can use, besides videotaping, that might work better for some clients or situations. We want to have an integrated supervision system, one that includes reviewing cases together; periodic review of our files, such as client progress notes and treatment plans; training that meets the needs of a variety of staff; and review of our client evaluation surveys. While I'm on that topic, we also want to receive more input from clients about how we're doing. There's a new tool we hope to incorporate that routinely asks for input from clients after each counseling session, and at the end of each day for our residential units.

AL: I have reservations about how useful information from clients might be. After all, for clients in early recovery, their brains are still foggy.

WALT: Good point Al. If we ask clients regularly, though, we should get useful information about our ability to address clients' needs and the quality of our relationships with them. This is helpful information when we link it to our direct observation and supervision. Sort of like watching a TV program and getting the Nielsen Ratings about the show at the same time.

[*Laughter.*]

[*In the discussion that follows, Walt acknowledges Al's concerns, and Al, Carrie, and Walt talk about those concerns. Walt asks how they can get past those concerns, how they can work together to have further client input into the process.*]

 Master Supervisor Note: At times it is necessary for a supervisor to openly address staff resistance. The skill is in knowing when to address and when to deflect the resistance. Sometimes, it is useful to talk about staff resistance, to soothe people's discomfort before launching into the specifics of how supervision will be accomplished. MI suggests that it is most helpful to "roll with resistance" by reflecting back to counselors both sides of their ambivalence about the new supervision format. Often it is best to return to the issue at a later time.

WALT: And that's what we want to see happen with an integrated system of supervision. It will help us identify what we need to learn, the skills and competencies. To start the process, each of us will bring in a counseling session that we think is going well, that we feel good about. How does that sound to each of you?

CARRIE: I like that: a chance for each of us to "show off" a bit.

AL: Well, if you go first, Walt, as you said. I'll go the week after Carrie. I have all kinds of sessions where I'm doing a good job.

[*Laughter.*]

CARRIE: I found it helpful in grad school for us to help each other, to avoid throwing anyone into the process alone. Will that be possible for us?

WALT: That's a great idea, Carrie. How did peer supervision work in grad school?

[*Carrie discusses how peer supervision and team coaching work.*]

 Master Supervisor Note: Peer supervision is an effective form of group supervision. Supervisees confer in the group, discuss key topics of their counseling, and suggest solutions for difficult situations. The participants learn better ways to manage clinical issues, thus increasing their professionalism.

Peer supervision and team coaching have the following advantages and disadvantages:

1. The strengths and success of peer group supervision depend on the composition of the group, the individual members' strengths, and the clarity of the peer group contract. Members must agree on the time, location, and frequency of meetings, as well as the organizational structure and goals of the meetings and limits of confidentiality. In these dimensions, peer supervision differs from occasional and unplanned peer consultation, a more informal process.

2. Peer group supervision decreases professional isolation, increases professional support and networking, normalizes the stress of clinical work, and offers multiple perspectives on any concern. Peer supervision has the added benefits of being of low or no cost, intellectually stimulating, and fun for supervisees.

3. Vague, ambiguous, or ambivalent goals and structure often lead to difficulties in peer supervision. As with individual or clinical supervision, an interpersonal atmosphere of reasonable safety (including respect, warmth, honesty, and a collaborative openness) are critical.

4. Effectiveness and supervisee enjoyment diminish when competitiveness, criticism, inconsistency of members, and absence of support are prevalent.

5. The success of peer group supervision is affected by supervisees' varying commitment and irregular attendance.

WALT: So, we've identified how this works. This is a new role for me, too, so I can use your feedback and suggestions. Supervision involves a different set of skills than being a counselor.

CARRIE: Right. I took a course in school on clinical supervision and that's exactly what the professor said.

How To Choose a Course on Clinical Supervision

Look for the following components:

1. The training should be approved by credentialing organizations to fulfill the requirements for certification as a clinical supervisor.

2. It should meet the minimum training requirements of 30 hours.

3. The training should be provided by a trainer with the following skills: Level 3 counselor, Level 3 supervisor, excellent training experience, and ability to provide information on both administrative and clinical supervisory issues.

4. The training should teach practical clinical supervisory skills through role-plays and demonstrations, video- and audiotapes of supervision sessions, and opportunities to practice clinical supervisory skills.

5. The training should be provided by a reputable training individual or organization.

6. Online courses are also available. However, an organization should first verify if online courses are approved by their State certification board.

WALT: Let's summarize what we've said. We're moving into new treatment program strategies. Each of us has an Individual Development Plan (IDP) stating our individual learning goals. Mentorship is an important aspect of helping us all meet our IDP goals.

[*Walt describes the process of mentorship, that each staff member will have a mentor. Some staff will mentor each other. Walt discusses the relationship between the IDPs, clinical supervision, and the mentorship system. Walt also discusses the issue of stages of readiness and how that affects the form and extent of mentorship each person will receive.*]

Master Supervisor Note: Mentorship is a formalized relationship between a skilled professional and a mentee and is established to enhance the mentee's career by building skills and knowledge. In a series of structured sessions, a person of greater experience instructs, guides, advises, provides feedback, and coaches someone of lesser experience.

WALT: One of my tasks is to ensure that all of us get training so that any one of you could take over for me if need be. I love to surround myself with people who can take over my job on a given day.

CARRIE: I'd be happy to both be mentored and serve as a mentor to others, if that's what you wish. I'm feeling a lot better than when we began this discussion today.

[*Walt starts a discussion on clinical issues that might be topics for discussion in supervision, such as caseload size and complexity, work with clients with co-occurring disorders, the impact of dual relationships with clients, and confidentiality. The session ends with the group establishing the times for their group supervision and the procedures for tape review and live observation.*]

Vignette 2—Defining and Building the Supervisory Alliance

Overview

This vignette illustrates the tasks of defining and building a supervisory alliance, particularly when working with an entry-level counselor with an academic background different from that of the supervisor. The dialog is the initial supervisory session. It illustrates how to introduce direct observation and the establishment of an IDP.

Background

Bill is a certified clinical supervisor who worked his way up through the ranks, starting as a substance abuse counselor 20 years ago, 3 years into his own sobriety. Ten years ago he enrolled in a part-time master's degree program in counseling and completed the degree in 5 years. Since receiving his master's degree, he has worked as a clinician and supervisor in a community-based substance abuse treatment program. In addition to his supervisory duties, he is director of the program's intensive outpatient program (IOP).

Jan is in her first month at the agency, right out of graduate school. She is a Level 1 counselor, her first employment since receiving her M.S.W. She had limited substance abuse treatment experience in a field work placement and sees her current employment as a stepping stone to private practice after she receives her social work license. Her supervision in the field placement assignment focused on social work skills and integrating field work learning with her academic program. She averaged ten cases during her second year of field work.

The agency is a private, nonprofit organization providing comprehensive addiction treatment and education services. Jan has been assigned to the IOP and is expected to participate in a structured internship program of 3 months wherein she will receive training in the substance abuse treatment field. The agency has a well-established system for clinical supervision.

Learning Goals

1. To illustrate how to initiate supervision with a new counselor.

2. To demonstrate how to establish a supportive supervisory relationship and build rapport.

3. To define goals and boundaries of supervision.

4. To demonstrate how to identify supervision expectations and goals of the supervisee.

5. To illustrate how to address the developmental needs of a new counselor.

6. To show the start of a discussion on an IDP.

[*After brief introductions, the discussion begins about what will occur in supervision.*]

BILL: We're excited to have you here, Jan. You may already know that supervision is an essential part of how we help counselors in the agency. Since this is our first session together, perhaps we can explore what you want from supervision and how I can help you. Building on your training and experience, maybe you can give me some ideas about the areas where you wish to grow professionally.

JAN: Well, I haven't thought about that yet. I had excellent training and experience at the EAP [Employee Assistance Program] in the county health clinic. I'm not sure where to begin or even what I need. I recognize the need for supervision, certainly for orientation to the agency. I'd like to know about how much supervision I'll get and the focus and style of supervision here. I also need supervision to meet the requirements for licensure as a social worker.

BILL: I can understand that you're really excited about starting a new job and career. You had an excellent experience in your placement at the health clinic. I'd love to hear more about it, so perhaps you might tell me something about that placement, what you learned, and what treatment models they used there.

JAN: Wow, there is so much to tell you about that. I averaged ten clients on my caseload. Some were just assessments, but I did get to work longer term with several clients. I sat in on several counseling sessions, observed the senior counselor conduct the sessions, and co-led a group and several family sessions. I had weekly clinical supervision with my supervisor and the senior counselors. We used process recordings in school and that was really sufficient because I would write the verbatim, give it to my supervisor, she'd make comments, and we'd talk about it. So I didn't really need to have her watch me work. I've heard from Margaret [another counselor in the agency] that in supervision you do direct observation of counselors here and that idea is new to me. Frankly, I'm not sure if I really need that. My model for counseling is eclectic, whatever is needed for the client. They used a lot of cognitive–behavioral counseling approaches at the EAP. I try to meet the clients where they are and focus my therapeutic approach to meet their needs.

[*Discussion continues about Jan's experience at her placement and academic training.*]

BILL: So, we have a good sense of your background and experience. If it's OK, I'd like to return to the earlier question about whether you have any thoughts about what you want from our supervision together.

JAN: I'm not sure. Do all counselors here get supervision and are they all observed? I'm not sure I need that observation, especially since the placement didn't do that.

BILL: I appreciate your concerns about supervision. All our counselors here receive supervision. Some agencies don't do much direct observation of staff, but we've found it very helpful for a number of reasons. Here, we see supervision as an essential aspect of all we do. We believe you have a right to supervision for your professional development. We have great respect for our counselors and their skills and also understand that we have a legal and ethical obligation to supervise, for the well-being of the clients.

 Master Supervisor Note: Notice how Bill is laying the foundation and rationale for why clinical supervision is essential to this agency. Whereas every agency needs to develop its own, unique clinical supervision approach, there are models and standards of clinical supervision, as discussed in Part 1, chapter 1, which seem to be most effective. Agencies might benefit from adapting aspects of these models.

JAN: So, everyone must have supervision and observation?

BILL: We take our legal and ethical obligations seriously. We want all of our counselors—even the most experienced ones—to grow professionally, to be the best counselors they can be, for their own development and for the welfare of the clients. As you probably learned in your M.S.W. program, vicarious liability is an emerging issue for agencies. Counselors are legally liable for their actions. Vicariously, so are the agency and the supervisor.

We need to make a "reasonable effort to supervise."

JAN: OK, so what do you expect of me?

BILL: I'd like to explore that with you. I'm really interested in both what you expect of yourself and what you expect of us.

JAN: Again, I never really thought about that. I want to grow as a counselor and to develop skills that I can use in my future employment. I understood when I took this position that you do an excellent job of providing training opportunities for staff, something I really liked about the organization.

BILL: In our agency, clinical supervision is part of a larger package of staff development efforts. We try to help counselors improve their skills by offering the opportunity to work with a variety of different clients, using a variety of treatment modalities, such as individual, group, couples therapy, family therapy, and psychoeducation. Also, we want staff to be able to obtain their social work or substance abuse license or certification in the future. We want counselors to develop new skills by attending training both in-house and in workshops around the State. We encourage and support any efforts you might make toward professional development, such as getting your various levels of social work licensure. Our philosophy is that one of our greatest assets is our clinical staff and as they develop, the agency grows too. We believe clinical supervision is critically important in this mix. We both—you and the agency—benefit as a result.

[A discussion continues about Jan's course work in school and her training in the field placement, and how she can continue that learning in the agency. She articulates her clinical strengths.]

BILL: That sounds good. Those are the skills we saw in you that we thought would be helpful to our agency. In what ways do you wish to grow professionally?

JAN: I could learn other counseling techniques beyond CBT. What do you think I need?

BILL: That's what we can explore in supervision. I'll need to have a sense of what you've learned and where you see your skills. In addition to talking about your skills, we find it helpful to learn through observation of our staff in action, by either sitting in with you on a session or by viewing videotapes of counseling sessions. That way, we can explore your specific learning objectives. We all learn from watching each other work, finding new ways of dealing with clinical issues. What do you think of that process?

JAN: As I said, I wasn't observed in my placement and find it anxiety provoking. I don't really like the idea of your taping my session. It feels a bit demeaning. After all, I do have my M.S.W. I don't recall anyone saying anything in my interview about being videotaped. Now, that's intimidating, to me and the clients.

BILL: Being anxious about being taped is a fairly common experience. Most counselors question how clients will accept it. You might speak with Margaret and some of your other coworkers about their early experiences with taping, what it was like for them, and how they feel about it now.

JAN: How often do we have to meet for supervision?

BILL: Generally I meet each counselor individually for an hour each week. Then we do weekly group supervision where each counselor, on a regular basis, gets a chance to present a case and videotape, and we, as a group, discuss the case, and talk about what the counselor did well and how other things might have been handled differently. When you present a case, we all grow and benefit.

JAN: I want to be a proficient therapist, ultimately, to work as a private practitioner. If supervision can help me professionally, that's good.

Master Supervisor Note: It is important for Bill to be aware of what feelings are arising within him, particularly concerning Jan's seeming desire to pass through and use the agency as a route to private practice. This has happened to Bill and the agency before. Bill acknowledges to himself his feelings of being used by these clinicians in the past. Bill's self-awareness of these feelings is critical and he does not respond out of anger or resentment but makes a conscious effort to remain present to what the issues are with Jan.

BILL: I'm glad you see the value of supervision. And I admire your professional goals of wanting to be in private practice although I must say that I have difficulties with people just "passing through our agency" on the way to something else. But, that's my issue, and I'll address those concerns if they come up in our relationship.

Master Supervisor Note: In his own supervision, Bill might explore his feelings about people passing through the agency, his anger or resentment, and how he can effectively address those feelings. For example, Bill's supervisor might wish to explore with Bill the following questions:

1. What feelings does Jan bring out in you? When have you had these similar feelings in the past?

2. How do you deal with negative feelings about a supervisee?

3. How do you keep from being drawn into a defensive posture where you are justifying the agency's use of direct methods?

JAN: Will I be criticized by others, perhaps those without as much formal training as I have? I understand you have several nondegreed counselors here—certified addictions professionals, with lots of life experience but without advanced degrees.

Master Supervisor Note: A Level 1 supervisor might respond angrily here. A Level 2 supervisor might get into an argument about the quality of counselors at the agency. Bill, as a Level 3 supervisor, does not react to Jan's seeming criticism of the nondegreed counselors. He responds in a supportive but direct manner, as you will see. But perhaps Jan is making this comment in response to Bill's previous statement that he has "difficulties with people just passing through" and this is another reason for Bill to address this in his own supervision.

As discussed in Part 1, chapter 1, just as there are levels of counselor development, there are also levels of supervisor development. Level 1 supervisors might have a tendency to be somewhat mechanical in their methods, perhaps needing to assert their leadership and position, and approaching situations somewhat anxiously. This is especially so for supervisors who have been promoted from within the organization. Their peers, with whom they have worked side-by-side before, know they do not know their strengths and limitations, and hence the new Level 1 supervisor may feel that she has to assert her authority (see vignette 6). A Level 2 supervisor is much like the Level 2 counselor, who is driven by alternating anxiety and self-confidence and who feels the need to be independent, even though she might not as yet be able to act independently. Finally,

Level 3 supervisors have balanced their levels of self-awareness, motivation, and autonomy. For further descriptive information on levels of counselors and supervisors, see Part 1, chapter 1, pp. 9–11.

BILL: Perhaps it would be a good idea if you began by observing in one of my groups. Then, when you're feeling more comfortable with it, we can discuss what times work best for you to be observed, and what cases you'd like me to observe. This will give you time to schedule the observation. The first time, maybe I could sit in when you're working on a case that you have confidence about so we can see how you accomplish the session's goals.

JAN: OK, that makes sense to me. I like the idea of talking to others and getting their impressions of the process and their suggestions on how to best make it work.

BILL: We also need to develop a learning plan for you, an IDP that all staff have, so that you can continue to learn. That's part of a supervision contract that we work on together. How does that sound?

 Master Supervisor Note: It is important to develop an IDP for each supervisee, and counselors should understand why an IDP is important for the supervisory relationship. Jan's IDP might focus on:

1. Increasing her understanding of addiction by reading texts on the subject and beginning the credentialing process.

2. Discussing this material in supervision, in reference to clients in treatment.

3. Finding a social worker within or outside the agency who can assist her in fulfilling the requirements for her social work licensure.

4. Beginning direct observation of her counseling sessions within 2–3 months with monthly videotaping and discussion of a session.

JAN: It will be a new experience for me but it sounds like it might be helpful. I'd appreciate your helping me look at my skills and growing as a social worker in substance abuse treatment.

BILL: I'll provide you with as much background in substance abuse treatment as I can and also try to help you develop as a social worker to meet your career goals.

 Master Supervisor Note: Bill is working with Jan to establish a supervisory alliance, through listening, reflection, and mutual goal setting.

JAN: Good. I hope it will broaden my skills and further my career goals. I can learn more about working with clients' substance abuse. I think I can learn from people in other disciplines.

BILL: Although each discipline has its unique perspective, we have a multidisciplinary team approach and value each staff member's contributions. We teach one another. For example, Margaret has worked in this unit for 10 years and has a lot of experience working with the kinds of clients you'll be treating. She is a useful resource for you to use to improve your skills so that you can be successful here and in your career. How will that work for you?

JAN: I've heard about Margaret. People have a high regard for her clinical skills. So I'm sure I can learn something from her. I still would like some more details about how the supervision works, who else is involved, and how do we do this together.

BILL: We do individual observation and group supervision where we find common issues in our counseling, using videotape and case presentation to trigger discussion of related issues. Everyone learns from the presenter's experience. Each counselor takes a turn presenting a case, including a videotape. We can cue the tape to the session segment you want us to discuss. After your brief introduction of the case, we discuss how the session went, what skills were effective, and what areas might be further developed. How does that sound?

JAN: That sounds great. Can I come to you at other times to review cases, especially while I am learning the ropes of how things are done here?

BILL: Yes. I appreciate your wanting immediate feedback. I have an open-door policy. Although I may look busy, I'll try to find time when we can discuss whatever you want. You can also meet with others if you feel comfortable doing so. We encourage teamwork. Does that seem reasonable?

JAN: Yeah. I'm pretty autonomous at this point. I think it's great that there are other counselors and social workers I can collaborate with. It will be really helpful for me especially since I'm new at the job, and it's good to be able to work together. I'm OK with supervision, and I like the fact that we're both going to have an agenda, so that's fine.

BILL: So, let's go back to your experience. I'd love to hear more details about your internship and what you learned there.

[*Jan explains her work experience in her internship.*]

JAN: In my second year I was at an EAP clinic. I had a great supervisor, Jackie. Several of my clients were alcoholics, my first introduction to substance abuse. There was something that attracted me, to understand more about the disorder and to contribute what I was learning in social work. Jackie was a social worker and a really good role model. I need to understand more about substance abuse treatment, and try to marry the social work and substance abuse fields.

[*Bill and Jan continue to discuss her experience with supervision, what worked best, what she found most useful and supportive.*]

JAN: I'm a little worried about how I'll meet my licensure requirements about being supervised by a social worker. Will that be a problem for me?

BILL: Not at all. Margaret is an LCSW and we can ask her to provide the supervision you need for social work licensure. This will allow Margaret to develop her supervision skills. I also think that an important part of developing a professional identity is receiving coaching from an experienced person, and perhaps Margaret can assist in that area too.

JAN: That sounds fair and helpful.

BILL: You mentioned that Jackie was a good supervisor. Can you tell me what she was like and what she did that made her a good supervisor?

JAN: She was really smart. I could learn from her. When I went to talk to her she always gave me good advice. She trusted that I knew what I was doing and didn't micromanage me. She was open about her theories and made linkages to issues. She trusted me to just go ahead and implement what I learned. She was easy to talk to. If I had a problem, I could say so.

BILL: It sounds like Jackie and I have a similar orientation as supervisors, and that should make the transition easier. I hope you'll observe from your perspective how the supervision is developing, and give me feedback on the relationship, the process, and the outcomes from your point of view. Our first step will be to expand your training by introducing you to a broad range of substance abuse issues. Perhaps at our next session we can start developing a learning plan to apply your studies to clinical work. What do you think of that?

How To Write a Supervision Contract

The following elements might be included:

1. The purpose, goals, and objectives of supervision.

2. The context of services to be provided.

3. The criteria and methods of evaluation and outcome measures.

4. The duties and responsibilities of the supervisor and supervisee.

5. Procedural considerations.

6. The supervisees' scope of practice and competence.

7. The rewards for fulfillment of the contract (such as clinical privileging or increased compensation).

8. The frequency and method of observation and length of supervision sessions.

9. The legal and ethical contexts of supervision as well as sanctions for noncompliance by either the supervisee or supervisor.

JAN: That'd be good. I like that you're interested in my experience, about who I am. I'd like to know a bit about you. Jackie would talk about who she was, her model of supervision, and why this work was important to her. I felt I could trust her because I knew where she was coming from. Would you tell me more about yourself?

Bill: I'd be happy to.

[*Bill provides an overview of his work, academic experiences, and primary model of counseling and supervision.*]

JAN: I have a beginning understanding of the type of supervisor you are. I like that you're direct so I don't have to guess at the agenda. So, we'll work on a training plan and I'll suggest times for you to observe a session and videotape. Is that correct?

BILL: That seems fair and clear. Any other concerns we should talk about today?

[*Further discussion follows about Jan's anxiety about supervision. They discuss how supervision would work to help reduce her anxiety about being scrutinized and critiqued.*]

BILL: So, although you're a bit nervous about the process, you're ready to begin. We'll start with your observation of me to give you an opportunity to get your feet wet. Then you can tell me when you're ready for me to come in and observe, maybe in the next 6 or 8 weeks.

JAN [*jokingly*] I think sometime in the next 6 months.

Master Supervisor Note: As a Level 3 supervisor, Bill doesn't react to this comment. A Level 1 supervisor might respond by saying "The timeframe is not negotiable. You'll begin the observation in 6 weeks." Another response might be to avoid the issue without affirming her. When she is noncompliant after 6–8 weeks, he'd blame her for her lack of follow through. Such responses might negatively affect the relationship. A supervision of supervision issue might be to explore what was happening for Bill and his possible ambivalence about Jan.

BILL: Thanks for your willingness to begin and try the process.

JAN: OK. So, I can pick the client?

BILL: Yes. You can pick the client or group. We'll meet every week for about an hour.

[Bill and Jan set the time for the next supervision session and discuss what is expected for the next session and end the discussion with both excited about the process.]

Vignette 3—Addressing Ethical Standards

Overview

This vignette illustrates the role of the supervisor as a monitor of ethical and professional standards for clinicians, with the goal of protecting the welfare of the client. The vignette begins with a discussion about a potential ethical boundary violation and illustrates how to address this issue in clinical supervision.

Background

Stan has provided clinical supervision for Eloise for 2 years. He's watched her grow professionally in her skills and in her professional identity. Lately, Stan's been concerned about Eloise's relationship with a younger female client, Alicia, who completed the 10-week IOP 2 months ago and participates weekly in a continuing care group. Alicia comes to the agency weekly to visit with her continuing care counselor. She also stops by Eloise's office to chat. Stan became aware of her visits after noticing her in the waiting room on numerous occasions. Earlier in the day, Stan saw Eloise greet Alicia with a hug in the hall and commented that she will see Alicia "at the barbecue." Stan is aware that Alicia and Eloise see each other at 12-Step meetings, as both are in recovery. Eloise feels she is offering a role model to Alicia who never had a mother figure in her life. Eloise expresses no reservations about the relationship. Stan sees the relationship between Eloise and Alicia as a potential boundary violation.

Learning Goals

1. To illustrate monitoring professional boundary issues of counselors in clinical supervision.

2. To demonstrate supervisory interventions to help the counselor find appropriate professional boundaries with clients.

3. To help counselors learn and integrate a process of ethical decisionmaking into their clinical practice.

4. To demonstrate skills in addressing transference and countertransference issues as they arise in clinical supervision.

[After brief introductory comments, the discussion begins with how Alicia is progressing in her recovery.]

STAN: If it's OK, I'd like to share some concerns I have about Alicia.

ELOISE: Sure, I'm always ready for feedback.

STAN: When I walked through the lobby a few minutes ago I heard you say something to Alicia about seeing her at a barbecue.

ELOISE: Right. Sarah is one of my sponsees in AA, and we're having a barbeque at her house for some people in recovery. She and Alicia have gotten really close, so Alicia will probably go, too.

STAN: And that's a barbecue you might be attending?

ELOISE: Yeah. I'm fairly active with all my 12-Step friends and sponsees.

STAN: I would like to raise a concern I have about your relationship with Alicia. You take great pride in working with recovering people, helping them, and doing everything you possibly can to ensure their recovery.

ELOISE: Yes, it means the world to me. Alicia reminds me of myself when I was in early recovery. When I see her and how hard she's working, it inspires me because I know that struggle.

STAN: I'm pleased that you care so much about your clients and that you can identify with their struggles. I do have concerns though, when I hear you are going to see her at a barbeque. It seems like a possible dual relationship issue for you, and I would like to know what you think about this?

ELOISE: Well, I certainly know not to sleep with my clients, or borrow money from them, or hire them to mow my lawn, or take them on trips. But seeing Alicia at a barbecue? Come on, Stan.

 Master Supervisor Note: At this point Stan might be feeling somewhat defensive and may need to restrain his urge to begin disciplinary action against Eloise for her attitude. A Level 1 supervisor might react angrily to Eloise's tone of voice, seeing this as a clear disciplinary issue. A Level 2 supervisor might get caught up in an argument with Eloise about the extent of the violation. The skill of a Level 3 supervisor is to be clear with Eloise about what a dual relationship is without responding out of anger. As shown below, Stan needs to help her identify what a boundary violation is, how to make ethical decisions, and how to have this discussion in the context of a supportive supervisory relationship. It is important for Stan to help her be more aware in future situations with similar clients and dynamics.

STAN: I'm glad we agree on those kinds of extremes because dual relationships are a big concern of our agency and staff. A dual relationship occurs when a counselor has two relationships with a client, one personal, one professional. Our mission is to provide professional clinical services to clients. Within those services there is a scope of practice. When a personal relationship with a client or former client intrudes on that professional clinical service, then we may have a relationship that is considered outside the parameters of what's considered solely professional.

ELOISE: What I understand about dual relationships is that it . . . well, help me here. For example, I know I'm not supposed to hire anybody for any personal services or any form of exchange of money or buy anything from a client. If they've been a client here, I can't contract with them for private practice or anything like that.

STAN: Let's talk about your relationship with Alicia and what the intent is now. You want to do everything you can to build a safety net for her recovery. I appreciate your concern for her recovery. One goal of recovery is for the client to achieve a sense of autonomy and make decisions on her own, to take care of herself. You play a role. So, if we can, let's discuss what that professional role is, and what it isn't. When I walked through the lobby and heard you say "I'll see you at the barbecue," I had some concerns.

ELOISE: You mean I shouldn't say that in a public place?

STAN: My concern is whether going to a barbecue with a client is appropriate behavior, to have a relationship with her outside your professional relationship as defined by our agency. When I heard your remark, I thought, "I wonder what Eloise's intent was and where that's going or what might that lead to? Let me check it out to see if I am being clear."

ELOISE: Are you saying I shouldn't see clients in other contexts? How reasonable is that? We live in a small town here and run into clients all the time in the supermarket and at 12-Step meetings. So what are you saying?

Master Supervisor Note: There is a difference between a dual quality to a relationship and a dual professional and personal relationship. Dual qualities are inevitable in certain communities. A dual relationship has the potential for the abusive use of power, where harm might be done to the client through manipulation or inappropriate self-disclosure. Actions in one context might be acceptable, whereas in another they might be harmful. A skillful supervisor would help Eloise see this distinction and help her be better able to make sound ethical decisions concerning the line between dual qualities and dual relationships.

STAN: Great observation. Yes, we find ourselves in situations that potentially have a dual quality to them. The difference between running into clients in the supermarket and going to social activities together involves the potential impact that action might have on the client and our use of the power we have in the relationship. You were her counselor.

ELOISE: Yes, but I'm not her counselor anymore. She's in continuing care now.

STAN: Okay, but she's still a client of the agency. The ethical question is how long is a client a client? According to our substance abuse counselor's code of ethics, once a client, always a client in terms of our professional responsibilities.

ELOISE: Yes, but she just stops by when she's here. She pops in just to say hi, for not more than 5 minutes. I don't counsel her anymore.

STAN: Okay, that might be reasonable. Perhaps we can discuss that relationship and the impact of seeing her outside the agency at functions.

ELOISE: Well, she goes to the women's AA meeting that I go to. And she knows some of my sponsees. What should we do, leave our home group because clients attend the meetings also?

STAN: It is inevitable that we will run into clients at meetings. When does that cross over the ethical boundary and become a dual relationship? I'd like to hear your ideas about where you see that line for you.

ELOISE: I don't want to do the wrong thing, Stan, to hurt her. My intent is to be helpful.

STAN: Again, I know you don't want to hurt her, and I know you're trying to help her in her recovery. We have to be mindful of not being drawn into relationships that hurt the client or that could be perceived as dual relationships.

ELOISE: She doesn't call me or come see me. I want you to know I'm not sponsoring her. But I didn't know that going to the barbecue was wrong. So, I won't go.

Master Supervisor Note: Stan really wants to keep the focus on the larger issue of dual relationships. Once Stan and Eloise have clarified this larger perspective, then it might be more appropriate to come back to the specific issue of the barbecue. A more inexperienced supervisor might be tempted to just establish the boundary about socializing with clients with a comment like "That would be a wise decision (not to attend the barbecue)" but would possibly lose the potential of helping Eloise develop more effective ethical decisionmaking skills in the process.

It would, in effect, run the risk of making the decision for Eloise, rather than helping her come to an ethical decision on her own.

STAN: With your permission, perhaps we can talk about how we make ethical decisions about the nature of a relationship with a client or a former client, and what's not professionally appropriate. If it's okay, let's use the conversation with Alicia in the agency lobby. How do you think that conversation might be perceived by anyone who is walking by who hears you say you'll meet at the barbecue?

ELOISE: I've never really thought about it. Well, I guess if it was someone who didn't know me, they might think that I was personal friends with her. That's not a perception I want others to have.

STAN: So, you want others to see you as a professional, upholding boundaries and your code of ethics?

ELOISE: Yes, of course.

STAN: I reread the code of ethics to help evaluate whether or not there might be an issue. I was reminded of the power differential in all counseling relationships and that as professionals in our field we need to be careful to not engage in social relationships (or relationships that might be seen by others as social relationships) with clients or former clients. You may recall we recently had a lawsuit over dual relationships that put the agency in jeopardy. It got resolved in our favor but we're particularly sensitive about our liability. It was a wake-up call to all of us. So how can we clarify this boundary issue with your relationship with Alicia?

ELOISE: Wow, I never saw going to the barbecue as pursuing a friendship, and I certainly would not want to jeopardize our agency's relationship with her. I certainly don't seek any personal gain from our time together. Although I must admit, she does remind me of myself when I was in early recovery. Besides, she has never had a strong, positive, maternal figure in her life. That's something I think I can help her with. What do you think?

STAN: I admire your concern for her and it sounds like you are becoming aware of some maternal feelings for her that might be coming close to stepping over that professional boundary. When our relationships with others, and particularly with clients or former clients, begin to even have the possibility of affecting their recovery in a potentially negative way, then we might be edging close to an ethical boundary violation.

ELOISE: I understand, but part of my recovery program is being in touch with other people in recovery, other people from meetings, like Alicia.

STAN: I agree. It's important for your own recovery that you stay connected to other people in recovery. So, the question is: What's the difference between seeing people in recovery at meetings, such as your sponsees or your sponsor, and relating to clients active in treatment at our agency whom you encounter at a meeting?

ELOISE: Do I have to cut off all my recovery relationships and not go for coffee after meetings?

 Master Supervisor Note: It is important for supervisors to take into account cultural variables that might affect clinical relationships, such as differences in ethnic, religious, and geographic factors and their impact on the counselor–client relationship. This is not to condone unethical behavior but to be mindful of cultural issues as they affect the context of counseling. For example, in some Latino cultures some form of socializing may be expected. In Asian cultures, it is not uncommon for a client to ask the counselor personal questions as a means of establishing trust. Skillful supervisors assist counselors in understanding cultural variables while continuing to make sound ethical decisions.

STAN: I understand the dilemma we find ourselves in as counselors. We have to go on living our lives in our small rural community. So, how do we reconcile our daily lives with the Federal laws, agency policies, and our code of ethics? We need to be mindful of those boundaries just because of the closeness of our community. The interesting thing is that the clients are not bound by the same rules as we are. So, they might not see it as a boundary violation. In fact, as often as not, clients and former clients are flattered by contact with their current or former counselor and invite such relationships. How will we reconcile these differences? How do we know what the ethical wall looks like before we hit it?

ELOISE: Well, I guess we need to be careful about what contexts we see clients in, whether they are actively being counseled by us or not. Is that what you're saying?

STAN: Yes, we do need to be mindful of the various relationships we develop with clients. I'd like to use the barbeque as an example to discuss. Okay?

ELOISE: Sure. First, I have six sponsees. They've all been in recovery for different lengths of time, and they like to get together every 3 months, all six of them, and do some kind of activity. And they invite over a bunch of people from the 12-Step group. Sarah was having this barbecue and asked me because we go to the same home group. She also invited Alicia. I'm not sponsoring Alicia. Does that mean I can't go?

 How To Perform Ethical Decisionmaking

Stan's task here is to help Eloise identify potential boundary issues in a broader context and aid her in her ethical decisionmaking. The following are steps to ethical decisionmaking:

1. Recognize the ethical issues by asking whether there is potentially something harmful personally, professionally, or clinically. In what way might this go beyond a personal issue to the agency, the profession?

2. Get the facts. What are the relevant facts? What facts are unknown to us at this time? Who has a stake in the decisionmaking? What are the options for action? Have all of the affected parties been consulted?

3. Evaluate alternative actions through an ethics lens. Which options will produce the most good and least harm? What action most respects the rights of all parties? What action treats everyone fairly?

4. Make a decision and test it. If you told someone you respected what you did, how would they react?

5. Act, then reflect again later on the decision. If you had to do it all over again, how would you react differently?

STAN: It might help to ask yourself what happens for you when you find yourself in such a dilemma, to be your own problemsolver.

ELOISE: Well, it's hard to not go to social activities in this small community when I'm invited. But I can see how some might see me in a different light because I'm a counselor. At one party, someone came up to me and started to ask questions about problems in their marriage. I guess she figured that since I'm a counselor, she could get some free assistance. I was really uncomfortable in that situation.

STAN: What did you do?

Master Supervisor Note: At this point Stan might:

1. Have Eloise consider her own solution.

2. Use her solution in a dialog to expand the context so she can generalize the solution to other situations she may encounter.

3. Conclude with Eloise's restatement of what she has learned for the future from this discussion.

ELOISE: I told her I could not be her counselor and was there at the activity in my "civilian" clothes. [*Chuckling*.] Ah, I see what you're getting at. It's hard to be in two relationships, a professional and a personal one, with the same person. And I can see what you mean by how a reasonable uninvolved person might view this situation. At the party, when that woman wanted free counseling, it was clear that that was not the context or the relationship for that. That's unprofessional. But Alicia is different.

STAN: So, you see that it is unprofessional to counsel someone outside of a professionally defined relationship. I'd like to hear how it is different with Alicia.

ELOISE: Well, I really care for her. She reminds me of myself when I was younger. I am the mother she never had. I feel bad for her that she's never had a positive female, maternal role model in her life.

[*Eloise cries as she expresses her concern for Alicia.*]

STAN: This is difficult for you. You care very deeply for her. I can understand that in some ways she reminds you of yourself at that point in your recovery.

ELOISE: Yes, she does.

[*Her crying continues, and Eloise speaks of her concern for Alicia. After a few minutes, the two sit quietly.*]

ELOISE: The last thing I want to do is to hurt her or to act in an unprofessional manner.

STAN: I value your concern for Alicia and your desire to be professional. It is difficult when we care so deeply for our clients. We're asked to show empathy and caring for clients, and sometimes it can be confusing if we care too deeply. It's like, as caring professionals, we're always living close to that ethical slippery slope. We can retreat into "professional white coats" and separate ourselves emotionally from clients. But that turns counseling into a sterile activity, and we're detached and removed from their pain. But, when we care deeply, we are drawn into the emotional world of our clients. And the boundaries can become fuzzy for us.

ELOISE: I see what you mean. I guess we can rationalize a lot of our behavior when we care so deeply. We call that enabling behavior, don't we, when family members do that with the person in substance abuse treatment? So, how do we walk close to that ethical slippery slope without falling over the edge?

STAN: That's an excellent question. Ethical decisionmaking can be difficult at times. Intent is an important part of ethical decisionmaking.

How To Ask Questions in Ethical Decisionmaking

The following are key questions to ask at this point:

1. What would a reasonable person, counselor, or colleague do in a similar situation?

2. What are the relevant issues regarding justice, fairness, self-advocacy, non-malfeasance?

3. How would a person discern his or her intentions? How do you keep yourself from self-deception about your motives, remembering that the best test for your motives is time?

ELOISE: What do you mean by "intent?" It was my intent with Alicia to be helpful, certainly not to hurt her in any way or to be disrespectful of our agency or of me as a professional.

STAN: When we commit to a professional relationship with a client, there is always a power differential. When someone like Alicia comes with her need for a maternal figure, as you well described, we need to be careful of our role in offering to fulfill that need. The power differential alone can create some opportunities for people to misperceive what's going on. What do you think?

ELOISE: Can it be that I took advantage of her because of my own need to be a mother figure in someone's life?

STAN: That is always a risk we have. It could be perceived that way.

ELOISE: I feel bad that I wasn't being very professional with her and my own needs came out.

Master Supervisor Note: It is important to remember the power differential between supervisor and supervisee. How might key audiences (colleagues, the community, board of directors, the press, peers) see or experience the counselor's behavior? What is the risk? There are many stakeholders involved who each view the situation from their own perspective. For example, stakeholders (such as the board of directors) might be concerned about the risks of legal liability for the agency, the media and community with the public image of the organization, and peers with the clinical implications of a possible boundary violation.

STAN: That's a key insight. It's great that you could step back from the situation and see how your caring deeply for her spilled over in other ways.

ELOISE: You think I had power over Alicia?

STAN: As I said, when you're a counselor to a client, there is always a power differential that we have to be very cautious and very aware of. It may not be something we do so much as the power that the client gives us. Now, if it is okay with you, I'd like to summarize a little.

[*Stan and Eloise review what has been discussed and what actions might be appropriate for Eloise to take at this point. They express their concerns about Alicia and how she might be hurt if Eloise abruptly cuts off the relationship with Alicia. They strategize on how to best handle the situation in a way that would be clinically supportive of Alicia.*]

STAN: I want to talk a little about ethical decisionmaking and how we can keep within certain guidelines. There are some questions to be asked, such as how that behavior is experienced by someone else. How would your actions be perceived by colleagues, the community, a supervisor, and clients?

ELOISE: I appreciate your saying that; I need to think about it. It makes sense.

STAN: I'd like to review what we've discussed and your understanding of the issues.

ELOISE: I have a clearer understanding of how my relationship with clients after they're discharged is as important as when they are my active clients. I need to think and give more consideration to how that's perceived, to consider my role with clients from their perspective. In my relationship with Alicia, I've thought of myself primarily as a recovering person, but I need to remember that she may perceive me primarily as her counselor. In other words, I am wearing two hats—a counselor and a person in recovery—and I need to be clear which hat I am wearing and when those hats are on.

STAN: So you have a sense of the potential conflict of interest depending on what hat you're wearing and how that might be perceived.

ELOISE: Yes. I need to think about how that reflects on the agency and how the community sees it.

[*The supervision session ends with Eloise making a commitment to rethink the relationship with Alicia and strategies for making ethical decisions in the future.*]

Vignette 4—Implementing an Evidence-Based Practice

Overview

This vignette portrays supervision of two counselors at different levels of experience and orientation to implement an evidence-based practice (EBP) into their clinical work. Both counselors have reservations about adapting the way they practice and have some resistance to undertaking the new EBP. The clinical supervisor has to address their resistance while achieving the mandate of the agency.

Background

The executive director (ED) of a mid-sized substance abuse treatment program has issued a statement to all staff that, according to State requirements, the agency must incorporate EBPs, now a necessity for State funding. Therefore, the ED has directed the three clinical supervisors to begin the implementation of MI as a primary treatment method for treatment staff, first on a pilot basis then agency-wide. Gloria, one of the supervisors, is meeting with Larry and Jaime, two program counselors, to discuss implementation of MI with their clients. Both Larry and Jaime are aware of the mandate but have not had an opportunity to discuss the change with Gloria until their regularly scheduled supervisory session this morning. Both have, in the last year, expressed some resistance to undertaking a new treatment approach when they were required to attend MI basic training.

Learning Goals

1. To demonstrate leadership by a clinical supervisor toward meeting agency goals and mission.

2. To demonstrate leadership in the face of staff who are resistant and reluctant to incorporate EBPs into their counseling.

3. To model MI in the supervisor/supervisee relationship.

4. To illustrate fostering a spirit of learning and professional development among counselors.

5. To illustrate how a clinical supervisor can help counselors build new clinical skills, especially those that are science-based practices.

6. To understand the resistance and impediments in the field to the implementation of EBPs.

GLORIA: I know you have some reservations about the MI implementation program. Today I want to spend time discussing your reservations and how MI can be good for our clients and for the agency. You have both done a tremendous service for our programs. We want to be responsive to your needs, not just impose something on you. When you've been doing a good job and you know that what you're doing works, it's hard to take on something new that you're uncomfortable with. I know that you're concerned that taking on something new could, at least initially, potentially interrupt the normal flow you have with clients.

So, there are several things that I think are important for us to consider today. First, let's review why we are implementing MI for staff as a tool in their counseling. Perhaps we can explore any concerns you might have, then review why it is important to implement MI.

Second, let's look at your concerns about how those changes might affect client care.

Third, let's focus on how we can keep the strengths you have with your clients and be sure they don't get lost in the transition process. One of the beauties of MI is that it integrates well with what good counselors do naturally: active listening, respect for others' views, an appreciation of the role of resistance, good goal setting practices, and the like. Most important, MI aids in establishing and enhancing the therapeutic alliance between the counselor and the client.

Finally, I want to spend a little time talking about where we go from here and how we are going to make the implementation process as smooth as possible.

How To Introduce Changes in Clinical Practices

Changes in counseling methods are difficult for staff who are attached to their model of counseling and know that it is working for them. When presenting new policies and directions to staff, it is important that you follow these guidelines:

1. Be respectful of staff's resistance. Instead of exhorting, arguing with, or threatening the counselor if they do not "play ball," seek to understand the counselor's concerns with words such as "Yes, this is difficult. So how can we resolve the issue?"

2. Show respect for counselors and for the experience each brings.

3. Depending on the individual counselor, you may need to be flexible yet firm in your approach with staff who are expressing resistance to or ambivalence about change, being clear that the change is needed yet allowing time for the person to adjust and providing the resources needed to aid the counselor in making that change.

4. Recall when you were in the counselor's role and perhaps how you experienced resistance to change in supervision.

5. Consider using self-disclosure to address defensiveness with supervisees. You can either give an example from your own training or experience, such as, "I know it was difficult for me too when I was a supervisee," or by describing your own ambivalence in the present, such as, "I also have concerns about the change we have to undertake and want to ensure that it works in the best way for clients, now—what can I do?" These self-involving statements can engage supervisees in the discussion and problemsolving.

LARRY: Well, Gloria, we've had the MI training, and I like its focus on active listening, the attention it gives to the relationship and respect for the client's perspective. But, you know, I'm basically a 12-Step facilitation guy. That works for me and for my clients. I don't see changing horses in the middle of the stream to achieve political correctness.

GLORIA: Your 12-Step approach works for you, and we heartily endorse it, too. 12-Step facilitation is an essential part of everything we do at the agency. And I definitely don't want to see us throw out the baby with the bathwater. As you know, counseling is an ever-evolving process, and I think our task is to be able to take what we do well and build on it with new approaches. I think MI can add to your repertoire. I think your concerns are realistic, and we need to consider that as we move into adopting new methods. What about you, Jaime?

Master Supervisor Note: At times a supervisor might feel caught in the middle, representing policies and procedures coming down from funding sources, yet posing implementation difficulties. An effective supervisor plays this dual role of advocating for both administrators and leadership and the line worker and client. Whether working on a factory floor or in a clinical setting, it is difficult being in the middle. To aid you in this position, it is helpful to:

1. Understand the rationale of both administrators and line staff.

2. Never lose sight of where you came from. At some point in your career, you were a supervisee. It is useful to remember what it felt like being in that position.

3. In the example of MI, practice reflective and active listening to understand the concerns of those above and below, and to empathize with each group's concerns.

JAIME: All of this discussion is really above me. I just want my Latino clients to get good care and for their treatment needs to be respected. My clients need decent jobs and to be accepted as Latino men being sober in their community. That's what's important to me. I just want to serve my clients. I know that may not be what you want to hear, but that's how I feel.

Master Supervisor Note: A Level 1 supervisor might respond either in a defensive or overly directive fashion here, telling Jaime that this is something he must do. A Level 2 supervisor might get into a struggle over what really matters, defending MI as good for Jaime's clients, or disrespecting his statement about what matters most to him, his clients. A Level 3 supervisor listens to Jaime's statement, affirms and supports him in that, and tries to engage Jaime in the discussion. Further, Gloria is working with two counselors at different levels of proficiency, so she has different expectations for their contributions and recognizes that they have different learning needs. An effective supervisor understands the stages of counselor development and varies the approach depending on the stage of each staff member.

GLORIA: Jaime, I respect your commitment to the Latino clients. Larry is clear about one of the things he knows works, 12-Step facilitation. In your experience, what works with Latino men?

JAIME: I'd agree with Larry, 12-Steps, because I go to AA myself, and I know AA works. But what's also important is jobs, not feeling discriminated against, not being asked for ID papers if you've lived here all your life. What helps is to be with a group of sober men. That's what helps my clients.

GLORIA: You both seem to be clear on what you see works for you and your clients. That's a good start for us. As you know from the recent ED's memo to staff, the State has required all agencies to implement an EBP to continue to receive State funds. There has been a lot of discussion at all levels about this. We've talked before about our desire to move from being a good agency to a great one, being one of the best in the State. Over the past year we've made incredible progress toward this goal, thanks to all the staff's efforts. And all through this process, we've been able to stay true to our 12-Step philosophy. Honestly, when I first heard about the new State policy, I, too, was skeptical, saying to myself, "Here we go again." But then I was reminded of the agency's mission to keep improving our skills for the well-being of the clients. So, discussing this together now is helpful. I'd like to hear more from you about your concerns regarding MI.

LARRY: I don't really give a darn about MI versus CBT versus 12-Step facilitation versus the next thing to come down the pike. I've been in the field for a long time, and I know what works is my relationship with people. I know 12-Step works, and I have to be convinced that this doesn't interfere with having a strong relationship with my clients. I think that's the most important thing. I'm not sure I need a new way to do this. I don't want to have to be worried about whether I have to use this science-based thing.

GLORIA: Wow, Larry! I really hear that the most important thing to you is building strong relationships with your clients, and it's not so important what method you use to build strong relationships, but that the method helps you accomplish that goal. Perhaps we can look at how MI's approach to active listening with clients and reflection enhances that relationship. If it builds the therapeutic alliance with the clients, that's good. I'm curious how you feel about that.

LARRY: What I want to be sure of is that we're not moving away from our roots: that this is not taking us away from 12-Step. That's what this agency is founded on, and that's what we stood for all these years. I need to hear that from you.

GLORIA: That's a really excellent point. How do MI and other approaches keep us close to our roots of 12-Step work? What do you think?

LARRY: If an approach builds the relationship with the client, I'm all for it. I know that 12-Step facilitation does that. And I know from the course I took on MI that it also emphasizes the counselor–client relationship. But it is also a new way of thinking and a whole new vocabulary and I don't want to get so bogged down in catchy phrases that I lose contact with my client.

GLORIA: Larry, I clearly hear your concerns about interfering with your relationship with your clients and about us losing our roots.

LARRY: Maybe Jaime can do the MI stuff and I can do my 12-Step facilitation.

JAIME: What?

GLORIA: There are several different ways we can approach the implementation. We may decide that MI works better with some client populations than others. A place to begin would be for us to learn more about how MI can be implemented in the program. I know you've been to the MI training. That's a great start. MI has some good strategies that are congruent with a variety of client populations.

LARRY: What I heard you just say is that it doesn't matter whether we're on board or not.

GLORIA: That's a dilemma. The State's said, "You have to do it." What they haven't said is how you have to do it. They said we have to do "something." We have something to say about how we're planning this, how we'll implement an EBP. I want to be sure that we hear and use your experience.

Master Supervisor Note: It is helpful to watch how Gloria handles the polarizing confrontation. A Level 1 supervisor might either come down hard on Larry for his suggestion, saying "No, we're not doing that." A Level 2 might argue about it. Note the Level 3 approach, not to confront the statement by Larry but to find a working alternative.

A master supervisor is able to manage staff confrontation and avoid becoming defensive. To do this, it is important for the supervisor to understand that struggle is a sign of staff ambivalence to change. Resistance and ambivalence are normal in any situation involving change. A master supervisor works with the resistance, using its energy to promote change, not taking it "head-on."

LARRY: I like the idea that we can implement the strategies that work best for our agency because that allows us to stay close to our roots of 12 Steps.

GLORIA: So you see the value of implementing an EBP approach such as MI as long as it stays close to our 12-Step roots. Moving ahead, I recognize that this is going to change some of our approaches, how we think about treatment, how clients experience us.

LARRY: How are we going to do this implementation anyway? Who's going to do the implementation, train us in MI?

GLORIA: Perhaps I can show a videotape of a counseling session I conduct when I think I am doing effective MI. What do you think of that idea? Would that help us all feel more comfortable with an EBP? I'm willing to stick my neck out if you're willing to give me feedback on what you see on the videotape.

Master Supervisor Note: A basic rule of supervision is "do not ask a supervisee to do something you're not willing to do first." A second rule is that "leaders bear pain, they don't inflict it." Master supervisors are willing to take a risk by demonstrating their skills first before asking staff to do so. Effective supervisors are able to establish trust by serving as a team leader, inspiring staff by encouragement and motivation, communicating enthusiasm and capability, and taking appropriate risks to initiate change. Leaders also demonstrate vision, drive, poise under pressure, and maturity of character. They inspire rather than command staff. Since leadership entails teaching, mentoring, and coaching, having the title "supervisor" does not necessarily make a person a leader. To earn respect, the supervisor should display qualities of honesty, responsibility, fairness, and understanding. In this vignette, Gloria provides direction and leadership by showing staff how they can implement MI together and how the training will work. She also gives them a say in the process and allows them to keep to their roots, learn new tools, and do so over time.

GLORIA: That's a good question about implementation. Any approach we use needs to be respectful and build on the counselor–client relationship. So let's start there. First, we want to implement MI over time. It's not something that we'll become instant experts at. I want to make sure that we're well prepared and understand what we're doing.

[*Larry and Jaime nod in agreement.*]

GLORIA: Again, let's be clear. We need to implement EBP for State funding. Remember when the agency went smoke free: How difficult that was, how much resistance some staff expressed? But, it was something we just needed to do, and in the end, being smoke free has had significant health benefits to staff and clients, and has reduced the health care premiums for all personnel. I'm interested whether you see the similarity to such changes.

LARRY: Yes, I do. The smoke-free campus has been a real benefit to all. I hope implementing an EBP is also.

GLORIA: I agree. Maybe we can return to the training issue you raised earlier. Larry and Jaime, with your help and support, I'd like to establish a year-long training plan. First, I'd like to have an advanced trainer come in and provide several days more of training that particularly addresses the needs and concerns of the staff. We'd also like to contract with the trainer to establish an MI coding system that will be part of what we do in our clinical supervision. Over the year, we'd continue our direct observation for supervision. Only now we'd look at the interactions through the MI lens. The coding system will help us in doing so.

JAIME: I remember hearing about coding in the basic MI course I attended. Can you tell me more about that?

GLORIA: Here is a coding sheet that the trainer of that course recommended. I like the form and find it simple and easy to use. I also think it's consistent with what we do as counselors, and it reinforces our efforts to listen better to clients. As in 12-Step facilitation, it helps to build an alliance with the client.

LARRY: So you're convinced this is a good thing? You're not just doing this to get State money?

GLORIA: From what I know about MI and have read about it, I think MI is a very useful tool for us. We're concerned about our funding, of course. But, client welfare always comes first. No, we would not be doing this simply for money. I believe this will help our clients, and that's the bottom line, isn't it? So, perhaps we can discuss the skills we have as a team and how to proceed.

JAIME: I think we work well together and we seem to have good stable funding that allows us to maintain the quality of care we offer to our clients.

LARRY: Yes, we have good teamwork and support each other. Jaime and I work well together. We've got a lot of respect for each other. We've had the basic MI training. That's a good start.

GLORIA: Teamwork is important.

LARRY: We do good treatment. Our clients respect us. We have good credibility out there. That's a plus.

GLORIA: I'd also add that we have experience at successfully implementing changes.

JAIME: Three years ago we had few Latino clients and no Latino program.

GLORIA: Implementing a Latino program was a major positive step forward. The other thing I like is that we have a good supervision system which helps us assess how we're doing when we implement any new practice or program, like the Latino program. It gives us a way of assessing quality.

LARRY: So, what's going to change here?

GLORIA: We do have time for more training. It's difficult jumping into a new approach if we don't feel like we're adequately prepared for the change. One solution would be for us to devote more time in our normal clinical supervision sessions (individually and in group) to MI practices, to use videotapes and role plays to continue our learning and practice our skills. We can phase in MI over time. I'm committed to supporting you in whatever you need to do your job effectively. More than 150 studies have shown that MI is effective; this will enhance our skills and give us better client outcomes. It might be helpful for us to talk to an agency that uses MI and ask how they did it. We need to do training, as I said earlier, so we can be consistent with our core approach. I want to integrate this in a way that makes sense for all of us. Perhaps between now and our next meeting you'd think about two things you can do to help us write the implementation plan that will show how we're going to do this. We have an excellent team and do good work. I value and trust the work that we do. Learning a new strategy requires training, mentoring, and coaching. Our relationships with the clients and each other are the most important because that's how we serve the clients.

[*A discussion follows when they discuss the training system, who might serve as a consultant for the advanced training, and how the coding system works and can be incorporated into the clinical supervision system. The session ends with a mutual commitment to move to the next stage of implementation.*]

Vignette 5—Maintaining Focus on Job Performance

Overview

In this supervisory session, a counselor with marital problems carries this stress into the workplace. She feels overwhelmed by the complexity of her caseload, misses work, and cancels patient appointments. Observe how the supervisor must address the counselor's job performance, provide emotional support for the counselor, and, at the same time, not get involved in the counselor's personal life.

Background

Juanita has worked as a counselor at the agency for over a year and brings a number of valuable attributes to her job. She is bilingual, understands the stresses and cultural dynamics faced by recent Central American immigrants living in the United States, works well with female clients, and gets along well with other staff. Her husband is a recovering alcoholic, and Juanita has been active in Spanish-speaking Al-Anon. She recently received her addiction counselor credential.

Since receiving her license as a substance abuse counselor, Juanita has been given new job assignments that involve working with more complex and difficult clients. She now conducts educational and support groups by herself, does intake interviews, provides individual counseling to her caseload, and has recently increased her caseload to accommodate the increased number of clients at the agency. She is also seeing several clients with co-occurring disorders.

While she is friendly and outgoing with others, her natural response to stress is to withdraw and isolate herself, rather than ask for help. To Melissa, her supervisor, Juanita seems more tentative and less energetic in their supervision sessions. She seems to be meeting most of her work performance goals established in the supervision, but the quality of discussion about her cases and her lack of vitality in the meetings concerns Melissa.

In the past month, Juanita has come late to work on a number of occasions and missed several client appointments. She has called in sick three times in the last 3 weeks. In supervision, she seems distracted, which is a change from her prior behavior. Melissa, in her concern, asked in supervision "is everything OK?" Juanita replied, "No, Jorge has been laid off his construction job, and he has been drinking." She explains that she is quite distressed, having trouble sleeping, and feeling overwhelmed. Though clearly worried, Juanita did not elaborate, and Melissa did not pursue the questioning. Juanita did ask if she could talk to Melissa at another time to discuss her personal problems and to seek Melissa's advice on how to handle her current situation at home. Melissa was uncomfortable agreeing to this but also was uncomfortable not responding to Juanita's distress. She hesitatingly said that they could discuss this at the next supervisory meeting.

In the upcoming supervisory session, Melissa feels it is important to clarify the differences between providing help for personal problems and maintaining supervision goals. Melissa also thinks it is important to address Juanita's job performance issues in the next meeting.

Learning Goals

1. To illustrate how work-related stresses and personal problems can interact and affect one another.

2. To demonstrate the boundary between clinical supervision and personal counseling.

3. To demonstrate how to help an employee get the help necessary to address personal (non–work-related) life problems that affect the work environment.

4. To illustrate how to monitor and maintain adequate clinical performance when an employee is facing difficult personal dilemmas that affect job performance.

5. To demonstrate awareness of and sensitivity to cultural issues that arise in the context of personal issues that affect job performance.

[*The vignette picks up with the beginning of the next clinical supervisory session.*]

MELISSA: Juanita, hi! Come on in. Before we start talking cases today, I would really like to go over some of what we discussed last week and see where things stand.

JUANITA: That's fine, but I think I owe you an apology about our last session. I really want to apologize for saying all those things to you about my family and how that is affecting me and all that, and I just want to apologize. I know it had nothing to do with anything work related. We were doing supervision and should just have talked about cases, and I just want to assure you that that will never happen again.

MELISSA: Well, Juanita, I'm sorry you have to cope with all that's going on, but I don't feel you need to apologize for anything last week. I know that what's happening is stressful to you. I hope we can work out a plan to help you get the help you need and also be sure that the pressures you are experiencing don't spill over into your work with clients.

How To Address Personal Issues That Affect Job Performance

Consider the following points when you need to confront a supervisee in clinical supervision with problems of job performance that are exacerbated by personal difficulties, such as emotional, familial, interpersonal, financial, health, or legal concerns:

1. You can help your supervisees see the relationship between their personal difficulties and work-related problems. The key question you need to return to is "How is this personal issue affecting your job performance?" This prevents you from becoming the counselor's counselor and turning supervision into therapy.

2. You can clarify the boundaries of what constitutes acceptable job performance, as some counselors may be uncertain where the boundaries lie.

3. You should continually focus on approaches to improve job performance, providing useful suggestions and recommendations for improvement. It is also

helpful to provide measurable benchmarks by which counselors can assess their own improvement.

4. You and your supervisee should develop a written work plan for how the employee will take the necessary steps to improve job performance.

5. You can help the counselor examine how personal stressors might affect interactions with coworkers or clients.

6. Finally, you and your supervisee can explore how you and the agency can support the employee in confronting and resolving personal issues that are affecting job performance, such as a referral to the EAP, use of personal or sick time, rescheduling of the counselor's time, and the like.

JUANITA: I appreciate that. I just want you to know that that's not me. That's not me.

MELISSA: And I appreciate that, and I want you to know that I value your work. You've worked hard. You've really worked hard in learning not only your job, but also as a professional counselor and you've made a valuable contribution to working with our clients.

JUANITA: I love my job. I love it.

MELISSA: Juanita, I want to be really clear with you that I am concerned about what is going on in your personal life, and I want to work with you to get help for that. I don't feel that it's something that we should address in supervision though, except to the extent that it affects your job performance. The goal of our supervision time is to help you to be the best counselor possible. When personal issues come up, those may keep you from being the best *person* you can be. These are important issues for you to address in your own personal counseling and therapy. I hope that distinction is clear for you. But I really want you to hear my concern for you.

 Master Supervisor Note: Although the distinction between personal counseling and supervision may be contingent on the supervisor's theoretical orientation, and both are interpersonal relationships, there are differences between the two, as summarized in the table below.

Personal Counseling	Supervision
1. The goal is personal growth and development, self-exploration, becoming a better person.	1. The goal is to make the counselor a better counselor.
2. Requires exploration of personal issues.	2. Requires monitoring of client care and facilitating professional training.
3. The focus of exploration is on the origins and manifestations of cognitions, affects, and behaviors associated with life issues and how these issues can be resolved.	3. The focus is on how issues may affect client care, the conceptualization of the client problems and counseling process, and accomplishment of client goals.

To help the counselor and the supervisor differentiate between therapy and supervision, the supervisor needs to continually ask him- or herself, "What does this have to do with your counseling functions? How is this affecting your relationship with clients?"

JUANITA: I'm still kind of worried that I told you about my personal life, but I do want to be the best counselor I can be.

MELISSA: I'm concerned about the time you have been missing from work and especially the times you have had to cancel patient appointments as a result of your situation at home.

JUANITA: I know I've missed a couple of sessions, but I called. The clients were okay with me rescheduling, and I've continued to meet with them. I don't think there's any problem. It was the first time I ever had to reschedule those clients, and we caught up on their visits later in the week.

MELISSA: I hear that you were concerned about missing some sessions so you made a strong effort to reconnect with your clients later. I really appreciate your effort. I had a chance to review a videotape of a session you did last week. I'm pleased with the skills you've developed in group counseling. In the middle of the session we videotaped, there were some issues that came up about men that I thought might be a concern and might illustrate what we're talking about. Can we view that section of the tape and discuss what was happening for you at that point?

JUANITA: Sure, if you have the tape there.

[*Together, Juanita and Melissa watch the tape, cued to the segment about clients actively drinking while in treatment. Juanita appears surprised to see her response to the client on tape and notes the impact she might be having on clients. For example, there was an interaction between Juanita and a male client in group where she saw herself being judgmental and overly critical. Melissa and Juanita continue to discuss the tape and the meaning of counter-transference in the counseling relationship. From the discussion of being angry at clients who continue to drink, Juanita becomes aware that the sessions she has cancelled with clients were all with drinking men.*]

MELISSA: I'm glad you can stand back objectively and see the relationship between your personal issues and your clinical functioning. So, what do you think you need to do now?

JUANITA: Well, first maybe I shouldn't see any more male patients?

MELISSA: That is an option. But I think we can find a better resolution. For right now, let's focus on what else needs to change.

JUANITA: Well, I just won't cancel any more appointments. I didn't realize rescheduling was such a problem. But I just won't do it anymore. And about the missed days, I think that is beyond me now. If I need a day off for personal reasons, I'll schedule them in advance from now on.

MELISSA: OK. I think I would like you to go through me for the next few months if you need either time off or if you have to cancel patient appointments. I know emergencies happen, but just let me know if you need time off and we'll see where we go from there.

JUANITA: I understand. I am so sorry that my personal life is intruding on my counseling. I never thought that would happen. And I'm going to get back to my work. I'm going to make sure I get the paperwork and everything done, and I will be on time tomorrow.

MELISSA: Let's put the paperwork aside and talk about your work with the clients and what you need to do to maintain your high level of work performance. Let's get back to the countertransference. I'd like to hear more about the clients you work with. Let's go back to the videotape and discuss what else is happening in the session.

JUANITA: Basically, I've moved into working with some of the more difficult clients in the last several months. It's been very challenging developing plans with them and encouraging their attendance and working with their treatment plans on a more active level because I'm definitely sensing the resistance.

MELISSA: So, not only are you working with more complex clients but you also have a higher caseload than you had not so long ago. So your job responsibility has increased significantly recently. I think you'll see some different features of supervision as you continue to see clients with more complex problems and as you begin to work in other treatment modalities, such as group. Let's discuss how you're dealing with the more complex clients.

[A discussion follows, using the videotape, about how Juanita has been working with these clients, some of her concerns about working with clients with more difficult co-occurring disorders, some specific points about counseling interventions and her countertransferential reactions to men who are drinking. She acknowledges that her reaction to the client who has relapsed is in part a response to her current life situation with her husband. Now that Juanita recognizes where her work is being impacted by her personal issues, Melissa returns to the issue of the EAP and re-introduces the possibility of a referral.]

 Master Supervisor Note: It is important for the supervisor and counselor to understand the impact of countertransference in a counseling relationship, including:

1. It can distract from the therapeutic relationship.

2. A counselor's personal issues may contaminate how he or she sees the client's issues.

3. The counselor may distance him- or herself or avoid discussion when the client's issues come too close to home, or conversely, the counselor may focus on client issues that resemble her own.

4. The counselor may have negative reactions to the client, based on the counselor's current life issues, as Juanita did with the men in her group who were actively drinking.

MELISSA: Juanita, you may remember that, as part of your professional development plan, we talked about a personal care plan: knowing when you need support and where you could get it. Your Al-Anon program has been a strong support for you, and you've used it in a very effective way. I'm wondering if you have used or would consider using our EAP to help you address the crisis you are experiencing now. I think it would be helpful if you had the opportunity to sit down with someone and assess how things are going and what could help. I hope you'll use our EAP for that. As you know, using the EAP is optional. I'm not mandating that you go. But if you think it would help, I hope you'll take advantage of it. This booklet has some information about the EAP and how to access their services. As you know, the EAP is strictly confidential, and nothing is reported back to the agency. I'm also wondering how I can be of support to you.

JUANITA: Just be there for these sessions. Just be there as the supervisor when I come and have questions. I'll call the EAP this afternoon. Do you think they would also be willing to help Jorge if he is willing to come with me?

MELISSA: The EAP is for the whole family, and I'm sure they would be available to see Jorge too, either with you or separately. I'm glad you are going to follow up on that.

Master Supervisor Note: Note that Melissa doesn't ask Juanita to report back to her about using the EAP. The EAP referral is to address personal life issues that are not the concern of her employer. It is Melissa's role to monitor job performance and to use all of the resources that are available to help Juanita improve her job performance. In most organizations, an employee's use of the EAP is not the concern of the supervisor. The focus of the supervisor needs to be on improving job performance. Statements such as "Let me know if you use the EAP" are not within the supervisor's scope. Remember, the goal of clinical supervision is not necessarily to make the supervisee a better person, but a better worker. It is tempting for clinical supervisors to focus on the personal issues of staff—after all that's what they do for a living. However, personal issues are a part of clinical supervision only insofar as they affect the counselor's interactions with clients.

[Melissa and Juanita continue to discuss some of her cases and her efforts to work with more challenging clients. At the end of the supervision session, Melissa and Juanita schedule two sessions in the coming week for Melissa to sit in on Juanita's sessions again. Melissa reaffirmed that she hoped Juanita would consider using the EAP to address some of the issues in her personal life.]

Vignette 6—Promoting a Counselor From Within

Overview

In this vignette, a counselor has been promoted from within a work group to a supervisor position over the counselors she worked with as a peer. Issues addressed include how the new supervisor handles staff resistance and works to build a new relationship with the counselors she will now be supervising.

Background

Kate has been a counselor at the agency for 3 years. She, Maggie, and Kevin have worked together as outpatient counselors, supervised by Gene, who left the agency last month to take another position. Kate has a master's degree in counseling, is licensed as a drug and alcohol counselor and, for the past year, has been taking continuing education courses to develop her supervisory skills, hoping that a supervisory position would open up in this or another agency. But the courses only gave brief reference as to how to work with and supervise counselors who last week were her peers.

Maggie has worked at the agency 2 years longer than Kate, is a licensed drug and alcohol counselor, recently completed her bachelor's degree and has started working on her master's degree. She understands that Kate got the promotion partly because of her advanced degree but still feels she was treated unfairly in the selection process because she has been with the agency longer.

Kevin, also a counselor, is in process of becoming licensed. He has a bachelor's degree and has worked in the field for about a year. He has concerns that someone who was a counselor and his peer last week can be an effective supervisor for him now. He likes Kate and has turned to her numerous times for advice and support, but wonders about her competence as a supervisor.

The agency director announced the promotion yesterday afternoon and suggested to Kate that she meet with Maggie and Kevin soon. The director offered to sit in on the meeting, but Kate declined, feeling that she would rather discuss the promotion and changes alone with Maggie and Kevin first. Since everyone had appointments already scheduled for the morning, lunchtime was the first available opportunity for the meeting.

Learning goals

1. To demonstrate how a new supervisor can establish a leadership position and demonstrate a leadership style with former peers.

2. To show how a new supervisor handles the potential conflict of her promotion over others with whom she has worked.

3. To give some guidance to recently promoted supervisors to clarify their roles, develop opportunities to learn new supervisory skills, and establish rapport with supervisees.

[*Kate, Maggie, and Kevin meet over lunch to discuss Kate's new position.*]

KATE: Thanks for being willing to sit down with me and discuss how we are going to proceed in face of the changes that were announced yesterday. I'm pleased with the promotion and excited about getting my feet wet in this new role. I hope we can work together to continue doing the good job we have been doing.

[*Long pause while Kevin and Maggie wait for Kate to proceed.*]

KATE: I hope you see this as an opportunity for all of us.

[*Another pause while Kate waits expectantly.*]

KEVIN: Well, Kate, it's going to be strange having you as a supervisor. Gene and I had a good relationship. He was my boss the entire time I've been here, and I learned a lot from him. I knew there were going to be changes. I guess I'd rather see you or Maggie get the promotion rather than having someone new come in from the outside. This is quite a shift. Two weeks ago, when Gene announced he was leaving, all three of us were in group supervision together. Now you're our boss.

[*Another pause.*]

KATE: Yes, Kevin, it seems strange for me too, I have to admit. I've enjoyed our collegial relationship. I've learned from you and appreciated your input too. I've even enjoyed our "grousing sessions" when we've felt overworked and underpaid. [*Laughter.*] And I know there is going to be a shift in our relationship, but I still want us to see ourselves, as well as new staff, as a team, focused on the best patient care we can offer.

 Master Supervisor Note: It is important for new supervisors who are promoted from inside not to try to be something they're not. Everyone knows you don't know the job. Don't try to fake it. Instead, acknowledge to staff that this is new, that you have things to learn, and that, with their assistance, you can work as a team. The worst mistake you can make as a new supervisor promoted from within is to try to take the reins of leadership abruptly and without consideration of staff reaction to your promotion.

KEVIN: I'd like to hear about any changes you are planning or how things might be different now that you are running the show.

KATE: Great question, Kevin. In the past, we've all sat around in the lunchroom and spoken of what needs to be different in the agency. Now, together, perhaps we have an opportunity to make some of those changes. For example, we've spoken before about how we'd like to streamline the paperwork process. I know we're all buried in forms. How can we reduce the strain of administrative tasks we all face? How do we deal with our burnout? So much is asked of us, and that places great strain on us. We've spoken about that together, how tired we can become. How can we take better care of ourselves and of the team?

But, I want that process to unfold together. I need your help and input. Also, I want a few weeks or a month of breaking in time before any changes are made. So, perhaps we can sit together as a group and think about what needs to be different. I will then "run those changes up the flagpole" with the director and do what needs to be done to bring about the changes we deem necessary. How does that sound to you?

 How To Demonstrate Leadership

It is important for a new supervisor to demonstrate leadership without being controlling or condescending, especially if promoted from within. Perceptions of quality leadership have shifted from the traditional hierarchical, command-and-control model to a networked, team-based approach that values participative leadership and staff empowerment, bottom-up management, team input, and collaboration. Qualities of this leadership style include:

1. Taking responsibility for decisions made, never blaming others for something you've done, and giving credit to others when things succeed.

2. Always putting the well-being of supervisees above personal accomplishments.

3. Not being afraid of taking appropriate risks that are in the best interests of the organization, staff, and clients.

4. Protecting and advocating for supervisees, defending them to senior administrators and buffering them from rapid changes.

5. Not playing favorites. Most important, not giving orders just to prove who's boss. If you have to prove who is the boss, you are not.

MAGGIE: I have to say that I'm not very happy about this. I met with Gene and Susan [the agency director] about ten days ago and expressed an interest in applying for the position. I didn't hear a word until I found out yesterday that you got the job. I want to be clear that I'm not upset with you. I'm glad for you, but I'm not happy about the way this was handled, especially how Susan made the announcement. It makes me wonder how decisions are really made around here.

KATE: I think if I were in your situation I'd be unhappy too. It doesn't feel very good when there's no communication. I understand that you were interested in the position. I am sorry about how the communication was handled.

MAGGIE: Like I said, I'm not upset with you, but with Gene and Susan. I felt disrespected after my years of service to the agency. That really doesn't feel very good, like not being valued.

KATE: Yes, it feels like you should have had some communication at the least, and not have been surprised by the decision.

MAGGIE: Yeah, it feels lousy. I wonder what my future is with the agency: if I'll be passed over for other promotions. And, quite honestly, I regret that I didn't go back to school and finish my degree years ago, if that's required for a supervisory job. It makes me angry though, because they never told me that education would be a deciding factor. I don't even know what the criteria were for the decision.

KATE: Maggie, I can sure understand your feeling that way. And to be honest with you, I think I would have felt much the same as you do if the decision had gone the other way. I'm sorry that's the way this happened. If it would be helpful to discuss your concerns with Susan, either together or alone, I'd be willing to help you with that.

 Master Supervisor Note: It would be easy for Kate at this point to triangulate the communication, making Gene and Susan "the bad guys." However, Kate skillfully identifies Maggie's feelings, provides self-reflection on how she'd feel if in a similar situation, without polarizing the process and the others involved.

KATE: In the future, perhaps we can make suggestions to administrators on how we'd prefer the process and communication to flow. How could this situation have been handled differently? What would have been more helpful to you, Maggie?

[*A healthy discussion follows between Kate, Kevin, and Maggie about how to improve the communication process in the future. Maggie feels like she has a voice in the process and feels listened to and understood. Kate asks Maggie what she needs now.*]

MAGGIE: Thanks for this conversation and for your concern. Let me think about what I want to do now and what I need. Can I get back to you on that?

KATE: Sure, we can discuss it when you're ready.

KEVIN: I'd still like to maintain our friendship. I understand it is going to be a little different, for instance, calling you "boss." But the three of us have had a good thing going here. It's been fun for this last year. I want to keep that.

MAGGIE: Our friendship has been fun: something I've treasured, too. As you say, things aren't going to be the same. Kate is the supervisor now. And when we hire a new counselor, you are no longer the new guy on the block. More is going to be expected of you.

KATE: I am going to miss some of what we have had together too. It would be hard to act as if we're peers and then have any objectivity when it comes to management decisions. We'd risk claims by others of favoritism. So, as hard as that will be for me, I'll need to stop doing as much socializing as I did before. I don't understand fully what I mean by that, but I know things will be different. I also will experience a sense of loss of some of my clinical duties. I'm giving up some of the real satisfaction that I found in counseling, working with clients. And I'm swapping that for new tasks. So I likely will also go through some grieving as well.

KEVIN: Thanks for your honesty, Kate. This means changes in a number of ways, for all of us. Kate, I have confidence you'll do a good job. Although you'll have to get a new wardrobe and dress more like a manager. [*Laughter.*]

KATE: Thank you so much for your patience and understanding. I was nervous coming into this meeting, given how this all unfolded. I feel like we're heading in the right direction. How do you feel we're doing so far?

MAGGIE: I appreciate your listening to my venting and I think you understand how I'm feeling.

KEVIN: I am cautiously optimistic, which, for me, is saying something positive. After all, you know what a cynic I am. [*Laughter.*]

KATE: You, a cynic, Kevin? No way! [*Laughter.*] There's one more thing I would like to address before we stop today: how we proceed. Gene had a really good system in place for clinical supervision. I would like to return to that system and schedule that includes the efforts Gene was making to improve our supervision process. What do you think?

[The discussion continues about what to do in clinical supervision, returning to the effective system formerly in place.]

 Master Supervisor Note: It is important to move forward, saving what was working before, not seeking to make radical, hasty, drastic changes. Also, this is an opportunity for Kate to demonstrate leadership by not languishing in the present situation, not "badmouthing" administrators for how this decision was made, while also acknowledging the emotional and professional concerns of staff.

[The session ends with a group decision to move forward in their clinical supervision.]

Vignette 7—Mentoring a Successor

Overview

This vignette illustrates the process of mentorship as a supervisor faces retirement and needs to mentor a successor from within the agency. Mentorship is an urgently needed process in the substance abuse field as a significant number of current leaders in the field face retirement in the near future.

Background

Margie is a certified clinical supervisor with 25 years' experience in the field. She is in her early 60s, has worked at the agency her entire career, and is, in fact, the longest term employee at the agency. She is approaching retirement in the next 2 years. It is agency policy to promote from within whenever possible.

Betty has been in the field for 10 years and has been employed by this agency for 3 years. She is an excellent counselor and is well respected by colleagues in the agency. She has the potential to be promoted to Margie's position as clinical supervisor. However, she has professional development issues that need to be addressed before she could be promoted. For example, she would need training in clinical supervision skills and eventually will need to get her certification as a supervisor. She also has a managerial style that needs to soften a bit. She sometimes comes off as too authoritarian and abrupt. Previous attempts by other supervisors to address this style have not been successful in changing the behavior. Margie has worked with Betty for 3 years as her clinical supervisor but without a mentorship training plan.

The vignette focuses on how Margie can mentor her successor and the next generation of personnel so they could be promoted upon her retirement. The vignette addresses the necessary systems of mentorship that can be involved, what ought to be in Betty's IDP, and the coaching Margie will provide to Betty.

The dialog begins with a discussion about current and future personnel issues and Margie's pending retirement. Margie's goals in this session are to begin to define Betty's learning needs, to establish a mentoring relationship, and to pave the way for Betty to be accepted as a supervisor by others in the agency. Margie's approach is to be a positive, supportive coach and to encourage Betty to begin the professional development and training required to be a supervisor.

Learning Goals

1. To illustrate how to design a mentorship program for personnel, including the writing of mutually agreed upon IDPs for potential successors and all clinical staff.

2. To illustrate the process of establishing a supervisory alliance that incorporates principles of mentorship and training.

3. To suggest how to develop and maintain a strong collaborative and professional supervisor–supervisee relationship.

MARGIE: Betty, as you know, I'm beginning to wind down my career and am looking forward to retirement in 2 years. Our agency strongly believes in the idea of fostering our own leaders and promoting people from within. You and I have had a great relationship over these past few years. I've seen your skills and feel you have great potential to grow professionally and as an important professional in this agency. Your clinical skills are excellent, you always complete your paperwork on time, and you're a joy to supervise.

 Master Supervisor Note: It takes a Level 3 supervisor to be able to mentor someone else. Level 1 and 2 supervisors might find it difficult to let go of the reins, to essentially work themselves out of a job, and might feel threatened by helping others develop to their own level of competence. A Level 3 supervisor needs superior vision: the ability to look ahead and see what's needed for the sake of the agency and staff. This requires maturity, serenity, and wisdom.

BETTY: Thanks so much, Margie. That really feels good. I really like my job and would like to continue working here.

MARGIE: I hope you continue working here. You're a great asset to the agency. You've just implemented some innovative ideas, and you're enthusiastic about the work. Whenever I ask you to take on an assignment, you're always the first to complete it. I like that. You've worked hard to become an excellent counselor. So, I'd like to have an idea where you want to be in 5 years. Would you be willing to discuss that with me?

BETTY: Sure. I hope I'm still here. I like the clients, my colleagues, and this agency. I like that I get to try new things. You've been supportive of that. This is a place where I'm able to make a contribution to my community.

MARGIE: So this is "home" for you: That is so evident. It's working really well for you. Perhaps we can discuss what's ahead for you. What would you like to be doing differently here in the future?

BETTY: I don't know. I'd like to continue to improve my counseling skills, maybe even advance up the ladder a bit. I think I have good individual and group counseling skills, but I also know administration involves another whole set of competencies.

MARGIE: You're right, there are different skills in administration and that's important to recognize. And I'm excited that you want to move up.

BETTY: Oh, that scares me a bit. I like seeing clients and wouldn't want to become a paper-pusher, not that that's all you do. [*Laughter.*]

MARGIE: I like that you want to stay anchored in clinical work. I think that is important and I appreciate your concern for clients. That's one reason you're so good at counseling. You have a real caring and compassionate nature for the people you work with.

[*A discussion follows about Margie's job and what it means to be in a supervisory position at that agency. Margie outlines the roles and requirements of being a supervisor.*]

MARGIE: Another way to look at your contribution to clients and legacy in counseling might be in the fancy word used by Erik Ericson, who spoke of "generativity": getting to a stage of life when you want to give something over to the next generation of people to follow you. You're having a great impact now on your clients. As you progress into a supervisory role, you have the potential of affecting even more clients and staff, as you train and supervise counselors.

BETTY: What do you mean?

MARGIE: Remember years ago in school? Can you recall any teachers that left their mark on you, people that helped you become the professional you are today?

BETTY: Yes, there were many.

[*A discussion follows about these mentors and how Betty benefited from their teaching.*]

MARGIE: As you supervise, you have the opportunity to touch more people's lives. Yes, there is more dreaded paperwork. But, at the end of my day, I go home with a rich sense of legacy that I've had the chance to touch even more people's lives as a result of being a supervisor, even more than I might have as a counselor alone.

BETTY: Yes, I see that in you. You've had a profound impact on my life and that of so many counselors here.

 Master Supervisor Note: One of the most effective ways to lead is by example. Mentorship should include something of attraction; people should see something in you that they want. "Whatever she has, whatever she does, I want to have and do that." People are imitative; they find role models they want to be like. So, when mentoring, use personal examples for the potential to grow and impact on others. It is important to identify the qualities and characteristics of a positive mentor and role model for staff, such as eliciting, rather than imposing, their judgment; drawing ideas from the supervisee, and being positive and affirming.

Mentorship is a special kind of professional growth opportunity, differing from other supervisory models. In mentorship, the mentee asks questions, shares concerns, and observes a more experienced professional in a safe learning environment. Through reflection and collaboration, the mentee can become more self-confident and competent in his or her integration and application of the knowledge and skills gained. Mentorship addresses the unique needs, personality, learning styles, expectations, and experiences of each person. Mentorship can be defined in numerous ways. One definition is a working alliance offering regular opportunities for discussion, training, and learning to occur between less experienced and more experienced people in various settings, addressing practical, hands-on work experience to enhance the knowledge, skills, attitudes, and competencies of everyone.

MARGIE: So, perhaps we can discuss how you can increase your skills, both clinically and in supervision. This is the beginning of our developing and updating your IDP. One place to start would be for you to attend clinical supervision training. There are online courses, self-study programs, and classroom programs. I have a list of upcoming training events. I'd encourage you to take a look at these options and see whether you'd be interested in one of them.

BETTY: Sure, of course. I'm always open to training, especially if it's held on the beach, in a nice location. [*Laughter.*] Will the agency pay for the training? You know a counselor's salary will only stretch so far.

MARGIE: Yes, it would be part of your IDP. We fund professional development as much as possible.

BETTY: Thanks for the vote of confidence.

MARGIE: Further, I'd like you to start doing more staff training, using your clinical experience and conducting sessions for other staff.

BETTY: You mean like some of the presentations I do in the community, to staff here? That's a little intimidating, presenting to my peers.

MARGIE: It can be intimidating, presenting to people you work with.

BETTY: I assume you'll help me with that?

MARGIE: Yes. I also think you have the potential to present at State and national conferences. This would expand your repertoire of material, hone your speaking skills, build your confidence, and help you become better known outside the agency. We know you're good. It's time for others outside to see in you what we see.

BETTY: Really?

MARGIE: Really. I have a call for papers for a counselors' conference in Cincinnati this fall. I think you should submit a proposal. The conference's theme is PTSD and substance use disorders. I've heard you present here at the agency on this topic. The people attending the conference will be your peers. That's a good place for us to take another step in the mentorship process, and you can begin with an area where we know you're especially strong. I'll attend the conference, too, and we can discuss afterward how it went for you. I'm interested if you've ever thought of being acknowledged outside of the agency for what we all know you know.

BETTY: If I'm really honest with you, yes. I've gone to conferences and thought "I can talk on that subject." But it's always seemed immodest to say that out loud.

MARGIE: Yes, it's difficult stepping forward, not wanting to seem arrogant, but also acknowledging that you might have something others would benefit from hearing. So, how about putting your thoughts together for a proposal? It's due in 3 weeks. You and I can review the proposal together. I'm confident it will be accepted for presentation. When it comes to your actual presentation, you can do the outline and slides and we can discuss your ideas.

BETTY: So is this what you meant by mentorship?

MARGIE: It's a good place to start. I'll never forget my mentor, Todd. He saw in me something I couldn't see in myself at the time. He believed in me when I was feeling uncertain and insecure about my abilities, when I wasn't even sure I wanted to stay in counseling for the rest of my life. He got me to do things I didn't think I could do. He made me really stretch and taught me some invaluable lessons I still remember. Perhaps I can discuss what I mean by mentorship. Would that be okay with you?

BETTY: Sure, I want to hear.

MARGIE: Well, this is my own view and from my own experience, but it seems to me that mentorship is when someone with more experience and professional maturity helps someone coming along to want to reach out for more and develop new skills. There are lots of new opportunities for mentorship that weren't available just a few years ago. Mentorship is different from our supervision relationship. Together we can identify areas of growth for you, and then we'll meet to discuss what we need to do so you can achieve your goals.

BETTY: I am honored (and a wee bit embarrassed) that you see that potential in me, and want to invest in my professional growth. I'm not sure anyone else has expressed that interest to me before. I'm really flattered.

MARGIE: It has been an honor for me to work with you these last 3 years. It also gives me great joy to see you grow professionally, and perhaps advance into supervisory and administrative positions here in the future. Speaking nationally will give you better exposure. We'll start with that, if that's okay. Then we'll move on into other areas that we identify together on your IDP.

BETTY: Okay, if you really think I can do this.

Master Supervisor Note: One of the four foci of supervision is supportive, which includes at times cheerleading and encouragement. Often counselors may lack the confidence in themselves to step forward. Supervision should build on strengths, nurture assets, and support and encourage all personnel to grow. Identifying staff with high potential for advancement is a key function of a supervisor. Through mentorship, personnel can grow professionally, and leadership succession can become a key aspect of the organization and field.

MARGIE: You can help our agency. We will see the scope and the focus of how you want to shape your career as it moves on.

BETTY: And you would be willing to make that kind of investment in me, Margie?

MARGIE: I sure am. The agency surely is.

BETTY: You know how exciting this is? I am fluttering inside.

MARGIE: It's exciting for me too. I enjoy seeing staff use their potential to the fullest. It's something I can leave behind when I retire that will last far beyond my years of service. It's like looking into the eyes of children and seeing the future in them that I will never realize myself. If I can help mentor you and others, that will be the icing on the cake of my career.

BETTY: If I can grow to become a representative of the agency and to work more closely with you and learn from your experience and your wisdom, I'd love that.

MARGIE: Here are some other ideas where you might consider growing professionally: learning about leadership, creating a vision, business and financial management, continuous quality improvement, organizational development, conflict resolution, and on and on. I know that might all sound rather intimidating at this point, but there are many areas we can address. I'll be there with you throughout the learning and mentorship process.

[*Discussion continues about the next steps for Betty. First, they arrange to begin to revise and update her IDP and the strategies to reach her learning goals. The supervision session then turns to the future needs of the agency and how Margie and Betty can be part of the evolving future. The session ends with an agreement to begin writing an IDP and decide on the next steps for their mentorship.*]

Resources on Mentorship

ATTC Leadership Institute (http://www.nattc.org/leaderInst/index.htm). After an assessment of leadership and management interests, values, and skills, participants attend a 5-day training session designed to present the necessary body of information. With their mentors, participants develop an individualized training plan and individualized project. They then return to their organizations for 6 months of mentoring and working on their projects.

Michael E. Townsend Leadership Academy (http://www.mhmr.ky.gov/mhsas/files/KSAODSCatalog.pdf). A 3-day onsite workshop continues in followup sessions throughout the year in this program sponsored by the Kentucky Division of Mental Health and Substance Abuse.

South Carolina Addiction Fellows Program (http://www.addictionrecoveryinstitute.com/Southcarolina/welcome.htm). Participants meet in six 3-day sessions during the year.

North Carolina Addiction Fellows Program (http://www.addictionfellows.com/). Twenty participants meet to create a group of leaders for the field in North Carolina.

Vignette 8—Making the Case for Clinical Supervision to Administrators

Overview

This vignette illustrates how a clinical supervisor can justify a system of supervision, along with time and resource allocations, to agency administrators in the light of recent pressures from the administration to increase billable hours. (Clinical supervision is not a billable expense at this agency.)

Background

Ella, a Level 2 supervisor, was recently hired to be the clinical supervisor of this agency, overseeing the work of six counselors. Jonathan is the agency's CEO and Ella's immediate boss. Jonathan has directed Ella to maintain supervisory functions "the way your predecessor did." Jonathan does not want to introduce any significant tasks into the workload, especially those that are not billable or revenue generating.

Ella, on the other hand, recently attended a 30-hour class on clinical supervision and is seeking her certification as a clinical supervisor. During the class she learned the importance of "making a reasonable effort to supervise," and the legal and ethical obligations of the agency to supervise. She learned about her and the agency's vicarious liability for the actions of the clinical staff. In the class, Ella was given the 20-to-1 guideline: for every 20 hours of client contact, staff should receive a minimum of 1 hour of clinical supervision.

Until now, staff has received primarily consultation and support with case management. To justify more in-depth clinical supervision, Ella needs the support and endorsement from Jonathan of the new supervision system. Given his emphasis on billable hours and reducing nonreimbursable activities, Ella knows that introducing these changes in the agency will not be easy, but she comes to Jonathan with her plan for supervision, asking for his endorsement.

Learning Goals

1. To describe the benefits and rationale of clinical supervision.

2. To design a system of supervision that is efficient and effective, without greatly increasing staff and supervisory time and resources.

3. To explore a system in which the supervisor can balance management and administrative duties, maintain a clinical caseload, conduct training, and perform other duties as assigned.

[*The vignette begins with a meeting between Jonathan and Ella to discuss her supervisory tasks and her plan. After a short introduction in which Ella discusses her feeling of being overwhelmed by her tasks, the dialog continues.*]

JONATHAN: The last time we met you were to look at how to improve the quality of our counseling and design a new plan for supervision. What did you come up with?

ELLA: Well, first I looked at what makes us a quality agency: our strengths and skills and our weaknesses and liabilities. We want to be the best agency possible. There are four issues that came to me. First, after the client suicide last year, concerns were raised about our liability as an agency. Even though we took the right action, we need to be mindful of our vicarious liability for what our staff does. I think we're both concerned about that issue.

Second, we're now required by the State to eventually have all counseling staff be certified addiction counselors. Our accrediting body is pushing us to provide better quality assurance systems with more clinical supervision.

Third, I know our organizational development plan calls for us to expand services in the near future. We need to attract high-quality counselors. That's difficult in a highly competitive market, with many agencies vying for good staff. We've had significant staff turnover in recent years for several reasons. I found that the average tenure of a counselor in our agency is 2 years, which, by the way, is consistent with the national average. We know from the exit interviews that the majority of staff who leave complain that we didn't provide as many good training and supervision opportunities as other agencies do to support their learning and self-care needs. It's costing us a lot of money to have such high staff turnover.

Finally, we need to increase our billable hours. Research tells us that the better the supervision, the better staff morale and in turn, the better the client services. This has a direct impact on our bottom line if we retain clients in treatment longer.

[*Ella gives Jonathan copies of various studies she's compiled from her training on the cost of staff turnover, the CSAT Manpower Study* (CSAT, 2003), *and a synopsis on staff development issues from the agency's development plan.*]

Master Supervisor Note: Notice how Ella is well prepared for her presentation to Jonathan, providing a rationale in language and terms that appeal to administrators: concerns about liability, credentialing of personnel as mandated by the State, staffing needs and turnover, and billable hours. When presenting a proposal for a clinical supervision system to senior administrators, it is wise to:

1. Use terms and language that apply and appeal to administrators

2. Be prepared with facts and figures (e.g., the CSAT Manpower Study)

3. Be clear, direct, and succinct; most administrators value clarity, directness, and results-oriented presentations

4. State clearly the goals, objectives, timelines, and costs for the system and have the data to support them

JONATHAN: Wow, I'm impressed. You've done your homework. So, what is it you're suggesting? You know money is a key issue right now.

ELLA: Money *is* an important issue. I'm suggesting that we look at our current supervision system and that we design and offer a new system that will help counselors become credentialed, meet the requirements of our accreditation body, reduce our high turnover rates, protect our liability concerns, improve morale, and in turn, bring more money into the agency.

JONATHAN: That's a tall order. And you're going to do this without spending any money? [*Laughing.*] Let me go back to what you said. I thought after last year's suicide that we beefed up our oversight.

ELLA: Yes, we trained staff on how to deal with suicidal ideation and what actions to take. We were really sensitive to suicidal symptoms and documentation of issues. We have done a good job addressing that issue. However, I have concerns about our liabilities in general. What is going on right now that we don't know about? What are our counselors actually doing behind closed doors? Is there another legal issue waiting for us that we don't know about? That's what I mean by our vicarious liability. Without a sound, consistent system of supervision, it will feel like we're constantly putting our fingers in the dike.

Master Supervisor Note: When conceptualizing, justifying, and implementing a new comprehensive supervision program each level of staff—agency administration, supervisory staff, counselors providing direct services, and support staff—have unique concerns about the needs and effects of clinical supervision. Administrative staff are most likely to be concerned about some of the issues noted below:

1. Legal and ethical requirements for supervision, such as vicarious liability, scope of competence and practice requirements, and recent court rulings requiring clinical supervision. It is useful to stress the agency's fiduciary responsibility to ensure the quality of services provided.

2. Relevant Federal, State, and credentialing or accreditation requirements for supervision.

3. Staffing costs, such as personnel retention and turnover rates, hiring costs and expenses associated with retraining of personnel, and impact on staff morale. It is useful to provide any research data available in the field or from your agency.

4. Costs associated with implementing a supervision system, such as material and time costs and the impact on billable hours.

5. The cost benefit for implementing a supervision system, addressing: "What's in it for the agency? Why should we do this? What are the ramifications and costs if we don't?"

6. A timeline for implementation, with dates and deliverables, including benchmarks to measure success.

It is important that support in the form of data or relevant resource materials supplement these points.

JONATHAN: I agree. Are you telling me we're not doing our job? That our supervisors are not supervising?

ELLA: Our counselors are working very hard. We have fine staff here. Yet, we've got to give them more tools to do a better job, to continue to enhance their skills, and to ensure they recognize what they don't know. And, as we grow, the skills needed by staff will also grow.

JONATHAN: We're not doing that now? We have money in the budget for training. We send people to summer institutes every year. We have weekly training sessions. Isn't that supposed to address those issues?

ELLA: It does, but only partly. Much of what we do in these sessions is administratively oriented, addressing new policies, procedures, and paperwork, compliance issues, and personnel concerns. We're not doing *clinical* supervision.

JONATHAN: I'm confused. Maybe I don't have a good understanding of what clinical supervision is. I thought that's what we were doing. Are we better off than we were a year ago? I need to assure the board of directors that we're doing a better job, that the legal concerns of last year have been addressed.

[*Ella presents a brief and clear description of what clinical supervision is and how it differs from what they have been doing, which is primarily case management.*]

ELLA: We've made significant progress. You can assure the board of that. We've minimized some of our legal risk. We've addressed compliance issues. That's good! When you asked me to look at a quality assurance plan, it was clear our weekly staff meetings and training sessions only address some of the needs. We must increase our clinical oversight of staff. That's not just administrative in nature. In the course on clinical supervision you sent me to, I found a definition that I think really makes my point. First, clinical supervision is a process where counseling principles are transformed into practical skills. Second, there are four focuses in clinical supervision: administrative, evaluative, supportive, and clinical/educational. We've addressed the administrative aspects of supervision well. We now need to increase the amount of evaluation we give staff, support them in their clinical duties, and train them by watching them work with our clients more closely.

 Master Supervisor Note: In many agencies, administrators may not have a clinical background and thus may not understand the differences between case management and clinical supervision. A skillful supervisor patiently educates administrators about the distinction and stresses clinical concerns.

JONATHAN: I think I understand the difference. I'm not a clinician so I am not always familiar with terminology. So what are you proposing we do?

ELLA: I need your endorsement and support for a system of supervision involving direct observation of counseling staff, so we shift the balance of our supervision from mostly administrative to include a clinical focus, too. The supervision will address each counselor's skills, what competencies they need to develop further, and how each can best address the needs of the clients.

 How To Demonstrate the Importance of Administrative Support for Clinical Supervision

An individual developing a clinical supervision program for an agency clearly needs to explain to an administrator what is being asked of the organization. It is essential that administrators understand and support the supervision system. Without that endorsement, supervision systems will not be successful. Critical steps in this process include:

1. The endorsement of supervision to all staff should be both verbal and in writing.

2. Clinical supervision systems need the support of staff at all levels of management and in a manner they will understand: how it will benefit them, the agency, and the clients.

3. Staff should hear a consistent message about supervision over time, lest they see the supervision system as the current "flavor of the month," and believe "this will pass as soon as another priority comes along." Staff need to hear that administrators have a long-term commitment to a consistent program of quality assurance in their supervision program.

4. It is essential that administrators understand that systemic change takes time. Although some immediate results will be seen, long-term results can best be measured over the long term. Many staff have settled into their ways of doing counseling and might take time to adjust to receiving clinical supervision and make noticeable improvements in their skills.

JONATHAN: This is making me nervous. It's sounding like money. [*Laughing.*] You know the pressure we're under to increase billable hours and decrease activities that don't generate revenue. Now you seem to be adding more activities and expenses. Where's the time coming from to do this?

ELLA: I understand the concern about increasing expenses. There are two answers. Remember the oil commercial years ago, that went something like: "Pay me now or pay me later, but you're eventually going to pay me." We're paying a lot for staff turnover and decreased productivity because people are feeling unsupported by administrators. Staff morale is lower, too. If we can provide better training and supervision, we can save the agency considerable expense. Second, if we can train our staff better, we can perhaps increase both the quality of our care and the number of clients we can serve. That goes right to the bottom line.

JONATHAN: Are you sure you didn't get an M.B.A. somewhere along the way? You sound like a business person. Are you saying we're not as productive as we might be? Isn't that an administrative issue if people are not doing their jobs?

ELLA: If we support them further, they could do an even better job. Our counselors are excellent at what they do. They work very hard and for long hours. Often that leads to burnout and eventually staff turnover. If we reduced that burnout through supervision, we'd keep them here longer, and their treatment of clients would improve. That would help our credibility in the community and eventually lead to more services and revenue. "Pay me now or pay me later." The choice is up to you.

JONATHAN: Okay. So what are you proposing, and what will it cost?

ELLA: For an agency our size, with only a few counselors, two clinical supervisors can do the job. At the same time, they can attend to some administrative issues too, in addition to their own clinical work. At the training, I learned of a system where a supervisor would spend about 3 hours a week supervising her counselors. Some of the time is observation, and the rest is individual and group supervision. I can show you the matrix we'd use to do this. Each counselor would be observed in action with a client at least once a month. The supervisor would meet with the team every week and review the case presented by the counselor of the week. We'd use videotape of counseling sessions to demonstrate the counselor's skills and actions. The group would view sections of the videotape, and we'd have an hour-long discussion of the tape. In some cases, instead of videotaping (it may not be appropriate to videotape some clients), the supervisor would sit in on the actual session and observe. They'd then follow the same individual in small group supervision discussion. To do this, I need you to provide funds to purchase video cameras, tripods, and DVDs. We need $1,000 for this purchase. That will ensure we're making a reasonable effort to supervise and will significantly increase our clinical supervision system here. What do you think?

How To Implement a Clinical Supervision System

To clarify the above statement by Ella, if a supervisor oversees the work of one to five counselors, it typically requires 2–3 hours per week (see Figure 3 on p. 11). This entails relying on group clinical supervision and direct observation through audio- or videotaping or live supervision. Supervisors might need to provide additional time for close supervision of trainees, interns, or counselors needing specific attention. The critical aspects in rolling out a clinical supervision system include:

1. Administrative support. This should be in the form of both written and oral communication to all personnel showing administrators' support for clinical supervision.

2. Training of supervisors. Credentialing organizations require a certain number of hours of training to be certified as clinical supervisors. Simply because

a person is a good counselor does not qualify them to be a supervisor. It requires another body of knowledge and skills to be a supervisor.

3. Educating staff about what quality supervision is and what to expect in the new system. A session for clinical staff should be held (1–2 hours duration), explaining the rationale for supervision, the policies, procedures, techniques, and expectations of supervision.

4. A system of supervision of supervision, monitoring the progress of supervisors in implementing the system, and providing feedback on how they are doing. This is sorely lacking for most supervisors, at least initially. This can be done through internal supervisors overseeing other supervisors, peer supervision of supervisors, or externally by contracting with a master supervisor to oversee the work of supervisors.

5. Consistency of the message that supervision is here to stay and that clinical supervision is a requirement of the agency.

6. Time to implement the system, acknowledging and working through staff resistance to change. Attitudes and behaviors about supervision change slowly. Thus, administrators need to understand that it takes time to work with personnel, to be clear about what's expected of them, and to overcome staff resistance.

JONATHAN: We can do that. That's a modest expense we can afford. How do I sell this to the board?

ELLA: What did the potential law suit cost us last year in legal fees? Surely more than the cost of three cameras. What does it cost us to train a new counselor when someone leaves? Surely more than the time we're investing in their training. Perhaps you could tell that board that if we can retain a staff member for 6–12 months longer, we'll save the agency far more than you've invested in supervision. By being careful, by providing quality supervision, in the long run, it will in fact save us money by being preventive.

JONATHAN: What else can I tell the board about this supervision system?

ELLA: You can tell them that when a counselor leaves, clients react and the quality of their care decreases. The board is interested in client satisfaction and treatment outcome. This supervision system will help with that.

JONATHAN: Okay, I'm sold. What's next?

ELLA: First, I want to submit to you this plan I've developed for the supervision system. I'd ask that you read it and next time we meet, if we concur, I'd like a written statement from you endorsing the plan. I'd also like you to introduce the program at our next all-staff meeting. How does that sound so far?

JONATHAN: That's fair. Then what?

ELLA: Second, we need funding for the equipment. Third, we need to identify potential supervisory candidates from within the organization. If none can be found, we will have to look outside the agency to recruit a qualified supervisor. Fourth, we will begin to train our supervisors in this model of supervision. This can be done through a number of low-cost media. Fifth, we will provide an in-service training for all staff on the supervision system. We need to be clear with staff that we're going to be observing them with videotape and/or direct observation. Some won't like that. Some staff will be quite resistant to the change. This will take time—likely about a year for everybody to be on board. You and I have to be consistent over time, reinforcing the message that this is how we're doing clinical supervision here, regardless of staff's credentials or years of experience. There's going to be a learning curve.

Master Supervisor Note: Again, it is important to be prepared for this presentation with a clear statement of funding requirements, training needs, mechanisms of how these needs will be met, and benchmarks for success. Further, it is essential to get a firm commitment to the plan from administrators before the supervisor proceeds. The supervisor should also stress the barriers and obstacles to be overcome and how those will be addressed.

JONATHAN: Some of the distinction between case management and clinical supervision will hopefully become clearer to me and staff as we implement the system. You're going to have to continue to educate me about it. I'd like to meet regularly with you, perhaps once a week during the roll-out, to discuss how we're doing. Since the State now requires our counselors to eventually be certified, will this help in that process?

ELLA: Absolutely. As you might recall, to be certified as an addiction counselor, the person must be supervised by a certified supervisor. This system will meet that requirement. It will help our counselors to be certified.

[*Jonathan and Ella summarize the advantages of a model for clinical supervision that includes workforce development and a means to implement evidence-based practices, address risk-management issues and vicarious liability, create consistency within the agency, minimize reactivity, address accreditation issues, and support counselor wellness.*]

JONATHAN: Can you bring me a budget for what this will cost in person hours and hardware by next week? Talk to our accountant if you need costing data. How are we going to train our supervisors? What will that cost? What's the most cost-effective way of conducting the staff and supervisor training? I'd like to see a 3-, 6-, and 12-month implementation and financial plan for this. Can you provide projections as to potential cost offsets and savings on the other end? Can you have that for me by next week?

ELLA: Yes, I can do that by next week. I'll also give ideas as to how supervisors can balance management and administrative duties, maintain a caseload, and perform other duties as assigned.

Clinical Supervision and Professional Development of the Substance Abuse Counselor

Part 2:
A Guide for Administrators

PART 2

Chapter 1

Clinical supervision should be an essential part of all substance abuse treatment programs. Every counselor, regardless of skill level and experience, needs and has a right to supervision. In addition, supervisors need and have a right to their own clinical supervision. For more on the essential nature of clinical supervision, see Appendix B, *New York State Office of Alcoholism and Substance Abuse Services Clinical Supervision Statement*. Unfortunately, many agencies place a higher priority on administrative tasks (such as case recordkeeping and crisis management), than on clinical supervision. This guide for administrators will assist in developing a rationale for and designing a clinical supervision system for your substance abuse treatment organization. Part 2 provides strategies and tools for implementing effective supervision along with advice on allocating resources for best results.

Benefits and Rationale

A successful clinical supervision program begins with the support of administrators. You communicate the value, benefits, and integral role of clinical supervision in quality care, staff morale and retention, and overall professional development within the context of the organization's mission, values, philosophy of care, and overall goals and objectives. Being able to discuss specific benefits of clinical supervision will increase the likelihood of internal support, enhance your organization's ability to deliver quality supervision, and add marketability for funding opportunities.

Administrative Benefits

Clinical supervision enables organizations to measure the quality of services. It ensures that employees follow agency policies and procedures and comply with regulatory accreditation standards while promoting the mission, values, and goals of the organization. Supervision provides administrators with tools to evaluate job performance, maintain communication between administrators and counselors, facilitate conflict resolution, and hold personnel accountable for quality job performance. Clinical supervision is a risk-management tool that increases an organiza-tion's ability to respond to risk, thereby reducing overall liability. It also addresses human resource issues, including staff satisfaction and retention of personnel. Finally, supervision provides marketing benefits by improving the overall reputation of the agency in the community and among other service providers.

Clinical Services Benefits

The goal of clinical supervision is to continuously improve quality client care. Supervision by trained and qualified supervisors helps staff understand and respond more effectively to all types of clinical situations and prevent clinical crises from escalating. It specifically addresses assessment, case conceptualization, treatment strategies, and discharge planning. Supervision aids in addressing the unique needs of each client. It provides a mechanism to ensure that clinical directives are followed and facilitates the implementation and improvement of evidence-based practices (EBPs). "Quality supervision will become a major factor in determining the degree to which EBPs are adopted in community settings" (CSAT, 2007, p. 12). Clinical supervision also enhances the cultural competence of an organization by consistently maintaining a multicultural perspective. "Supervision encourages supervisees to examine their views regarding culture, race, values, religion, gender, sexual orientation, and potential biases" (CSAT, 2007, p. 27).

CSAT's Technical Assistance Publication (TAP) 21-A, *Competencies for Substance Abuse Treatment Clinical Supervisors*, defines supervision as a "social influence process that occurs over time in which the supervisor participates with supervisees to ensure quality care. Effective supervisors observe, mentor, coach, evaluate, inspire, and create an atmosphere that promotes self-motivation, learning, and professional development" (CSAT, 2007, p. 3). Also, supervision can improve client outcomes (Carroll, Ball, Nich, Martino, Frankforter, Farentinos, et al., 2006). Finally, supervision increases staff members' sensitivity and responsiveness to diversity issues among staff, with clients, and between staff and clients.

Professional Development Benefits

Quality clinical supervision has been shown to increase staff retention through professional skills development and increased competency (Bernard & Goodyear, 2004). Supervision provides the forum for expanding current clinical practices, intellectual stimulation, emotional support, and improvement in critical thinking (see CSAT, 2007). Supervision is part of an organization's career ladder, as it supports staff in obtaining and maintaining professional credentials. It also provides information and guidance about key contextual factors that may influence their work performance such as culture, lifestyles, and beliefs.

Workforce Development Benefits

Supervision by trained and qualified supervisors is an essential tool in the recruitment and retention of personnel, as counselors often rate training and development as critical factors in their selection of employment. In addition, supervision has been shown to improve staff morale and motivation by making staff feel valued and appreciated (Bernard & Goodyear, 2004). It also assists in promoting counselor wellness, and promotes the overall development of the substance abuse treatment field by upgrading the credentials, knowledge, skills, and attitudes of personnel.

Program Evaluation and Research Benefits

Implementation of program evaluation and/or research is often misunderstood by counselors and viewed as more work that is unrelated to quality client care. Supervision can mediate in this area by providing staff with the rationale for the initiative, connecting it to client outcomes, and communicating achievements and challenges to the evaluators. Clinical supervision can also provide the mechanism for data gathering and information retrieval in support of the new projects and programmatic innovations.

Key Issues for Administrators in Clinical Supervision

Administrative and Clinical Tasks of Supervisors

Supervisors wear many hats. In most organizations, the administrative and clinical supervisor is the same person (see also the section that follows, Administrative and Clinical Supervision, p. 89). Most clinical supervisors still carry a client caseload (albeit reduced somewhat from that of a line counselor), perform administrative duties, write grant proposals, serve as project managers, and supervise the clinical performance of counselors. Each role involves different expectations and goals. It is important for administrators to be aware of each of these roles and for supervisors to be prepared to perform effectively in administrative, organizational, and clinical roles.

Kadushin (1976) outlines multiple administrative tasks for a clinical supervisor: staff recruitment and selection; orientation and placement of employees; work planning and assignments; monitoring, coordinating, reviewing, and evaluating work; staff communication both up and down the chain of command; advocating for client and clinician needs; acting as a buffer between administrators and counselors; and acting as a change agent and community liaison. Munson states, "As part of their administrative responsibilities, supervisors are often required to manage program transitions and modifications. Departments and programs can be altered, restructured and merged" (1979, p. 72).

Assessing Organizational Structure and Readiness for Clinical Supervision

In implementing a clinical supervision program, an important first step will be to evaluate the agency's preparedness to support the functions of clinical supervision by identifying the agency's culture and organizational structure. Organizational readiness scales and attitude inventories can be helpful in the process of assessing and adopting EBPs. You need to assess the following:

- How decisions are made within the organization (centralized versus decentralized, vertical or horizontal).
- How authority is defined and handled (top down, bottom up, through the chain of command, or ad hoc).
- How power is defined and handled (reward, coercion, legitimate power through status, prestige, titles, expert power through skills and experience, or referent power through respect for an individual—or all of the above).
- How information is communicated (structured/formal/informal, on a need-to-know basis, bidirectional feedback and communication).
- How the organizational structure influences supervisory relationships, process, and outcome.
- The overall cultural proficiency of the organization.

The following organizational issues should be considered by an agency before a clinical supervision system is implemented:

- *Organizational context.* How consistently do staff adhere to agency philosophy and culture? To what extent will clinical supervisors teach and support this philosophy?
- *Clinical competence.* What specific knowledge, skills, and attitudes are expected of substance abuse counselors? What is each counselor's baseline competence and learning style? What is the level of cultural competence of staff?
- *Motivation.* How should the staff's motivation and morale be characterized?
- *Supervisory relationships.* What is the nature of relationships between administrators and front-line workers? How healthy or unhealthy are those relationships?
- *Environmental variables.* To what extent do administrators expect supervisors to proactively teach ethical and professional values? Do staff have a common set of goals? How does the organization promote professional development? How is progress toward those goals monitored and supported? What is the cultural, racial, religious, gender, and sexual orientation mix of the clients served by the organization?

- *Methods and techniques.* How familiar is the organization with individual, group, and peer supervision? How familiar is the organization with case progress note review, case consultation methods, direct observation, live supervision, audio- or videotaping, and role playing?

Assessing an organization's readiness for a clinical supervision system may also include such questions as: "What stage of readiness for implementing a clinical supervision system are the board of directors, other administrative staff and clinical supervisory staff (if any), direct care staff, and support personnel? What are some of the organizational, administrative, and clinical barriers to implementing a clinical supervision system?" Potential barriers include lack of familiarity with supervision methods and techniques, the need for further training of supervisors, and lack of technical equipment such as video cameras. It is helpful to develop a timeframe for addressing the most important barriers. What would you as an administrator like to see happen and who should be part of the process for implementing clinical supervision? (See Tools 1 and 2 in chapter 2.)

Administrative and Clinical Supervision

This section is a comprehensive look at the issues facing supervisors in their dual roles. In the substance abuse treatment field, one of the major challenges facing supervision is the reality that most supervisors perform both administrative and clinical supervisory functions. The numerous conflicts and ambiguity that result from these roles can pose serious problems for administrators, supervisors, and supervisees. Determining the distinction between the roles of clinical and administrative supervision can be difficult because there are no uniform definitions of these functions. Most writing on administrative supervision is in the context of the evaluative and record-keeping functions of a supervisor.

To the extent possible, administrative supervision should be distinguished from clinical supervision. Bradley and Ladany (2001) state that administrative supervisors "help the supervisee function effectively as a part of the organization," with an emphasis on "organizational accountability, case records, referrals, and performance evaluations" (p. 5). In contrast, clinical supervisors focus on the services received by the client, including the therapeutic relationship, assessment, interventions, and client welfare. While these tasks may be seen as substantially different, many are complementary. Therefore, you and the supervisors need to be mindful of the different roles and of the inherent ethical, relational, and role conflict issues. Best supervision practices will work to keep the dual roles as clear as possible.

Legal and Ethical Issues for Administrators

You play a vital role in clarifying legal and ethical issues for your organization, especially for clinical supervisors and counseling personnel. You are invaluable in providing information and support for supervisors and staff.

You and your supervisors need to define and document (in writing) the legal and ethical standards for the agency. You can draw from the staff's professional codes of ethics as well as accepted best practices. All personnel should be consistently and continually trained in the agency's legal and ethical standards, as well as in changing case law and legislation affecting clinical practice. You need to reinforce your support for supervisors who face situations where legal and ethical issues may arise. You should help supervisors develop a process for ethical decisionmaking as supervisors as well as a process for teaching ethical decisionmaking to counselors.

Among the key issues for you and your supervisors are the following:

- *Direct and vicarious liability.* Important factors affecting liability include the supervisor's power of control; the counselor's duty to perform a clinical service; the time, place, and purpose of the service; the motivation for responding the way the counselor responded; and the supervisor's expectations for action. Critical legal questions for administrators are: Did you make a reasonable effort to supervise? Was there any dereliction of duty? Did treatment create any harm, wrongdoing, or damage to the client, the organization, or the community? Did you and the supervisor give appropriate advice concerning the counselor's actions? Were

tasks assigned to staff that were outside their scope of competence?

Confidentiality. Has the organization adhered to all laws of confidentiality (i.e., the Health Insurance Privacy and Portability Act [HIPAA], 42 CFR, Part 2)? To what extent has the organization balanced the counselor's and client's right to privacy and performance review? Has the organization adhered to its duty to warn, to report, and to protect?

- *Informed consent and due process.* This requires that supervisees and clients be fully informed as to the approach and procedures of the agency's actions (see Tools 4 and 19). Have the clients and counselors been informed about treatment parameters and supervision requirements? Have all required forms and documents been read and signed by all relevant parties? Is there a fair process that encourages conflict resolution and ensures the person a process of appeals?
- *Supervisor and counselor scope of competence.* Are supervisors and counselors operating within their scope of practice and competence? Are supervisors and counselors meeting minimal standards of competence regarding cultural and contextual awareness, knowledge, and skills? Are they effectively working within the wider client systems and networking appropriately with wider community services and institutions?
- *Dual relationships.* A dual relationship exists when a supervisor and supervisee or counselor and client have an additional relationship outside the primary professional relationship. Guidelines for supervisory relationships prohibit supervising current or former clients (a difficult issue in the substance abuse field where it is not uncommon for an agency to hire and supervise former clients in recovery). Do any supervisors have current or former romantic or sexual partners, business associates, family members, or friends among their supervisees? Is the distinction clear between the teaching and supervisory roles when students are being supervised? Are supervisors mindful of crossing over from the supervisory relationship to social activities with supervisees that may impair objectivity? Do supervisors avoid excessive self-disclosure in supervision and avoid comments or actions that might be interpreted as sexual? Do you and your supervisors respect and recognize professional boundaries in all aspects of

your relationships? When in doubt, do you consult with colleagues?

You should provide comprehensive legal and ethical orientation to all employees, review codes of ethics at the time of hire, and require employees to sign a statement that they will abide by these codes. You will want to review agency adherence to these codes periodically under the umbrella of a quality assurance or compliance program. Clinical supervisors should be proactive and provide documentation that describe and conceptualize client problems addressing potential legal and ethical dilemmas, document all clinical directives given, and offer counselors a written summary of recommendations. Finally, you should review liability insurance coverage and suggest that supervisors and counselors maintain their own personal professional liability and malpractice insurance.

For further legal and ethical issues, the reader is referred to the forms in this section.

Diversity and Cultural Competence

An important responsibility for supervisors is to continually improve their cultural competence in order to teach and support staff. Cultural competence is gained through education and training, supervised clinical work, and ongoing exposure to the population being served. All potential supervisors should be required to receive training in cultural competence. It is the supervisor's responsibility to initiate discussions of differences in race, ethnicity, gender, religion, socioeconomic status, sexual orientation, or disability regarding both clinical work with clients and supervisory and team relationships. This promotes the acceptance of diversity and cultural issues as appropriate topics of discussion and allows the supervisor the opportunity to model culturally competent behaviors.

To appreciate the importance of cultural competence, counselors must first recognize "the power of their own cultural assumptions to influence their thinking and their interactions with others" (Bernard & Goodyear, 2004, p. 118). From there, supervisors can help supervisees understand how their own diversity variables affect their interactions with clients. Administrators should be watchful for problems that can arise in the supervisory relationship when supervisors are of a different race, culture, or ethnicity than their supervisees. Fong and Lease (1997) have identified four areas that might present challenges:

1. *Unintentional racism.* Well-intentioned supervisors who are unaware of how their racial identity affects their relationships with supervisees may avoid talking about race or culture.
2. *Power dynamics.* The power differential in the supervisory relationship may be exaggerated in dyads where the supervisor is part of the dominant group and the supervisee is a member of a minority group.
3. *Trust and vulnerability.* Supervisees who are in a vulnerable position are, at the same time, encouraged to trust their supervisors, when they may have little reason to do so.
4. *Communication issues.* Differing communication styles among cultural groups can result in misunderstandings.

An excellent exercise for you and your supervisors is to evaluate how supervisors measure up to multicultural supervision competencies. Bradley and Ladany (2001) list the following in what they term the "supervisor-focused personal development" domain:

- "Supervisors actively explore and challenge their own biases, values, and worldview and how these relate to conducting supervision;
- Supervisors actively explore and challenge their attitudes and biases toward diverse supervisees;
- Supervisors are knowledgeable about their own cultural background and its influence on their attitudes, values, and behaviors;.
- Supervisors possess knowledge about the background, experiences, worldview, and history of culturally diverse groups; and
- Supervisors are knowledgeable about alternative helping approaches other than those based in a North American and Northern European context" (pp. 80–81).

Developing a Model for Clinical Supervision

An organization must develop a model for clinical supervision that best fits its needs. What are its underlying needs, goals, and objectives? What models are available to assist in reaching your organizational goals? The model should be selected in light of the organization's mission, philosophy of treatment, and orientation. You need to assess the organization's readiness for implementing a supervision system and barriers that might impede the process. What are the organization's capacities for implementation? Once implemented, how will the program's quality be evaluated? How will continuous quality improvement strategies be incorporated into the supervision model? And if the program is successful, how will it be sustained?

An effective model for clinical supervision will keep the target clear: ensuring that the client receives better treatment as a result of the clinical supervision system. In addition:

- It will begin with the supervisors' unique management or leadership style, their levels of proficiency in supervision, the organization's philosophy about clinical supervision, and the specialized client needs for clinical services.
- It will improve counselor competence, make work more manageable, encourage staff to stretch beyond their current capabilities, build mastery and growth, and meet the needs of the client, counselor, agency, and credentialing bodies.
- It will encourage supervisees to grow professionally in their understanding of culture, race, religion, gender, and sexual orientation as these issues are present clinically.

Implementing a Clinical Supervision Program

TAP 21-A (CSAT, 2007) describes the importance of using a clearly articulated process for implementing a new model of clinical supervision in both State and local agency settings as follows: "If agencies are to improve their supervisory practices by adding activities identified as clinical supervision competencies, a set of guidelines is needed to support the develop-

ment of an implementation plan" (p. 7). To ensure a smooth transition to the new supervision program, an agency will need to perform the following tasks: [d]efining or clarifying the rationale, purpose and methods for delivering clinical supervision; [e]nsuring that agency management fully understands and supports the changes that need to be made; [p]roviding training and support in supervisory knowledge and skill development; and [o]rienting clinicians to the new supervision rationale and procedures" (p. 7). These tasks are part of an implementation process whereby the changes are introduced over a limited period of time that allows for procedures to be developed and tested and clinicians to provide feedback and adjust to the supervisory process. "The broad goal is to create a continuous learning culture within the agency that encourages professional development, service improvement, and a quality of care that maximizes benefits to the agency's clients" (p. 8).

More detailed guidelines for implementing and phasing a clinical supervision system into existing processes include:

1. You need to be clear as to the organization's goals of supervision, viewing supervision as a way of supporting and reaching the agency's mission.
2. You should be familiar with the skills and competencies outlined in TAP 21-A (CSAT, 2007) and other experience and/or credentialing requirements. The competence of the designated supervisors is central to the successful design and implementation of the program. In some cases, agencies will need to invest in additional training for potential clinical supervisors. Ask yourself the following about your supervisors:
   - Has the supervisor had formal training and is he or she credentialed in counseling, substance abuse, and clinical supervision?
   - At what level of supervision proficiency are the clinical supervisors?
   - Has the supervisor received supervision of his or her clinical skills?
   - What is the supervisor's relationship with staff?
   - What is his or her level of cultural proficiency and ability to work with culturally diverse clients?
3. It is essential that a clear statement of support from senior administration be provided both verbally and in writing to all levels of administra-

tion, counselors, and support staff. This statement should provide a rationale (see p. 95) for implementing clinical supervision. The importance of this step cannot be overemphasized.

4. The next step in implementing a clinical supervision system is to create a Change Team from within your organization to spearhead the effort. Selecting the appropriate agency representatives to be the link between you and the supervision system will ensure internal communication and support. The Team should comprise individuals committed to quality care and the supervision process. They need to be somewhat familiar with the process of supervision and have a clinical background. Supervisors need to have a thorough understanding of the agency's model and techniques of supervision. The Change Team leader will ensure participation and followup with the organization's clinical supervisors. Planning specific steps to ensure sustainability of the system is integral to long-term success.

5. You, the Change Team, and clinical supervisors should read and understand the importance of the standards outlined in TAPs 21 (CSAT, 2006) and 21-A (CSAT, 2007). Each counselor should have a copy of TAP 21 (*Addiction Counseling Competencies—The Knowledge, Skills, and Attitudes of Professional Practice* [CSAT, 2006]). It is important for clinical supervisors to meet with the Change Team to discuss the skills and competencies in TAP 21-A, and to identify both the organization's strengths and areas needing improvement. The Team should draft formal policies and procedures to articulate expectations and guidelines.

6. An all-staff meeting should feature the organization's view of clinical supervision and how it will implement the supervision system. The formal policy and procedure should be distributed and discussed. All clinical staff involved in the system should attend this briefing, presented by the Change Team leader and key clinical supervisors.

7. Provide necessary training, time, and funding for supervisors. Because the training requirement for credentialing as clinical supervisors is typically participation in a 30-hour class on supervision, you need to ensure that all supervisors receive training before proceeding to comprehensive implementation.

8. If the organization is sizable or the clinical staff is large, it is sometimes helpful to initiate a pilot supervision system in selected units of the organization. This is an issue that can be addressed by the Change Team. If organizational staff are particularly resistant to implementing the supervision program, it may be helpful to demonstrate the efficacy of a quality supervision program via a pilot program.

9. Supervisors should prioritize discussing the supervisory agreement or contract with each supervisee and invest time to determine the training needs and goals for each counselor. This is the beginning of an Individual Development Plan (IDP), outlining the counselor's knowledge, skills, attitudes, and cultural competence. It is essential that the supervisor observe the counselor in action before rating her or his abilities. Rating scales provide the baseline from which to begin supervision. Both supervisors and counselors should develop and complete rating scales and IDPs. Dialog on areas of agreement and disagreement at the outset form a vital part of the supervision process. This discussion also provides the supervisor with an opportunity to praise staff members for their strengths.

10. Supervisors should schedule formal, frequent, and regular individual supervisory sessions. These sessions, similar to individual sessions with clients, need to be respected and protected from unnecessary interruptions or distractions. The supervisory sessions should be documented and follow the prescribed focus outlined in the IDP.

11. To begin direct observation, design an implementation strategy (assuming the organization has recognized the value of direct observation; see Part 1, chapter 1), and establish a weekly rotation schedule for the observation of each counselor over the next 3 months. Initially, the clinical supervisor can provide direct observation feedback to counselors individually and then move toward a group supervision model whenever practical and possible to promote team building and efficiency. To help with sustainability, the supervisor should discuss supervision at every opportunity. Staff needs to see that supervision will be conducted on a regular basis, and that frequency will be determined by the agency's needs and those of the individual counselor and team.

12. Provide feedback and review the IDP. Through the observation, the supervisor and counselor can discuss the strengths and challenges of the counselor's performance. The developing IDP should outline in detail the areas for improvement and how these changes will be further observed and monitored. Learning goals evolve as continued observation leads to further suggestions for improving performance.

13. Supervisors should document their direct observation using various forms that exist for this purpose. The documentation should include times of meetings and observation, a brief statement of the content of the clinical session observed, review procedures (audio or video tape), feedback provided, and mentoring and teaching offered.

14. Incentive plans can be developed to encourage counselors to become seriously involved in their professional development.

15. Create a sustainable treatment team. Over time, some staff will leave and others will join the team. It is important for you and your supervisors to work with the team to create an atmosphere of learning that supports the agency's commitment to clinical supervision. This means including the clinical supervision policy and procedures in the orientation of new staff. It definitely means that the team will continue to meet for supervision on a regular basis.

16. Develop a system of supervision of clinical supervisors, particularly for those who are new to their role. Supervisors need to continually build and improve their supervisory skills as well as have a forum to discuss staff challenges. Some agencies have created supervisory peer groups where the supervisors present and receive feedback on their supervision, other agencies hire a consultant to provide supervision, while some regional coalitions have established monthly forums.

Some of the primary elements in a supervision of supervisors system include:

- *Direct observation.* This may best be done by periodically (e.g., once a calendar quarter) videotaping a supervision session and having the supervisor's supervisor review the videotape. They then discuss what occurred during the supervision, with the supervisor's supervisor providing feedback and recommendations.

- *Competencies.* It is important that the supervisors of supervisors be Level 3 counselors and preferably Level 3 supervisors (see Figures 5 and 6 in Part 1, chapter 1). They need to be certified clinical supervisors and to have had supervision as supervisors themselves so they have experience with this type of supervision. Administrators should give them the responsibility and authority to perform this task and to require that tapes be provided for review in a timely fashion. Supervisors should develop the competencies sufficient to attain their credentials as a certified clinical supervisor.

- *Record-keeping system.* A logging system should maintain records on the initial counselor–supervisor sessions and the supervision of supervisors sessions.

- *Recruiting personnel.* If your agency does not have an internal person to provide the supervisor's supervision, it is recommended that you contract for such services with external sources. Over time, the external supervisor should train an internal person to assume this role.

Phasing in a Clinical Supervision System

The steps below have been found to be helpful in phasing in clinical supervision systems in an orderly manner. Although the list is provided sequentially, the needs of an agency will determine the timeframe and selection of objectives.

Phase I: Organization and Creation of a Structure

- Assess and describe the agency culture (including assets and deficits), selecting assets to build on and/or deficits for remediation regarding clinical supervision.
- Assess the facility's policies and procedures to determine the feasibility and practicality of a clinical supervision system (i.e., presence of clinical supervisory staff, availability of direct observation technology, etc.).
- Examine job descriptions to determine staff scope of practice and competence.

- Reach consensus among the Change Team about the definition of clinical supervision and its key components for that agency.
- Publicize this consensus statement to all personnel, introducing staff to the new supervisory model and clearly communicating expectations for the delivery and outcomes of clinical supervision before program implementation.
- With all personnel, discuss and introduce clinical supervision policies and procedures.
- Review the organization's cultural competence as it relates to the client populations served.
- Develop documentation and accountability systems.

Phase II: Implementation

- Implement a supervisory contract, including informed consent, with all staff to improve the supervisory working alliance.
- Assess the quality of the supervisory relationship and devise interventions to strengthen the learning alliance.
- Conduct counselor assessments to establish competency baselines.
- Design initial supervisory goals and measurable objectives for each counselor.
- Use strengths-based approaches where appropriate and possible in clinical supervision, supporting counselors' positive actions with clients.
- Develop a system of supervision of supervision. Some programs use the same taping and monitoring systems for supervisors that are used between counselors and clients, with supervisors expected to videotape their supervision sessions at least once a month, and receive supervision of their supervision by the team of supervisors and/or their supervisor.

Phase III: Establishing a Training Plan and Learning Goals

- Complete a written IDP for each counselor.
- Provide focused, on-the-job training.
- Identify clinical supervision quality indicators to monitor the quality assurance program for the agency.
- Periodically review job descriptions and evaluation procedures to ensure that counselor competencies

are sound. Review the counselor's ability to perform the TAP 21 competencies, the activities and functions performed by a substance abuse counselor that form the basis of the standards required in many States for credentialing. Also see the Northwest Frontier Addiction Technology Transfer Center Performance Rubric at http://www.nfattc.org.

Phase IV: Improving Performance

Proficiency in the Addiction Counseling Competencies (CSAT, 2006) and the International Certification and Reciprocity Consortiums 12 Core Functions should be the subject of continuous assessment and professional development during clinical supervision. Additional specific performance concerns include:

- Continually align the clinical supervision goals to the agency's mission, values, and approach;
- Create risk management policies and practices and monitor adherence;
- Address the cultural competence of personnel in supervision;
- Consistently address a deepening of counselor knowledge, skills, and attitudes about legal and ethical issues;
- Use formative and summative evaluation and feedback procedures to inform the clinical supervision process;
- Develop quality improvement plans for the agency, including clinical supervisory procedures;
- Overtly address and encourage counselor and staff wellness programs;
- Invest in counselor and staff training; and
- Foster your staff from within, continually seeking individuals with the potential to become tomorrow's supervisors.

Documentation and Record Keeping

Overseeing documentation and record keeping is an essential administrative task, as maintaining a supervisory record has multiple purposes for administrators, supervisors, and counselors. One of the primary purposes of documentation is to serve as the legal record for the delivery of supervision: a reasonable effort was made to supervise. The supervisory record is also important in developing a thoughtful plan for both quality client care and professional development. The supervisory record serves to:

- Improve client care.
- Model good record-keeping procedures for personnel.
- Afford and enhance ethical and legal protection.
- Provide a reliable source of data in evaluating the competencies of counselors.
- Provide information concerning staff ability to assess and treat clients.
- Reflect staff understanding of the dynamics of behavior and the nature and extent of the problems treated.
- Assess staff cultural competence and proficiency.
- Provide information about the clinical supervisor's ability to assess counselor competencies and the nature of the clinical supervisory relationship.
- Provide information about the clinical supervisor's clinical and supervisory competence.

A good clinical supervision record should include the following elements:

- Requirements for counselor credentialing (certification/licensure) and the extent to which each counselor meets those requirements.
- The counselor's regularly updated resume and a brief summary of his or her background and clinical expertise.
- A copy of the informed consent document, signed by the supervisor and the supervisee.
- A copy of the clinical supervision contract, signed by the supervisor and the supervisee.
- The IDP, updated minimally twice a year and preferably every 3 months.
- A copy of the formative and summative evaluations the supervisor has given to the supervisee and all relevant updates to these evaluations.
- A log of clinical supervision sessions, dates, times; a brief summary of key issues discussed; recommendations given by the supervisor and actions taken by the counselor; documentation of cancelled or missed sessions by either the supervisor or supervisee; and actions taken by the supervisor when supervision sessions are missed.
- A brief summary of each supervision session, including specific examples that support learning goals and objectives.

- A risk management review summary, including concerns about confidentiality, duty to warn situations, crises, and the recommendations of the supervisor concerning these situations.

The entire documentation record can be brief and in summary form. (See Tools 10–12 in Part 2, chapter 2, including checklists and summary statements to reduce the volume of work for the supervisor.)

Evaluation

Although training in how to conduct productive and constructive evaluations of personnel is rare, evaluation of personnel is a critical administrative task of supervisors and administrators. The goals of evaluation include, but are not limited to, reviewing job performance; assessing progress toward professional development goals; eliciting future learning goals; assessing fitness for duty and scope of competence; and providing feedback to staff on adherence to agency policies, procedures, and values.

There are a number of issues that shape the feedback process, including:

- How does the agency define a "good" counselor? What knowledge, skills, and attitudes are critical? What level of cultural competence is needed?
- How does a supervisor measure general affective qualities, such as counselor's empathy, respect, genuineness, concreteness for clients?
- What standardized tools will be used to support the evaluation? There are few evaluation instruments with psychometric validity or reliability.

The IDP can be the basis for evaluation. Each counselor should have a development plan that takes into consideration her or his counseling developmental level (see Stoltenberg, McNeill, & Delworth, 1998), learning needs and styles, job requirements, client needs, and the agency's overall goals and objectives. A sample IDP is provided in chapter 2 (Tool 15).

How do administrators and supervisors evaluate personnel and assess job performance? There are two forms of evaluation: formative and summative. Formative evaluation focuses on progress, is regularly provided, and gives feedback to the employee regarding his or her attainment of the knowledge, skills, and attitudes necessary to the job. It addresses the question, "Are you going in the right direction?" The quality of the supervisory relationship determines the success of the formative evaluation process. Summative evaluation is a formal process that rates employees' overall ability to do their job and their fitness for duty. It answers the question, "Does the employee measure up?" In substance abuse counseling, summative evaluation takes into account many variables: the range and number of clients seen, the issues and problems addressed by the counselor, the general themes in training and supervision, skill development, self-awareness, how learning goals have been translated into practice, and the employee's strengths, expertise, limitations, and areas for future development. Summative evaluation also addresses the nature of the supervisory relationship and goals for future training.

The best evaluations occur when there is open exchange of information and ideas between the supervisor and counselor, where specific examples are gleaned from the ongoing supervisory documentation, and expectations are again reviewed and agreed upon. Some organizations have moved to 360-degree assessments, with input from many layers of the organization. Tool 13 in chapter 2 is a counselor evaluation of a supervisor. The quality and quantity of feedback from a supervisor is an important part of supervision, according to supervisees (Bernard & Goodyear, 2004). Formalized feedback and evaluation is designed to review the ongoing, frequent feedback provided over time in a supervisory system (see Tool 14).

Conducting an evaluation involves exercising authority and power. When supervisors evaluate counselors, they are also evaluating themselves and their effectiveness as supervisors with particular supervisees. The evaluation process brings up many emotions for both parties. In providing feedback, supervisors should:

Provide positive, as well as constructive, feedback:

- Differentiate between data-based and qualitative judgments about job performance.
- State observations clearly and directly.
- Prioritize key areas for review rather than flood the counselor with an all-inclusive review.

Supervisees prefer:

- Clear explanations.
- Written feedback whenever possible.
- Feedback matched to their counseling development level.
- Encouragement, support, and opportunities for self-evaluation.
- Specific suggestions for change.

Feedback should be:

- Frequent.
- As objective as possible.
- Consistent.
- Credible.
- Balanced.
- Specific, measurable, attainable, realistic, and timely: SMART.
- Reduced to a few main points.

Supporting Clinical Supervisors in Their Jobs

Being a supervisor in any setting is a difficult job. The supervisor represents the concerns of administrators, counselors, and clients. Supervisors advocate on behalf of those above and below them in the organization chart. Hence, it is imperative that you provide support for the clinical supervisor in the agency and in the job.

To show support for clinical supervision, review the organization's receptivity to supervision: Is its climate for change, tolerance, and commitment conducive to efficient implementation of a clinical supervision system? Also, assess the magnitude of the proposed supervision system and the critical factors needed for success. "The agency structure and the supervisory program within it define the parameters of the supervisory relationship. Decision-making processes, autonomy within units, communication norms, and evaluative structures are all relevant to the supervisory function" (Holloway, 1995, p. 98).

To assess the organization's receptivity to supervision, you should address the following issues:

1. To what degree does the organization value accountability and have clear expectations of its personnel?

2. How is supervision tied to an employee's ongoing performance improvement plan or performance incentive program?

3. To what extent does the organization have efficient and effective systems in place to manage day-to-day operations?

4. To what extent does the organization view itself as a learning environment, encouraging inquisitiveness, creativity, innovation, and professional development?

5. To what extent does the organization value upward and downward communication and relationships by creating opportunities for staff to be heard? Does the organization understand that the learning alliance and relationship is key to successful supervision?

6. In what ways is the organization a dynamic, growing organism that values everyone's contribution?

7. To what extent does the organization "provide diversity training and other experiences that empower [a counselor] to become an advocate for the organization's target population and an agent of organizational change" ? (CSAT, 2007, p. 31)

8. How does the organization view teamwork, and what structures are in place to support the team-building process?

9. How do lines of authority and communication operate in the organization? How do formal and informal decisionmaking processes that influence the supervisors' functions work?

10. To what extent do administrators know about and understand the process and practices of clinical supervision? What training do they need in this regard?

11. What is the common ground in understanding the relationship between the administrative and clinical functions of the supervisor?

12. If the organization does not have trained and motivated clinical supervisors, what is your plan for recruiting new supervisors and/or training current supervisors who will be able to take on this new responsibility?

13. Are the job descriptions and roles clear, current, and accurate for all personnel?

14. How much supervision of their supervision will the supervisors receive from administrators or other consultants?

You support clinical supervision when you help supervisors build an organizational climate in which they can do quality work. This entails the following factors:

1. Allocating time for clinical supervision. Since supervision is not (in most cases) a revenue-generating activity, administrators may tend to minimize the importance of quality clinical supervision and fail to provide the needed time to "make a reasonable effort to supervise." A matrix presented in Part 1, chapter 1 gives guidelines to supervisors for organizing their time and providing quality supervision.

2. Making clinical supervision an agency priority. You can support the clinical supervisor with a clear statement of the importance of supervision and provide the resources needed to perform this function. This might include the acquisition of taping equipment, provision of one-way mirrors, etc. Staff need to hear unequivocally that supervision is a necessity and a requirement for all personnel, regardless of years of experience, academic background, skill and counselor developmental levels, and status within the organization. Supervisors also need supervision.

3. Supporting creative methods for supervision. As this TIP advocates for direct methods of supervision through one-way mirrors, video/audio taping, and live observation, you can state clearly that "at our agency we observe." Other methods for clinical supervision might include group or peer supervision models (see Part 1, chapter 1).

4. Building and supporting a record-keeping process for clinical supervision. This entails providing time and tools for the documentation related to clinical supervisory and administrative functions. Supervisory notes need to be integrated with clinical notes and human resource files. One good documentation system is the Focused Risk Management Supervision System (FoRMSS; Falvey, Caldwell, & Cohen, 2002). Assisting in organizing the supervisory process by investing in activities that will increase productivity over time, setting and adhering to priorities, and increasing coping skills repertoire to manage multiple tasks through cross-training and team building. You also need to periodically review job descriptions, personnel strengths and aptitudes, and cultural competence, and reorganize work-

loads accordingly. You should periodically review the purpose and function of every meeting and seek to streamline meeting times for economy and efficiency.

5. Assisting supervisors in implementing agency priorities, such as the adaptation of EBPs to fit the agency's goals and objectives. Hence, if an organization is implementing an EBP, it is imperative that supervisors also be trained in how to supervise that practice, perhaps even before counselors are trained.

6. Assisting supervisors in other personnel functions, such as working with impaired professionals and providing an employee assistance program (EAP) as a resource to supervisors and supervisees. You and your supervisors need to work together when staff are involved in ethical or legal issues that might impair the organization's function and credibility, and the supervisor needs to keep the administrator informed of all actions taken throughout the process.

7. Supporting supervisors in developing cultural competence within the organization. This entails hiring culturally competent clinical supervisors and staff and providing personnel training on cultural issues. It also requires supporting supervisors in developing and improving cultural competence in counselors.

Professional Development of Supervisors

You both support clinical supervisors in their function and monitor their professional development and performance by:

- Building a system to monitor, evaluate, and provide feedback to clinical supervisors. Supervision of one's supervision is lacking in many organizations. Every clinical supervisor is entitled to and needs to have some form of supervision of their supervision, either live or online.

- Creating IDPs with all supervisors. Even as every client needs a treatment plan and every staff member needs an IDP, every clinical supervisor also needs an IDP. Supervisors' IDPs are jointly developed and monitored by the clinical supervisor and his or her supervisor.

- Helping supervisors develop a professional identity as a supervisor. This entails encouraging the supervisor to be credentialed as a clinical supervisor. They should also receive ongoing training required for recertification.

- Providing time for them to work with a mentor (either someone within the organization or an outside consultant).

- Requiring an annual minimum number of clinical supervision training hours.

- Offering time and resources for supervisors to participate in State or local support groups for supervisors.

- Providing job performance evaluations on a regular and timely basis.

Chapter 2

Introduction

Your clinical supervision system needs to match the unique issues and contextual factors of your agency, and your agency needs to have a clear vision of what it wishes to accomplish with its clinical supervision system and actively determine and understand the processes by which it will get there. The tools presented in this chapter are designed to make the tasks associated with implementing a clinical supervision system easier. You will want to take advantage of the experience of well-established supervision programs and adapt the tools that have worked for them to suit the specific needs of your program.

The resources presented in this chapter are organized to be parallel to Part 2, chapter 1. These tools should be considered as prototypes and, in some cases, might even be used as is, provided they fit the context of your organization. These tools can be used by both clinical supervisors and administrators as part of a comprehensive clinical supervision system.

The Change Book: A Blueprint for Technology Transfer (Addiction Technology Transfer Center [ATTC] National Office, 2004) provides the basis for the organizational change process presented here. You may wish to consult with colleagues who have implemented a clinical supervision system for their organizations, especially if the agency is similar to yours. Managing organizational change is very similar to working with a client in a clinical setting. Your understanding of the recovery process and of the counselor's personal qualities and skills that facilitate recovery are invaluable resources as you apply the tools presented in this chapter.

Assessing Organizational Readiness

You will need to determine the state of readiness of your organization and its personnel to implement a clinical supervision system. This assessment should include agency contextual variables, competence of supervisory staff, clinical competence of counseling staff and organizational integrity, motivation of personnel, the nature of your relationships with staff, environmental variables (such as current or recent organizational changes, financial issues, accreditation, and legislative mandates), and the best methods and techniques to be used (see Tool 1). Tool 2 will help in assessing organizational readiness to change and identifying and prioritizing barriers to change. Just as a clinician might assess a client's stage of readiness to change, these principles can be applied to implementing a clinical supervision system or other types of organizational change. Tool 3 will help you reach agreement with staff on the goals of supervision.

Tool 1. Initial Organizational Assessment Organizational Context					
Conditions	Not at All 1	A Little 2	Possibly 3	Very Likely 4	Definitely 5
Staff have a common set of goals. A goal of the organization is that clinical supervision is valued and should be provided.					
Administrators model a norm of collegiality. Although a supervisee's performance evaluation implies a hierarchy, the organization demonstrates an openness ensuring that each person will be respected and treated as a valuable member of the team.					
The organization promotes professional development. Continuous education and professional growth are promoted for supervisors as well as counselors.					
Progress toward goals is monitored actively and does not wait for outcome evaluation. Ongoing monitoring is valued. Obstacles are identified and handled as an organizational challenge, instead of allowing a situation to deteriorate and be judged as demonstrating a lack of competence of particular staff members.					
Support for clinical supervision is appropriately generous. Allotment of time and resources is critical.					

Priority Focus_____

Secondary Focus _____

Source: Based on Bernard & Goodyear, 1998; Adapted from Porter & Gallon, 2006.

Tool 2. Organizational Stage of Readiness To Change
Implementing a Clinical Supervision Program in Your Agency

Stages of Change

Precontemplation	Unaware of issue
Contemplation	Considering the issue
Preparation	Designing a plan of action
Action	Implementing the action plan
Maintenance	Maintaining the change

	Stage of Readiness	Incentives to Change	Obstacles to Change	Resources for Change
Board of Directors				
Administration				
Supervisors				
Direct Care Staff				
Support Staff				

Primary Group—Focus of Change   Expected Outcome and Timeframe

_____   _____

_____   _____

Secondary Group—Focus of Change   Expected Outcome and Timeframe

_____   _____

_____   _____

This part of Tool 2 is designed for use by administrators and supervisors to identify the current barriers in the organization to implementing a comprehensive supervision system. Administrators and supervisors should fill this out separately, and then discuss answers in an executive team meeting.

Tool 2. Organizational Stage of Readiness To Change Implementing a Clinical Supervision Program in Your Agency Current Barriers to Change			
Organizational	**Administrative**	**Clinical**	**Other**

List the most important barriers to address within the next 3 months.

_____

_____

_____

What would you like to have happen?

_____

_____

_____

Who do you need to help participate in the change?

_____

_____

_____

Source: Adapted from Porter & Gallon, 2006.

Tool 3. Goals for Supervision

Organizational Context

How does the organization support counselors and supervisors in achieving the organization's mission statement? What steps are needed to gain consensus between administration and direct service personnel to achieve the mission statement? What are the specific steps we can take as administrators to achieve this goal of consensus regarding the philosophy of the organization and its relationship to clinical work?

GOAL: _____
_____
_____

Cultural Competence

What cultural and contextual factors are unique to this agency? What factors need to be addressed in clinical supervision?

GOAL: _____
_____
_____

Clinical Competence

What specific knowledge, skills, and attitudes do we expect from our counselors? How do we acknowledge and address the individual counselor's baseline competence and learning style?

GOAL: _____
_____
_____

Motivation

How can we ensure that the clinical supervisor will help motivate counselors to participate in clinical supervision and perform clinical tasks?

GOAL: _____
_____
_____

Supervisory Relationship

How can we support and validate the supervisory relationship both informally and formally?
Do we believe that the supervisory relationship is an important variable in the supervisory process? How can we support and validate the supervisory relationship both informally and formally?

GOAL: _____
_____
_____

Ethics and Professional Values

How much do we expect that clinical supervisors will proactively teach ethics and professional values?

GOAL: _____
_____
_____

Source: Adapted from Mattel, 2007

Legal and Ethical Issues of Supervision

Legal and ethical considerations should be paramount as you implement a supervision system. The goal is to know how to operate within the boundaries of legal and ethical codes and regulations for the protection of all parties, including the agency, administration, staff, and clients. Legal and ethical issues of supervision include direct and vicarious liability, confidentiality, informed consent and due process, supervisor and supervisee scope of competence and practice, and dual relationships (see discussion of these issues in Part 2, chapter 1).

The Association for Counselor Education and Supervision (ACES) has standards for counseling supervisors that can serve as guidelines for the substance abuse field (available online at http://www.acesonline.net/ethical_guidelines.asp). ACES also has ethical guidelines for supervisors that address issues such as protecting client welfare and rights, supervisory roles, and program administration roles. The National Board for Certified Counselors, Inc., has a Code of Ethics pertaining to the practice of professional counseling and clinical supervision. This code, like the ACES code, is reproduced in TAP 21-A (*Competencies for Substance Abuse Treatment Clinical Supervisors* [CSAT, 2007]). Other professions also have similar guidelines, such as the Association of State and Provincial Psychology Boards (reprinted in Falvey, 2002*b*), the National Association of Social Workers (NASW, *Guidelines for Clinical Social Work Supervision,* 1994), and the American Association for Marriage and Family Therapy (*AAMFT Supervisor Designation: Standards and Responsibilities Handbook,* 1999).

Informed consent is important for several reasons: (1) clients are entitled to know and agree to what processes support quality treatment, who will be reviewing information about them, and how this information will be used; (2) counselors are entitled to know how their work will be evaluated, the process of the supervision, and how this information will be used to support both quality care and their professional development; and (3) the administration is entitled to know that supervisory processes are articulated to support quality care and address legal and ethical standards.

Tool 4 is one of a number of sample informed consent for supervision forms that are available.

Tool 4. Informed Consent Template

The consent should include:

The purpose of supervision: the structure and mutual understanding of supervision

- Goals of supervision
- How goals will be evaluated and the specific timeframes
- Specific expectations of the supervisor and the supervisee
- Integration of theoretical models

Professional disclosure: information about the supervisor that includes credentials and qualifications and approach to supervision

- Educational background
- Training experiences
- Theoretical orientation
- Clinical competence with various issues, models, techniques, populations
- Sense of mission or purpose in the field
- Educational plans and professional goals

Supervision process: methods and format of supervision

- Individual, group, peer, dyadic
- Method of direct observation
- Permission to record sessions on audio- or videotape

Due Process: includes written procedures to be followed when a grievance or complaint has been made against the administration, the supervisor, or the counselor. It ensures that all sides are heard and that the complaint and response to the complaint receive due consideration. In this case, informed consent means that all parties are aware of the process for lodging a complaint.

Tool 4. Informed Consent Template (continued)
Ethical and legal issues: policies, regulations, and laws regarding supervisory and therapeutic relationships

- Number of supervisees for which the supervisor will be responsible
- Emergency and back-up procedures (e.g., supervisor accessibility)
- Ethical codes of conduct
- Process for discussing ethical dilemmas
- Confidentiality regarding information discussed in supervision
- Confidentiality issues when more than one supervisee is involved
- Dual roles and relationships
- Process for addressing supervisee issues (e.g., burnout, countertransference)

Statement of agreement

Signed acknowledgement by all parties that they understand and agree to comply with the contract

Source: Adapted from Falvey, 2007.

Selection and Competencies of Supervisors

When hiring or appointing a person as a clinical supervisor, you will need to understand the scope of practice and competence of a supervisor. Consult TAP 21-A (CSAT, 2007) and the International Certification and Reciprocity Consortium [IC&RC] Role Delineation Study for Clinical Supervisors (2000).

Administrators can use checklists such as Tool 5 to determine the competencies of a potential clinical supervisor.

Tool 5. Checklist for Supervisor Competencies					
Competencies	Poor	Below Average	Average	Above Average	Excellent
Knowledge					
Has knowledge of theory and intervention strategies					
Has knowledge of screening, assessment, and diagnostic standards					
Understands cultural and ethnic issues					
Has knowledge of resources in the community					
Has knowledge of current ethical guidelines and legal issues					
Practice					
Demonstrates mastery of intervention techniques					
Is timely and thorough in documentation					
Is able to develop rapport					
Is able to conceptualize problems					
Can respond to multicultural issues					
Is able to formulate treatment goals					

Tool 5. Checklist for Supervisor Competencies (continued)					
Competencies	Poor	Below Average	Average	Above Average	Excellent
Personal					
Demonstrates ethical behavior					
Demonstrates use of good judgment and counseling skills					
Is interpersonally competent					
Is able to identify own strengths and weaknesses					
Is able to accept and learn from feedback					
Is an asset to the profession					
Source: Adapted from Campbell, 2000. Permission pending.					

Other sources to consult on the same topic include:
- Bernard and Goodyear, 2004: Evaluation Questionnaires and Scales (pp. 316–339).
- Falvey, 2004*b*: Ethical Mandates for Professional Competence, Standards for Clinical Supervisor Competence (pp. 25, 28).
- Powell and Brodsky, 2004: ACES Supervision Interest Network, Competencies of Supervisors (pp. 327–332).
- Campbell, 2000 (pp. 257–285).

Substance Abuse Policy

As an administrator, you have ultimate responsibility for enforcing policies and procedures for maintaining a safe workplace. Under provisions of the Drug-Free Workplace Act of 1988, all agencies receiving Federal and/or State funds are required to have a substance abuse policy. This policy should state how the organization maintains a safe workplace so as to provide the highest quality service to its clients. The procedures should address how the agency will deal with issues related to alcohol and drugs in the workplace, fitness-for-duty concerns, testing of employees, drug-related convictions, searches, and violations of policies. Tool 6 is a sample substance abuse policy. Other administrative issues can be addressed, such as gambling and tobacco in the workplace, pornography in the work-place, and abuse of Internet access and use in the workplace. Tool 6 is an example of a substance abuse policy.

Tool 6. Sample Policy on Substance Abuse
This organization is committed to maintaining a safe workplace and to providing high-quality service to its clients. Successful attainment of these goals depends on the establishment and maintenance of a workplace that is free from the adverse effects of drug use and alcohol abuse.

Alcohol

1. The use, possession, or being under the influence of alcohol while on duty or on the premises is strictly forbidden. This prohibition precludes an employee from consuming alcohol at meal times during work hours, even off premises.
2. Employees are prohibited from working with the smell of alcohol on their breath, regardless of when or where alcohol was consumed.

Drugs

1. The use, possession, being under the influence of, manufacture, sale, dispensation, or distribution of illegal or unauthorized drugs or drug paraphernalia while on duty or on the premises is forbidden.
2. An employee's involvement with illegal or unauthorized drugs off duty and/or off premises may result in discipline, up to and including discharge, where such involvement may have an adverse effect on the organization's reputation.

Tool 6. Sample Policy on Substance Abuse

3. Employees who are taking prescribed medications must keep them in a secure location, completely inaccessible to anyone but themselves, while on the premises. It is expected that employees will follow all safety precautions associated with consumption of that drug (i.e., regarding operating machinery or driving vehicles).

Fitness for Duty

1. Employees are required to be fit for duty.
2. An employee is unfit for duty if, while on duty or on the premises, he or she is under the influence of or affected by illegal or unauthorized alcohol and/or has an impermissible level of illegal or legally prescribed drugs or alcohol in his or her system and/or is affected to a degree that the employee cannot perform work because of the legally prescribed drugs.
3. Unfitness for duty can be determined through a variety of means, separately or in conjunction with each other, depending on the circumstances, such as direct observation and/or drug and/or alcohol testing.
4. An employee will be terminated if he or she is unfit for duty because of drugs and/or alcohol.

Testing of Employees

1. *Reasonable Suspicion.* An employee may be required to submit to drug and/or alcohol testing whenever there is reason to believe because of physical, behavioral, or performance indicators, that the employee is under the influence of or is affected by illegal or legally prescribed drugs and/or alcohol while on duty or on the premises.
2. *Post-Accident.* An employee may be tested for drugs and/or alcohol after any accident that could have been caused by human error or carelessness. An accident is defined as an event resulting in medical treatment by a professional or property damage in excess of $500.
3. *Medication Control.* If prescribed medication or controlled substances dispensed by the organization disappear or cannot otherwise be accounted for, all employees who may have had access to such medication or substances will be tested for illegal drugs.
4. *Positive Test Result.* An employee who tests positive for an illegal drug or unauthorized or illegally obtained legal drug and/or alcohol is unfit for duty and may be disciplined.

Drug-Related Convictions

An employee who is convicted of a drug-related offense occurring in or out of the workplace is in violation of this policy. A conviction includes a guilty plea, a plea of nolo contendere, or any court-supervised program or court-imposed sentence.

Searches

The organization reserves the right to search an employee, his or her possessions, work area, or vehicle while on the premises to determine if illegal drugs or alcohol are present.

Failure to Cooperate

An employee who refuses to provide a specimen at the date and time requested, who refuses to provide written consent to testing, who provides a false or tampered specimen, or refuses to consent to a search of his or her person, possessions, work area, or vehicle may be discharged.

Supervision Guidelines

Supervision guidelines describe the organization's commitment to clinical supervision, working terms, principles of supervision at that organization, and required documentation of clinical sessions and clinical supervision. The guidelines should clearly state the frequency of supervision, ongoing feedback procedures, and commitment to ongoing professional development. Tool 7 is an example of such a document.

Tool 7. Clinical Supervision Policy and Procedure

Underlying Principles

Clinical supervision is a powerful tool for managing and ensuring continuous improvement in service delivery. Clinical supervision is comprised of balancing four distinct functions: administrative, evaluative, supportive, and clinical. Fundamental structures include a positive working relationship, client-centered approach, commitment to professional development, and accountability. The following principles ensure high-quality clinical supervision:

- A safe, trusting working relationship that promotes a learning alliance.
- A counselor-centered program with a culturally and contextually responsive focus.
- Active promotion of professional growth and development.
- Shared clinical responsibility ensuring that the client's treatment goals are addressed.
- A rigorous process that ensures ethical and legal responsibility.
- An individualized approach based on the learning needs and style of the supervisee.
- Congruence with the values and philosophy of the agency.

Terms

A healthy **working relationship** is built on shared vision and goals, clear expectations, and the belief in the good intentions of staff members. It demonstrates reciprocal communication where all parties provide comprehensive, timely information that is respectful. Each person is responsible for providing relevant information critical to his or her job function and the mission of the agency. The working relationship recognizes the importance of the chain of command throughout all agency levels. The agency expects that this chain of command supports structure, appropriate boundaries, and decisionmaking at all levels. The chain of command is followed to ensure effective and efficient communication.

Trust is central to the working relationship. This is manifested in several ways: (1) people are accountable to their work and job responsibilities, (2) confidentiality is maintained, (3) decisions are respected, and (4) misunderstandings are pursued to clarify miscommunication, seek to understand the other person, air emotions, and reach resolution.

The **learning alliance** is based on the belief that the supervisee has specific learning needs and styles that must be attended to in supervision. The relationship between supervisor and supervisee is best formulated and maintained when this frame of reference is predominant. Supervisees participate in a mutual assessment based on a combination of direct and indirect observations.

Guidelines for Clinical Supervision

The principles of clinical supervision are made explicit by a clear contract of expectations, ongoing review and feedback, and a commitment to professional development.

Clear contract of expectations
It is critical that both the supervisor and supervisee share their expectations about the process, method, and content of clinical supervision. This can advance the development and maintenance of a trusting, safe relationship. The following information should be discussed early in the working relationship:
- Models of supervision and treatment.
- Supervision methods and content.
- Frequency and length of supervisory meetings.
- Ethical, legal, and regulatory guidelines.
- Access to supervision in emergencies.
- Alternative sources of supervision when the primary supervisor is unavailable.

The supervisee will be provided with a job description that outlines essential duties and performance indicators. Additionally, each supervisee will receive an assessment of core counseling skills based on the TAP 21 competencies and other appropriate standards.

Documentation
Supervisory sessions are recorded as notes that indicate the focus of the session, the issues discussed, solutions suggested, and agreed upon actions. Supervisors will maintain a folder for each of their supervisees. The folder will contain the IDP, clinical supervision summaries, and personnel actions (e.g., memos, commendations, other issues). Supervisees are allowed full access to the folders.

Tool 7. Clinical Supervision Policy and Procedure (continued)

Clinical supervision frequency
Each supervisee will receive 4 hours of supervision monthly. A combination of individual and group supervision may be used. Supervisors are to ensure that a minimum of 50 percent of this time is devoted to clinical, as opposed to administrative, supervision.

Ongoing review and feedback
The supervisee will be given an annual performance evaluation that reviews both job expectations and the clinical skills learning plan. Written records of the supervisee will be reviewed on a regular basis. Supervisees will be given specific written feedback regarding their strengths and areas for improvement. The supervision system operates through direct observation of clinical work. This ensures that direct, focused feedback will be provided, increases the degree of trust and safety, and provides an accurate evaluation of skills development progress. Observations will be pre-arranged and take the form of sitting in on a session, co-facilitating, or videotaping. The supervisee will present a case at a minimum of once per month.

Commitment to ongoing professional development
The supervisee's learning plan should document goals, objectives, and methods to promote professional development. The plan should be completed within the first 6 months of employment and updated annually. Ongoing supervision should focus on achieving the identified goals. The agency supports supervisees' participation in training to achieve their professional development goals.

Source: Adapted from unpublished Basics, Inc. materials

The Supervision Contract

A supervision contract protects the rights of the agency, the supervisor, and supervisee. A written contract between supervisor and supervisee, stating the purpose, goals, and objectives of supervision is important. Tool 8 is a template for supervision contracts. In addition to the contract, for the purposes of informed consent, it is useful to have a supervision consent form signed by both the supervisor and supervisee, indicating the supervisee's awareness and agreement to be supervised (see Tool 4).

Tool 8. Supervision Contract Template

This document serves as a description of the supervision provided by (supervisor name, credentials, title) to (supervisee, credentials, title).

Primary Purpose, Goals, and Objectives

- Monitor and ensure client welfare
- Facilitate professional development
- Evaluate job performance

Provision

- (Frequency) of individual supervision at (day and time)
- (Supervision model and case review format) will be used
- Clients of the counselor will give informed consent for supervision of their case
- Counselor will have a minimum of (amount) of supervision for every (number) of client contact hours
- All client cases will be reviewed on a rotating basis based on need

Documentation

- (Form name) will be used to document the content and progress of the supervision
- Informal feedback will be provided at the end of each session
- Written formal evaluation will be provided (frequency)
- Supervision notes will be shared (at the supervisor's discretion or at request of counselor)

Tool 8. Supervision Contract Template (continued)

Duties and Responsibilities

The supervisor at a minimum will:

- Review all psychosocial histories, progress notes, treatment plans, and discharge plans.
- Question the counselor to justify approach and techniques used.
- Present and model appropriate clinical interventions.
- Intervene directly if client welfare is at risk.
- Ensure that ethical guidelines and legal statutes are upheld.
- Monitor proficiencies in working with community resources and networking with community agencies.

The counselor at a minimum will:

- Uphold all ethical guidelines and legal statutes.
- Be prepared to discuss all client cases.
- Discuss approaches and techniques used and any boundary issues or violations that occur.
- Consult supervisor or designee in emergencies.
- Implement supervisor directives.
- Adhere to all agency policies and procedures.

Procedural Consideration

- The Individual Development Plan's goals and objectives will be discussed and amended if necessary.
- The quality of the supervisory relationship will be discussed and conflicts resolved.
- If conflicts cannot be resolved, (name) will be consulted.
- In the event of an emergency, the counselor is to contact the supervisor. If unavailable, contact (alternate's name, title, and other relevant back-up information).
- Crises or emergency consultations will be documented.
- Due process procedures (as explained in the agency's policy and procedure handbook) have been reviewed and will be discussed as needed.

Supervisor's Scope of Competence

- Title/date of credentials/licensure.
- Formal supervisory training and credentials.
- Years providing supervision.
- Current supervisory responsibilities.

This agreement is subject to revision at any time on request of either person. Revision will be made only with consent of the counselor and approval of the supervisor. We agree to uphold the directives outlined in this agreement to the best of our ability and to conduct our professional behavior according to the ethical principles and codes of conduct of our professional associations.

Supervisor_____ Title_____ Date_____

Supervisee_____ Title_____ Date_____

This agreement is in effect from (current date) to (annual date of review or termination)

Source: Mattel, 2007

Another sample supervision contract form can be found in Campbell (2000), p. 285.

The Initial Supervision Sessions

An initial supervision sessions checklist documents the topics to be covered in initial sessions by the supervisor and supervisee. The goal is that as part of establishing the supervisory relationship, the supervisor and supervisee should discuss the basic issues in substance abuse counseling and in supervision. For new supervisors and for administrators to monitor the implementation of supervision, a checklist, such as Tool 9, can ensure that the important issues are discussed. The example below can aid in setting a preliminary structure for supervision, clarifying goals and expectations, and incorporating feedback so as to promote a sense of openness, trust, and safety. It is understood that not all of these topics can be covered in the first few sessions, but these topics are important considerations in initiating clinical supervision.

Documentation and Recordkeeping

Documentation is unquestionably a crucial risk-management tool for clinical supervisors and is no longer optional in supervision. Legal precedents suggest that organizations are both ethically and legally responsible for quality control of their work, and the supervision evaluation, documentation, and record-keeping systems are a useful and necessary part of that professional accountability. However, in contrast with the myriad clinical forms and documentation required, there is a paucity of tools for documentation in supervision. Most organizations rely on the personal style and records of individual supervisors, and do not have an organization-wide standardized system of record keeping for supervision. Documenting supervision should not be burdensome, but it should be systematic and careful. Key components of what should be documented and how it should be documented are provided in the following paragraphs.

A record of supervision sessions needs to be maintained that documents: when supervision was conducted, what was discussed, what recommendations were provided by the supervisor, and what actions resulted. A supervisor should maintain a separate file on each counselor supervised, including:

- Caseloads.
- Notes on particular cases.
- Supervisory recommendations and impressions.
- The supervision contract.
- A brief summary of the supervisee's experience, training, learning needs, and learning styles.
- The individual development plan.
- A summary of all performance evaluations.
- Notations of supervision sessions, particularly concerning duty-to-warn situations, cases discussed, and significant decisions made.
- Notations of canceled or missed supervision sessions.
- Significant issues encountered in supervision and how they were resolved.

By far, the most comprehensive documentation system for clinical supervisors is Falvey's FoRMSS system (2002*a*), which includes emergency contact information, supervisee profiles, a log sheet for supervision, an initial case overview, a supervision record, and a termination summary that records the circumstances of client termination, client status at termination, and any followup or referrals needed. The FoRMSS system alerts supervisors to potential clinical, ethical, or legal risks associated with cases.

Records of supervision must be retained for the period required by the State and pertinent accreditation bodies. The American Psychological Association's guidelines (2007) recommend retaining clinical and supervisory records for at least 7 years after the last services were delivered. Organization policy may differ from this. Administrators should check with local and State statutes regarding record-keeping requirements. It is prudent for an organization and supervisor to retain supervision records for at least as long as required by the State and accreditation bodies.

PART 2

Tool 9. Initial Supervision Sessions Checklist

Education, Training, and Clinical Experience

_____ Educational background

_____ Training experience

_____ Setting(s), number of years

_____ Theoretical orientation

_____ Clinical competence with various issues, models, techniques, populations, presenting problems, treatment modalities

_____ Sense of mission and purpose in the field

_____ Educational plans and professional goals of the supervisee

_____ Training and awareness of cultural and contextual issues in counseling

_____ Training and awareness of community networking in counseling

Philosophy of Supervision

_____ Philosophy of therapy and change

_____ Purpose of supervision

Previous Supervision Experiences

_____ Previous supervision experiences (e.g., format, setting)

_____ Strengths and weaknesses as counselor and as supervisee

_____ Supervisee's competence with stages of counseling process

_____ Supervisee's level of development in terms of case planning, notes, collateral support, and networking

_____ Supervisory competence with various issues, models, techniques, populations, therapy groups, and modalities

_____ Methods for managing supervisor-supervisee differences

Supervision Goals

_____ Goals (personal and professional)

_____ Process of goal evaluation and timeframe

_____ Requirements for which supervisee is seeking supervision (e.g., licensure, professional certification)

_____ Requirements to be met by supervision (e.g., total hours, individual or group supervision)

Supervision Style and Techniques

_____ Specific expectations the supervisee or supervisor has of the parties involved (e.g., roles, hierarchy)

_____ Type of supervision that would facilitate clinical growth of the supervisee

_____ Preferred supervision style (didactic, experiential, collegial)

_____ Parallels between therapy and supervision models

_____ Supervision focus (e.g., counselor's development, cases)

_____ Manner of case review (e.g., crisis management, in-depth focus)

_____ Method (e.g., audio- or videotaping, direct observation)

Theoretical Orientation

_____ Models and specific theories in which supervisee and supervisor have been trained, practice, and or conduct supervision

_____ Extent to which these models have been used clinically

_____ Populations, presenting problems, and/or family forms with which the models have been most effective

_____ Interest in learning new approaches

Tool 9. Initial Supervision Sessions Checklist (continued)

Legal and Ethical Considerations

_____ Ultimate responsibility for clients discussed in supervision in different contexts (e.g., licensed vs. unlicensed counselor, private practice vs. public agency)

_____ Number of cases for which the supervisor will be responsible

_____ Emergency and back-up procedures

_____ Awareness of professional ethical codes

_____ Confidentiality regarding the information discussed in supervision

_____ Confidentiality issues when more than one supervisee is involved

_____ Specific issues in situations where dual relationships exist (e.g., former client)

_____ Process for addressing supervisee issues (e.g., burnout, countertransference)

Other

What do we need to know about each other that we have not already discussed?

Source: Adapted from Falvey, 2002b. Permission pending.

Tools 10–12 are sample documentation forms. (See also Campbell, 2000.)

Tool 10. Supervision Note Sample Professional Development Plan Current Focus		
Goal/TAP Competencies	Objective	Date of Expected Completion

Supervision Content			
Issue	Discussion	Recommendation/ Action	Followup
Progress on Professional Development Plan Objectives _____ _____			
Other_____			
Supervisor_____ Counselor_____ Date_____			

Source: Porter and Gallon, 2006.

Tool 11. Current Risk-Management Review

Case:_____   Date::_____

ISSUES	
☐ Informed Consent	☐ Supervisee Expertise
☐ Parental Consent	☐ Supervisor Expertise
☐ Confidentiality	☐ Institutional Conflict
☐ Recordkeeping	☐ Dual Relationship
☐ Records Security	☐ Sexual Misconduct
☐ Child Abuse/Neglect	☐ Releases Needed
☐ Risk of Significant Harm	☐ Voluntary/Involuntary Hospitalization
☐ Duty to Warn	☐ Utilization Review Discharge/Termination
☐ Medical Exam Needed	

Discussion:

_____

_____

_____

Recommendation:

_____

_____

_____

Action:

_____

_____

_____

Signature_____Date_____

Title_____

Source: Based on Falvey, 2002b.

Tool 12. Supervisory Interview Observations		
STATEMENTS/BEHAVIORS		**COMMENTS**
Step 1 SET AGENDA Decrease anxiety Involve counselor		
Step 2 GIVE FEEDBACK Empower Individualize		
Step 3 TEACH and NEGOTIATE Share agenda Clarify knowledge, skills, attitude Identify learning steps Agree upon methods of learning		
Step 4 SECURE COMMITMENT Clarify expectations Clarify responsibility Create mutual accountability		

LOOK FOR	OBSERVATIONS, BEHAVIORS, NOTES
SUMMARY OBSERVATIONS	
Interview structure followed?	
Time managed effectively?	
Established nurturing and supportive environment?	
Stayed on course?	
Resistance? Power struggle?	
Agreement secured?	
Followup plan created?	
NOTES:	

Source: Based on Porter & Gallon, 2006.

PART 2

Evaluation of Counselors and Supervisors

Evaluation of counselors and supervisors is both formative (ongoing and evolving over time) and summative (periodic and formal). Nowhere else in supervision does the power differential between the supervisor and supervisee become more evident than in the evaluation process. Feedback and evaluation are necessary and important in an organization's risk-management procedures. Agencies need a formal procedure and criteria for staff evaluation. When supervisors conduct supervisee evaluations, counselors need to understand there is a level of subjectivity in the process. There is no psychometrically valid tool to assess counselor competence. An element of the supervisor's judgment is always involved.

Most evaluation guidelines and tools identify general areas of competence to assess—knowledge, skills, and attitudes—but specific criteria for making an evaluation are left to the individual supervisor and the organization. It is important that the evaluation of staff be closely linked to job descriptions, the supervision contract, and the specific needs of the agency. Levels of competence and fitness for duty should be established by the individual organization, with consideration given to the credentialing and accreditation requirements of the agency. Supervisee triads also offer another option to assist in the evaluation process. A grievance and appeals process should be defined. Finally, supervisors need to be reminded that they are the gatekeepers for the agency, providing feedback, remediation as needed, and dismissal of personnel if indicated.

Tools 13 and 14 aid the supervisee in evaluating the supervisor and the supervisor in assessing the counselor.

Tool 13. Counselor Evaluation of the Supervisor	
This evaluation form gives the supervisor valuable feedback while it gives the counselor a sense of responsibility and involvement in the design and development of supervision. Use a 7-point rating scale where: 1 = strongly disagree 4 = neither agree nor disagree 7 = strongly agree	
	Rating
1. Provides useful feedback regarding counselor behavior	
2. Promotes an easy, relaxed feeling in supervision	
3. Makes supervision a constructive learning process	
4. Provides specific help in areas needing work	
5. Addresses issues relevant to current clinical conditions	
6. Focuses on alternative counseling strategies to be used with clients	
7. Focuses on counseling behavior	
8. Encourages the use of alternative counseling skills	
9. Structures supervision appropriately	
10. Emphasizes the development of strengths and capabilities	
11. Brainstorms solutions, responses, and techniques that would be helpful in future counseling situations	
12. Involves the counselor in the supervision process	
13. Helps the supervisee feel accepted and respected as a person	
14. Appropriately deals with affect and behavior	
15. Motivates the counselor to assess counseling behavior	

Tool 13. Counselor Evaluation of the Supervisor (continued)	
This evaluation form gives the supervisor valuable feedback while it gives the counselor a sense of responsibility and involvement in the design and development of supervision. Use a 7-point rating scale where: 1 = strongly disagree 4 = neither agree nor disagree 7 = strongly agree	
	Rating
16. Conveys a sense of competence	
17. Helps to use tests constructively in counseling	
18. Appropriately addresses interpersonal dynamics between self and counselor	
19. Can accept feedback from counselor	
20. Helps reduce defensiveness in supervision	
21. Encourages expression of opinions, questions, and concerns about counseling	
22. Prepares the counselor adequately for the next counseling session	
23. Helps clarify counseling objectives	
24. Provides an opportunity to discuss adequately the major difficulties the counselor is facing with clients	
25. Encourages client conceptualization in new ways	
26. Motivates and encourages the counselor	
27. Challenges the counselor to perceive accurately the thoughts, feelings, and goals of the client	
28. Gives the counselor the chance to discuss personal issues as they relate to counseling	
29. Is flexible enough to encourage spontaneity and creativity	
30. Focuses on the implications and consequences of specific counseling behaviors	
31. Provides suggestions for developing counseling skills	
32. Encourages the use of new and different techniques	
33. Helps define and achieve specific, concrete goals	
34. Gives useful feedback	
35. Helps organize relevant case data in planning goals and strategies with clients	
36. Helps develop skills in critiquing and gaining insight from counseling tapes	
37. Allows and encourages self-evaluation	
38. Explains the criteria for evaluation clearly and in behavioral terms	
39. Applies criteria fairly in evaluating counseling performance	
40. Addresses cultural issues of supervisee in a helpful manner.	
41. Discusses cultural and contextual issues of the client, family, and wider systems that open up new resources and avenues for support.	
Source: Adapted from Powell and Brodsky, 2004.	

PART 2

Tool 14. Counselor Competency Assessment
Based on TAP 21, Addiction Counseling Competencies:
The Knowledge, Skills, and Attitudes of Professional Practice (CSAT, 2006)

Competency Area	Needs Improvement	Able to Perform Skill	Proficient	Consistent Mastery
Understand Substance Use Disorders • Models and theories • Recognize complex context of substance abuse				
Treatment Knowledge • Philosophies • Practices • Outcomes				
Application to Practice • DSM-IV-TR • Repertoire of helping strategies • Familiar with medical and pharmacological resources				
Diversity and Cultural Competence • Understand diversity • Use client resources • Select appropriate strategies				
Clinical Evaluation • Screening • Assessment				
Assess Co-Occurring Disorders • Symptomatology • Course of treatment				
Treatment Planning • Based on assessment • Individualized • Ensure mutuality • Reassessment • Team participation				
Referral and Followup • Evaluate referrals • Ongoing contact • Evaluate outcome				
Case Management				

Tool 14. Counselor Competency Assessment (continued) Based on TAP 21, Addiction Counseling Competencies: The Knowledge, Skills, and Attitudes of Professional Practice (CSAT, 2006)				
Competency Area	**Needs Improvement**	**Able to Perform Skill**	**Proficient**	**Consistent Mastery**
Group Counseling • Group theory • Describe, select, and use appropriate strategies • Understand and work with process and content • Facilitate group growth				
Family, Couples Counseling • Theory and models • Understand characteristics and dynamics • Describe, select, and use appropriate strategies				
Individual Counseling • Theory of individual counseling • Describe, select, and use appropriate strategies • Understand functions and techniques of individual counseling				
Client, Family, and Community Education • Culturally relevant • Provide current information • Teach life skills				
Documentation • Knowledge of regulations • Prepare accurate, concise notes • Write comprehensive, clear psychosocial narrative • Record client progress in relation to treatment goals • Discharge summaries				
Professional and Ethical Responsibilities • Adhere to code of ethics • Apply to practice • Participate in supervision • Participate in performance evaluations • Ongoing professional education				

Source: Porter & Gallon, 2006.

Other useful resources are:

- Bernard and Goodyear, 2004: Supervision Instruments (pp. 317–326).
- Campbell, 2000: Generic Rating Sheet and Evaluation Form, Supervisee's Basic Skills and Techniques (p. 263); Sample Generic Supervisee Evaluation Form (p. 275).
- Powell and Brodsky, 2004: Evaluation of the Counselor, adapted from Stoltenberg and Delworth, 1987 (p. 351).
- Powell and Brodsky, 2004: Counselor Assessment Forms (p. 373–379).
- Northwest Frontier Addiction Technology Transfer Center Performance Rubric available online at http://www.nfattc.org.

Individual Development Plan

After the supervisor and counselor have agreed on goals, they should formulate an individual development plan (IDP) or professional development plan. It should address the expectations for supervision, the counselor's experience and readiness for the position, procedures to be used to observe and assess the counselor's competencies, and the counselor's professional development goals. Some IDP formats follow the 12 Core Functions taking into account the stage of development of the counselor. Other formats might use the competencies in TAP 21. Tool 15 outlines the generic knowledge, skills, and attitudes to be addressed as part of one's professional development plan. Whatever format is adopted, the IDP should provide the counselor with a road map for learning goals.

Tool 15. Professional Development Plan				
Staff_____ Position _____ Date _____				
Practice Dimension: _____				
Competency number and page from TAP 21: _____				
Present level of competence from TAP 21 Rating Form:				
1 Understands	2 Developing	3 Competent	4 Skilled	5 Master
1 = Understands 2 = Developing 3 = Competent 4 = Skilled 5 = Master		Comprehends the tasks and functions of counseling Applies knowledge and skills inconsistently Consistent performance in routine situations Effective counselor in most situations Skillful in complex counseling situations		
Describe the counselor's strengths and challenges for this rating: _____ _____ _____				
Expected level of competency to be achieved with this learning plan:				
1 Understands	2 Developing	3 Competent	4 Skilled	5 Master
Describe the goal for this learning plan in observable terms:_____ _____				

Tool 15. Professional Development Plan (continued)

List the Knowledge, Skills, and Attitudes relevant to achieving the target competency.

Knowledge_____

_____

Skills _____

_____

Attitudes _____

_____

State the performance goal in specific behavioral terms: _____

_____

What activities will the counselor complete in order to achieve the stated goal? _____

How will progress be evaluated? How will proficiency be demonstrated? _____

Supervisor Signature _____ Date _____

Counselor Signature _____ Date _____

UPDATE

Date of "re-observation" _____

Demonstration of knowledge and skills successful? _____ Yes _____ No

If "No," demonstration needs the following correction and followup demonstration rescheduled:

Supervisor Signature _____ Date _____

Counselor Signature _____ Date _____

Source: Adapted from Porter & Gallon, 2006.

Outline for Case Presentations

Counselors often need to be taught how to present cases in supervision. The counselor needs to think about the goals he or she would like to achieve for the client and his or her particular concerns about the case. It is possible to use the case presentation format for a variety of purposes: to explore the client's clinical needs, to aid in case conceptualization, to process relational issues in counseling (transference and countertransference), to identify and plan how to use specific clinical strategies, and to promote self-awareness for the counselor. In the beginning, the supervisor should structure the case presentation procedures to ensure consistency and conformity to agency guidelines. Tool 16 can be adapted to the particular theoretical model of the agency and the specific needs of the supervisee and organization.

Tool 16. Sample Case Consultation Format

Name of presenter:_____

Date:_____

Identifying data about the client (age, marital status, number of marriages, number and ages of children, occupation, employment status)

Presenting problem:_____

Short summary of the session:_____

_____

Important history or environmental factors (especially cultural or diversity issues):_____

_____

Tentative assessment or problem conceptualization (diagnosis):_____

_____

Plan of action and goals for treatment (treatment plan):_____

_____

Intervention strategies:_____

_____

Concerns or problems surrounding this case (e.g., ethical concerns, relationship issues):_____

_____

Source: Adapted from Campbell, 2000.

Audio- and Videotaping

To ensure competence, the agency should provide instruction on audio- and videotaping to all staff. Instruction should include the overall purpose of taping, how to inform the client about the taping procedure, how to use the recording equipment, the placement of taping devices, how to ensure client confidentiality and obtain signed releases, how to begin the actual session while recording, and how to process the tapes after recording. Tool 17 provides helpful hints for successful audio- and/or videotaping.

Tool 17. Instructions for Audio and Videotaping

1. **Use quality equipment.** Check the sound quality, volume, and clarity. It is best to use equipment with separate clip-on microphones unless you are in a sound studio with a boom microphone. Clip-on microphones are inexpensive and easy to obtain.

2. **Buy good quality tapes**. It is not necessary to buy top-of-the-line tapes, but avoid the cheapest. Better tapes give better sound and picture and can be reused.

3. **Placement of equipment matters**. Use a tripod for the video camera. Check the angle of camera, seating, volume, and the stability of the picture.

Tool 17. Instructions for Audio and Videotaping (continued)

4. **Check the background sound and volume.** Choose a quiet, private place to do this, both to protect confidentiality and to improve recording quality. Do not use an open space, an office with windows facing the street, or a place subject to interruption. Loud air-conditioning fans, ringing phones and pagers, street noise, and office conversations all disrupt the quality of taping.

5. **Know how to use the equipment.** Conduct a dry run. Be sure to check the placement of chairs, video camera angles, and picture quality before you begin. If the supervisee is especially anxious or unfamiliar with the equipment, have him or her make a practice tape. Be sure those in the picture are the persons agreed on by the supervisor and supervisee.

6. **Protect the confidentiality** of the supervisee and the client. Choose a private, controlled space for taping. Keep the tapes in a locked cabinet and don't include identifying data on the outside of the tape. When finished with supervision, erase the tape completely before reusing; do not just tape over the previous session.

7. **Process with the supervisee any anxiety** or concern generated by taping. Three areas of potential anxiety are the technical aspects (equipment and room availability), concern for the client (confidentiality), and the effect of taping on the session (critical evaluation of performance by the supervisor).

8. **Explain taping,** its goals, and its purpose to the client at least one session before proceeding. Review with the client any concerns about confidentiality. Remember that the more comfortable and enthusiastic the supervisor and the supervisee are with the value of taping, the more comfortable the client will be. Sometimes just reassuring the client that the tape can be turned off at any point if the client is uncomfortable increases a sense of control and reduces anxiety. Usually after the first few minutes of taping, both the client and counselor forget its presence, and this option is rarely used. If the client appears resistant, a decision should be made as to the appropriateness of using this particular method of supervision in this situation.

9. **Get a written release** from the client. Be sure the release includes a description of the purpose of the tape, limits of confidentiality, identities of those viewing the tape, and assurance of erasure of the tape afterward. If the tape is to be used in group supervision or a staffing seminar, the client should be informed of that fact.

10. Before beginning the actual session, **check the equipment** by making a short practice tape covering background material on the client. Then, rewind the tape and play it to check sound, volume, camera angle, and picture. When satisfied, begin the actual session.

Source: Adapted from Campbell, 2000.

PART 2

Further, it is essential that an organization provide documentation to protect the confidentiality of information and to preserve patients' rights. This is especially important if direct observation of clinical sessions is to occur using audio or videotaping. Tool 18 explains the benefits and procedures of taping and can be read by the counselor to the client. The consent form, Tool 19, should be signed and dated prior to taping.

Tool 18. Confidentiality and Audio- or Videotaping

Video recording of clinical processes will be conducted with the client's written, informed consent for each taping. Clients understand that no taping will occur without their consent. A process already in place will ensure the security and destruction of DVDs or erasure of VHS tapes.

The purpose of videotaping is to improve counselors' clinical skills through supervision and teaching.

Counselor benefits of videotaping include:
- Improving therapeutic skills.
- Improving treatment team cohesion.
- Improving assessment, treatment planning, and delivery of services.
- Improving clinical supervision.

Procedure:

The client's counselor will explain and fully disclose the reason, policy, and procedure for videotaping the client. Both will sign a specific videotaping release form. The counselor should also explain that refusal to be taped will not affect the client's treatment at the agency.

1. The client must be 18 years old to sign the consent. Those under 18 must have a parent's signature in addition to their own.
2. Respecting the client's concerns is always the priority. Should any client or family member show or verbalize concerns about taping, those concerns need to be addressed.
3. All taping devices will be fully visible to clients and staff while in use.
4. A video camera will be set up on a tripod, consistent with safety standards and in full view of each client. Clients will be notified when the camcorder is on or off.
5. The tape will be labeled when the session is completed, and no copies will be made.
6. Clinical review for supervision or training: The treatment team will review the tape and assess clinical skills for the purpose of improving clinical techniques.
7. The tape will be turned over to the Medical Records Department (if available) for sign out.
8. Tapes and DVDs will be stored in a locked drawer in the Medical Records Department. Within 2 weeks of taping, tapes will be erased and DVDs destroyed in the presence of two clinical staff members who attest to this destruction on a form to be kept for 3 years.
9. Tapes and DVDs may not be taken off premises.

Tool 19. Audio or Video Recording Consent

I, _____, consent to be recorded or filmed for supervision purposes. I also agree to allow the clinical staff to review the film as a resource to facilitate staff development for the enhancement of clinical procedures. I understand that any film in which I am a participant will be erased within 2 weeks of the date of filming. I understand that no copies will be made of such film.

Patient Signature _____ Date _____

Witness Signature _____ Date _____

Appendix A: Bibliography

Addiction Technology Transfer Center. (2004). *The Change Book: A Blueprint for Technology Transfer*. (2nd ed.) Kansas City, MO: Author. Retrieved February 5, 2008 from http://www.nattc.org/resPubs/changeBook.html

American Psychological Association. (2007). Record keeping guidelines. *American Psychologist, 62,* 993–1004.

Anderson, C. E. (2000). Supervision of substance abuse counselors using the integrated developmental model. *Clinical Supervisor, 19,* 185–195.

Beauchamp, T. L. & Childress, J. F. (2001). *Principles of Biomedical Ethics*. (5th ed.) New York: Oxford University Press.

Bernard, J. M. & Goodyear, R. K. (2004). *Fundamentals of Clinical Supervision*. Boston, MA: Pearson Education.

Borders, L. D., & Brown, L. L. (2005). *The New Handbook of Counseling Supervision*. Mahwah, NJ: Lawrence Erlbaum Associates.

Bradley, L. J. & Ladany, N. (Eds.) (2001). *Counselor Supervision: Principles, Process, and Practice*. (3rd ed.) Philadelphia: Brunner-Routledge.

Burke, P. A., Carruth, B., & Prichard, D. (2006). Counselor self-care in work with traumatized, addicted people. In Carruth, B. (Ed.). *Psychological Trauma and Addiction Treatment* (pp. 283–301). New York: Haworth Press.

Campbell, J. M. (2000). *Becoming an Effective Supervisor: A Workbook for Counselors and Psychotherapists*. Philadelphia: Accelerated Development.

Carroll, K. M., Ball, S. A., Nich, C., Martino, S., Frankforter, T. L., Farentinos, C. et al. (2006). Motivational interviewing to improve treatment engagement and outcome in individuals seeking treatment for substance abuse: A multisite effectiveness study. *Drug and Alcohol Dependence, 81,* 301–312.

Center for Substance Abuse Treatment. (1993*a*). *Improving Treatment for Drug-Exposed Infants*. Treatment Improvement Protocol (TIP) Series 5. (HHS Publication No. (SMA) 95-3057). Rockville, MD: Substance Abuse and Mental Health Services Administration.

Center for Substance Abuse Treatment. (1993*b*). *Pregnant, Substance-Using Women*. Treatment Improvement Protocol (TIP) Series 2. (HHS Publication No. (SMA) 93-1998). Rockville, MD: Substance Abuse and Mental Health Services Administration.

Center for Substance Abuse Treatment. (1993c). *Screening for Infectious Diseases Among Substance Abusers*. Treatment Improvement Protocol (TIP) Series 6. (HHS Publication No. (SMA) 95-3060). Rockville, MD: Substance Abuse and Mental Health Services Administration.

Center for Substance Abuse Treatment. (1994). *Simple Screening Instruments for Outreach for Alcohol and Other Drug Abuse and Infectious Diseases.* Treatment Improvement Protocol (TIP) Series 11. (HHS Publication No. (SMA) 94-2094). Rockville, MD: Substance Abuse and Mental Health Services Administration.

Center for Substance Abuse Treatment. (1995a). *Alcohol and Other Drug Screening of Hospitalized Trauma Patients.* Treatment Improvement Protocol (TIP) Series 16. (HHS Publication No. (SMA) 95-3041). Rockville, MD: Substance Abuse and Mental Health Services Administration.

Center for Substance Abuse Treatment. (1995b). *Combining Alcohol and Other Drug Treatment With Diversion for Juveniles in the Justice System.* Treatment Improvement Protocol (TIP) Series 21. (HHS Publication No. (SMA) 95-3051). Rockville, MD: Substance Abuse and Mental Health Services Administration.

Center for Substance Abuse Treatment. (1995c). *Developing State Outcomes Monitoring Systems for Alcohol and Other Drug Abuse Treatment.* Treatment Improvement Protocol (TIP) Series 14. (HHS Publication No. (SMA) 95-3031). Rockville, MD: Substance Abuse and Mental Health Services Administration.

Center for Substance Abuse Treatment. (1995d). *The Role and Current Status of Patient Placement Criteria in the Treatment of Substance Use Disorders.* Treatment Improvement Protocol (TIP) Series 13. (HHS Publication No. (SMA) 95-3021). Rockville, MD: Substance Abuse and Mental Health Services Administration.

Center for Substance Abuse Treatment. (1995e). *The Tuberculosis Epidemic: Legal and Ethical Issues for Alcohol and Other Drug Abuse Treatment Providers.* Treatment Improvement Protocol (TIP) Series 18. (HHS Publication No. (SMA) 95-3047). Rockville, MD: Substance Abuse and Mental Health Services Administration.

Center for Substance Abuse Treatment. (1996). *Treatment Drug Courts: Integrating Substance Abuse Treatment with Legal Case Processing.* Treatment Improvement Protocol (TIP) Series 23. (HHS Publication No. (SMA) 96-3113). Rockville, MD: Substance Abuse and Mental Health Services Administration.

Center for Substance Abuse Treatment. (1997a). *A Guide to Substance Abuse Services for Primary Care Clinicians.* Treatment Improvement Protocol (TIP) Series 24. (HHS Publication No. (SMA) 97-3139). Rockville, MD: Substance Abuse and Mental Health Services Administration.

Center for Substance Abuse Treatment. (1997b). *Substance Abuse Treatment and Domestic Violence.* Treatment Improvement Protocol (TIP) Series 25. (HHS Publication No. (SMA) 97-3163). Rockville, MD: Substance Abuse and Mental Health Services Administration.

Center for Substance Abuse Treatment. (1998a). *Comprehensive Case Management for Substance Abuse Treatment.* Treatment Improvement Protocol (TIP) Series 27. (HHS Publication No. (SMA) 98-3222). Rockville, MD: Substance Abuse and Mental Health Services Administration.

Center for Substance Abuse Treatment. (1998b). *Continuity of Offender Treatment for Substance Use Disorders from Institution to Community.* Treatment Improvement Protocol (TIP) Series 30. (HHS Publication No. (SMA) 98-3245). Rockville, MD: Substance Abuse and Mental Health Services Administration.

Center for Substance Abuse Treatment. (1998c). *Naltrexone and Alcoholism Treatment.* Treatment Improvement Protocol (TIP) Series 28. (HHS Publication No. (SMA) 98-3206). Rockville, MD: Substance Abuse and Mental Health Services Administration.

Center for Substance Abuse Treatment. (1998d). *Substance Abuse Among Older Adults.* Treatment Improvement Protocol (TIP) Series 26. (HHS Publication No. (SMA) 98-3179). Rockville, MD: Substance Abuse and Mental Health Services Administration.

Center for Substance Abuse Treatment. (1998e). *Substance Use Disorder Treatment for People With Physical and Cognitive Disabilities.* Treatment Improvement Protocol (TIP) Series 29. (HHS Publication No. (SMA) 98-3249). Rockville, MD: Substance Abuse and Mental Health Services Administration.

Center for Substance Abuse Treatment. (1999a). *Brief Interventions and Brief Therapies for Substance Abuse.* Treatment Improvement Protocol (TIP) Series 34. (HHS Publication No. (SMA) 99-3353). Rockville, MD: Substance Abuse and Mental Health Services Administration.

Center for Substance Abuse Treatment. (1999b). *Enhancing Motivation for Change in Substance Abuse Treatment.* Treatment Improvement Protocol (TIP) Series 35. (HHS Publication No. (SMA) 99-3354). Rockville, MD: Substance Abuse and Mental Health Services Administration.

Center for Substance Abuse Treatment. (1999c). *Screening and Assessing Adolescents for Substance Use Disorders.* Treatment Improvement Protocol (TIP) Series 31. (HHS Publication No. (SMA) 99-3282). Rockville, MD: Substance Abuse and Mental Health Services Administration.

Center for Substance Abuse Treatment. (1999d). *Treatment of Adolescents With Substance Use Disorders.* Treatment Improvement Protocol (TIP) Series 32. (HHS Publication No. (SMA) 99-3283). Rockville, MD: Substance Abuse and Mental Health Services Administration.

Center for Substance Abuse Treatment. (1999e). *Treatment for Stimulant Use Disorders.* Treatment Improvement Protocol (TIP) Series 33. (HHS Publication No. (SMA) 99-3296). Rockville, MD: Substance Abuse and Mental Health Services Administration.

Center for Substance Abuse Treatment. (2000a). *Integrating Substance Abuse Treatment and Vocational Services.* Treatment Improvement Protocol (TIP) Series 38. (HHS Publication No. (SMA) 00-3470). Rockville, MD: Substance Abuse and Mental Health Services Administration.

Center for Substance Abuse Treatment. (2000b). *Substance Abuse Treatment for Persons With Child Abuse and Neglect Issues.* Treatment Improvement Protocol (TIP) Series 36. (HHS Publication No. (SMA) 00-3357). Rockville, MD: Substance Abuse and Mental Health Services Administration.

Center for Substance Abuse Treatment. (2000c). *Substance Abuse Treatment for Persons With HIV/AIDS.* Treatment Improvement Protocol (TIP) Series 37. (HHS Publication No. (SMA) 00-3459). Rockville, MD: Substance Abuse and Mental Health Services Administration.

Center for Substance Abuse Treatment (2003). *Manpower Development Study.* Bethesda, MD: Department of Health and Human Services.

Center for Substance Abuse Treatment. (2004*a*). *Clinical Guidelines for the Use of Buprenorphine in the Treatment of Opioid Addiction*. Treatment Improvement Protocol (TIP) Series 40. (HHS Publication No. (SMA) 04-3939). Rockville, MD: Substance Abuse and Mental Health Services Administration.

Center for Substance Abuse Treatment. (2004*b*). *Substance Abuse Treatment and Family Therapy*. Treatment Improvement Protocol (TIP) Series 39. (HHS Publication No. (SMA) 04-3957). Rockville, MD: Substance Abuse and Mental Health Services Administration.

Center for Substance Abuse Treatment. (2005*a*). *Medication-Assisted Treatment for Opioid Addiction*. Treatment Improvement Protocol (TIP) Series 43. (HHS Publication No. SMA 05-4048). Rockville, MD: Substance Abuse and Mental Health Services Administration.

Center for Substance Abuse Treatment. (2005*b*). *Substance Abuse Treatment for Adults in the Criminal Justice System*. Treatment Improvement Protocol (TIP) Series 44. (DHHS Publication No. (SMA) 05-4056). Rockville, MD: Substance Abuse and Mental Health Services Administration.

Center for Substance Abuse Treatment. (2005*c*). *Substance Abuse Treatment: Group Therapy*. Treatment Improvement Protocol (TIP) Series 41. (HHS Publication No. SMA 05-4056). Rockville, MD: Substance Abuse and Mental Health Services Administration.

Center for Substance Abuse Treatment. (2005*d*). *Substance Abuse Treatment for Persons With Co-Occurring Disorders*. Treatment Improvement Protocol (TIP) Series 42. (HHS Publication No. SMA 05-3992). Rockville, MD: Substance Abuse and Mental Health Services Administration.

Center for Substance Abuse Treatment. (2006). *Addiction Counseling Competencies: The Knowledge, Skills, and Attitudes of Professional Practice*. Technical Assistance Publication (TAP) Series 21 (Rep. No. HHS Publication No. (SMA) 07-4243). Rockville, MD: Substance Abuse and Mental Health Services Administration.

Center for Substance Abuse Treatment. (2006*a*). *Detoxification and Substance Abuse Treatment*. Treatment Improvement Protocol (TIP) Series 45. (HHS Publication No. SMA 06-4131). Rockville, MD: Substance Abuse and Mental Health Services Administration.

Center for Substance Abuse Treatment. (2006*b*). *Substance Abuse: Administrative Issues in Intensive Outpatient Treatment*. Treatment Improvement Protocol (TIP) Series 46. (HHS Publication No. SMA 06-4151). Rockville, MD: Substance Abuse and Mental Health Services Administration.

Center for Substance Abuse Treatment. (2006*c*). *Substance Abuse: Clinical Issues in Intensive Outpatient Treatment*. Treatment Improvement Protocol (TIP) Series 47. (HHS Publication No. 06-4182). Rockville, MD: Substance Abuse and Mental Health Services Administration.

Center for Substance Abuse Treatment (2007). *Competencies for Substance Abuse Treatment Clinical Supervisors*. Technical Assistance Publication (TAP) Series 21-A (Rep. No. HHS Publication No. (SMA) 07-4243). Rockville, MD: Substance Abuse and Mental Health Services Administration.

Center for Substance Abuse Treatment (2008). *Managing Depressive Symptoms in Substance Abuse Clients During Early Recovery*. Treatment Improvement Protocol (TIP) Series 48. Rockville, MD: Substance Abuse and Mental Health Services Administration.

Center for Substance Abuse Treatment (2009). *Addressing Suicidal Thoughts and Behaviors in Substance Abuse Treatment*. Treatment Improvement Protocol (TIP) Series 50. Rockville, MD: Substance Abuse and Mental Health Services Administration.

Center for Substance Abuse Treatment (2009). *Incorporating Alcohol Pharmacotherapies Into Medical Practice.* Treatment Improvement Protocol (TIP) Series 49. Rockville, MD: Substance Abuse and Mental Health Services Administration.

Center for Substance Abuse Treatment (2009). *Substance Abuse Treatment: Addressing the Specific Needs of Women.* Treatment Improvement Protocol (TIP) Series 51. Rockville, MD: Substance Abuse and Mental Health Services Administration.

Center for Substance Abuse Treatment (in development a). *Addressing Viral Hepatitis in People With Substance Use Disorders.* Treatment Improvement Protocol (TIP) Series. Rockville, MD: Substance Abuse and Mental Health Services Administration.

Center for Substance Abuse Treatment (in development b). *Improving Cultural Competence in Substance Abuse Treatment.* Treatment Improvement Protocol (TIP) Series. Rockville, MD: Substance Abuse and Mental Health Services Administration.

Center for Substance Abuse Treatment (in development c). *Management of Chronic Pain in People With or in Recovery From Substance Use Disorders.* Treatment Improvement Protocol (TIP) Series. Rockville, MD: Substance Abuse and Mental Health Services Administration.

Center for Substance Abuse Treatment (in development d). *Relapse Prevention and Recovery Promotion.* Treatment Improvement Protocol (TIP) Series. Rockville, MD: Substance Abuse and Mental Health Services Administration.

Center for Substance Abuse Treatment (in development e). *Substance Abuse Treatment for Native Americans and Alaska Natives.* Treatment Improvement Protocol (TIP) Series. Rockville, MD: Substance Abuse and Mental Health Services Administration.

Center for Substance Abuse Treatment (in development f). *Substance Abuse Treatment: Men's Issues.* Treatment Improvement Protocol (TIP) Series. Rockville, MD: Substance Abuse and Mental Health Services Administration.

Center for Substance Abuse Treatment (in development g). *Substance Abuse Treatment for People Who Are Homeless.* Treatment Improvement Protocol (TIP) Series. Rockville, MD: Substance Abuse and Mental Health Services Administration.

Center for Substance Abuse Treatment (in development h). *Substance Abuse and Trauma.* Treatment Improvement Protocol (TIP) Series. Rockville, MD: Substance Abuse and Mental Health Services Administration.

Constantine, M. G. (2003). Multicultural competence in supervision: Issues, processes, and outcomes. In Pope-Davis, D. B., Coleman, H. L. K., Liu, W. M., & Toporek, R. L. (Eds.), *Handbook of Multicultural Competencies: In Counseling & Psychology* (pp. 383–391). Thousand Oaks, CA: Sage Publications.

Cross, T. L., Bazron, B. J., Dennis, K. W., and Isaacs, M. R. (1989). *Towards a Culturally Competent System of Care: A Monograph on Effective Services for Minority Children Who Are Severely Emotionally Disturbed.* Volume 1. Washington, DC: Georgetown University Child Development Center.

Delaney, D. J. (1972). A behavioral model for the supervision of counselor candidates. *Counselor Education and Supervision 12,* 46–50.

Dixon, G. D. (2004). *Clinical Supervision: A Key to Treatment Success.* Southern Coast Beacon Tallahassee, FL: Southern Coast ATTC. Retrieved August 14, 2007, from http://www.scattc.org/pdf_upload/Beacon004.pdf

Falender, C. A., & Shafranske, E. P. (2004). *Clinical supervision: A Competency-Based Approach*. Washington, DC: American Psychological Association.

Falvey, J. E. (2002*a*). *Documentation in Supervision: The Focused Risk Management Supervision System (FoRMSS)*. Pacific Grove, CA: Brooks/Cole.

Falvey, J. E. (2002*b*). *Managing Clinical Supervision: Ethical Practice and Legal Risk Management*. Pacific Grove, CA: Brooks/Cole-Thomson Learning.

Fong, M. L., & Lease, S. H. (1997). Cross-cultural supervision: Issues for the white supervisor. In D. B. Pope-Davis & H. L. K. Coleman (Eds.), *Multicultural Counseling Competencies: Assessment, Education and Training and Supervision* (pp. 387–405). Thousand Oaks, CA: Sage.

Glenn, E., & Serovich, J. M. (1994). Documentation of family therapy supervision: A rationale and method. *American Journal of Family Therapy, 22,* 345–355.

Herman, K. C. (1993). Reassessing predictors of therapist competence. *Journal of Counseling & Development, 72,* 29–32.

Hogan, R. A. (1964). Issues and approaches in supervision. *Psychotherapy: Theory, Research, Practice, Training, 1,* 139–141.

Holloway, E. (1995). *Clinical Supervision: A Systems Approach*. Thousand Oaks, CA: Sage Publications.

Hubble, M. A., Duncan, B. L., and Miller, S. D. (Eds.). (1999). *The Heart and Soul of Change: What Works in Therapy*. Washington, DC: American Psychological Association.

International Certification & Reciprocity Consortium. (2000). *Clinical Supervisor of Alcohol and Other Drug Abuse Counselors Role Delineation Study*. Research Triangle Park, NC: CASTLE Worldwide, Inc.

Kadushin A. (1976). *Supervision in Social Work*. New York: Columbia University Press.

Lambie, G. (2006). Burnout prevention: A humanistic perspective and structured group supervision activity. *Journal of Humanistic Counseling, Education & Development, 45,* 32–44.

Lindbloom, G., Ten Eyck, T. G., & Gallon, S. L. (2004). *Clinical Supervision I: Building Chemical Dependency Counselor Skills: Instructor Guide*. Salem, Oregon: Northwest Frontier Addiction Technology Transfer Center. Retrieved August 14, 2007, from http://www.mattc.org/_media/publications/pdf/Clinical_InstructorGuide1-05_3rd_ed.pdf

Loganbill, C., Hardy, E., & Delworth, U. (1982). Supervision: A conceptual model. *Counseling Psychologist, 10,* 3–42.

Mattel, P. (2007). Designing and implementing clinical supervision. Unpublished manuscript.

Munson, C. E. (1979). *Social Work Supervision*. New York: Free Press.

Munson, C. E. (1993). *Clinical Social Work Supervision*. (2nd ed.) New York: Haworth Press.

NAADAC, The Association for Addiction Professionals (2003). *NAADAC, The Association for Addiction Professionals Practitioner Services Network Year 2 Final Report: A Survey of Early Career Substance Abuse Counselors*. Washington, DC: NAADAC, The Association for Addiction Professionals. Retrieved August 14, 2007, from http://naadac.org/pressroom/ files/Year2SurveyReport.pdf

Nichols, W. C., Nichols, D. P., & Hardy, K. V. (1990). Supervision in family therapy: A decade restudy. *Journal of Marital & Family Therapy, 16,* 275–285.

Pope, K. S., Sonne, J. L., & Greene, B. (2006). *What Therapists Don't Talk About and Why: Understanding Taboos That Hurt Us and Our Clients.* (2d ed.). Washington, DC: American Psychological Association.

Pope-Davis, D. B. & Coleman, H. L. K. (Eds.) *Multicultural Counseling Competencies: Assessment, Education and Training, and Supervision* (1997). Thousand Oaks, CA: Sage Publications.

Porter, J. & Gallon, S. L. (2006). *Clinical Supervision II: Addressing Supervisory Problems in Addictions Treatment.* Salem, OR: Northwest Frontier Addiction Technology Transfer Center.

Powell, D. J., & Brodsky, A. (2004). *Clinical Supervision in Alcohol and Drug Abuse Counseling: Principles, Models, Methods.* (Rev. ed.). San Francisco: Jossey-Bass.

Reamer, F. G. (2006). *Social Work Values and Ethics.* (3rd ed.) New York: Columbia University Press.

Remley, T. P., & Herlihy, B. (2007). *Ethical, Legal, and Professional Issues in Counseling.* (Updated 2nd ed.). Upper Saddle River, NJ: Pearson Merrill Prentice Hall.

Rigazio-DiGilio, S. A. (1997). Integrative supervision: Approaches to tailoring the supervisory process. In T. Todd and C. Storm (Eds.) *The Complete Systemic Supervisor: Context, Philosophy, and Methods* (pp. 195-217). Needham Heights, MA: Allyn and Bacon.

Roche, A. M., Todd, C. L., & O'Connor, J. (2007). Clinical supervision in the alcohol and other drugs field: An imperative or an option? *Drug and Alcohol Review, 26,* 241–249.

Shoptaw, S., Stein, J., & Rawson, R. (2000). Burnout in substance abuse counselors: Impact of environment, attitudes, and clients with HIV. *Journal of Substance Abuse Treatment, 19,* 117–126.

Skovholt, T. M., & Ronnestad, M. H. (1992). *The Evolving Professional Self: Stages and Theories in Therapist and Counselor Development.* New York: Wiley.

Spice, C. G., Jr. & Spice, W. H. (1976). A triadic method of supervision in the training counselors and counseling supervisors. *Counselor Education and Supervision, 15,* 251–258

Stoltenberg, C. D. & Delworth, U. (1987). *Supervising Counselors and Therapists: A Developmental Approach.* San Francisco: Jossey-Bass.

Stoltenberg, C. D., McNeill, B., & Delworth, U. (1998). *IDM Supervision: An Integrated Developmental Model for Supervising Counselors and Therapists.* (1st ed.) San Francisco: Jossey-Bass Publishers.

Swenson, L. C. (1997). *Psychology and Law for the Helping Professions* (2nd ed.). Pacific Grove, CA: Brooks/Cole Pub. Co.

Tromski-Klingshirn, D. (2006). Should the clinical supervisor be the administrative supervisor? The ethics versus the reality, *The Clinical Supervisor, 25,* 53–67.

U.S. Department of Health and Human Services (2003). *Developing Cultural Competence in Disaster Mental Health Programs: Guiding Principles and Recommendations.* (Rep. No. HHS Pub. No. SMA 3828). Rockville, MD: Center for Mental Health Services, Substance Abuse and Mental Health Services Administration.

White, W. L. & Popovits, R. M. (2001). *Critical incidents: Ethical Issues in the Prevention and Treatment of Addiction*. (2nd ed.). Bloomington, IL: Chestnut Health Systems.

Williams, L. (1994). A tool for training supervisors: Using the supervision feedback form (SFF). *Journal of Marital and Family Therapy, 20,* 311–315.

Appendix B: New York State Office of Alcoholism and Substance Abuse Services Clinical Supervision Vision Statement

To position clinical supervision, within the system of prevention, treatment, and recovery-oriented services, as integral to a continuous learning culture that encourages professional development, service improvement, and quality of care, maximizing benefits to the client.

Clinical supervision is defined as "a social influence process that occurs over time in which the supervisor participates with the supervisees to ensure quality clinical care. Effective supervisors observe, mentor, coach, evaluate, inspire, and create an atmosphere that promotes self-motivation, learning, and professional development. They build teams, create cohesion, resolve conflict, and shape agency culture, while attending to ethical and diversity issues in all aspects of the process. Such supervision is key to both quality improvement and the successful implementation of consensus and evidence-based practices" (TAP 21A).

Highlights

✓ Clinical supervision is a valuable and necessary strategy to ensure continuous staff and program development.

✓ The supervisory relationship must be supportive and culturally competent, provide direct oversight, and prioritize skill development and counselor wellness.

✓ Clinical supervision is a formal process that is provided frequently and employs direct observation techniques.

✓ Clinical supervisors are specifically trained and invest in continuing professional development.

✓ Fully integrated clinical supervision is expected to result in improved staff retention, counselor skills, and clinical outcomes.

The integration of clinical supervision is both a short-term and long-term strategy for ongoing quality improvement and increased successful client outcomes. The proficiency and integrity of the workforce, and subsequently the caliber of services, are strengthened through gatekeeping functions, direct oversight, teaching, training, infusion of diversity-cultural competence and sensitivity, and the morale-boosting benefits inherent in quality clinical supervision.

Research and expert consensus links clinical supervision with a wide variety of actual and potential outcomes, including improved quality of services to clients, professional development of staff, better adherence to codes of ethical conduct, increased staff retention, improved morale and wellness, fidelity to evidenced-based practices, improved regulatory compliance and risk management, and enhanced perception of recovery-oriented systems of care by consumers, professionals, and the community. Though more empirical work is needed, there is enough reliable evidence to indicate that clinical supervision is a highly efficient practice key to the growth and future of the field

Skilled clinical supervisors help staff gain advanced competency through both formal training and education supported by ongoing feedback and guidance throughout their professional career. Values inherent in clinical supervision are articulated in the acronym ASPECT:

Accountability – upholding the promise to deliver quality services.

Stewardship – mindful use of all available resources.

Professionalism – consistent and ethical role modeling and application.

Excellence – the relentless pursuit to provide the best quality care.

Continuous Learning – steadfast commitment to ongoing development.

Teamwork – active support of collective wisdom and energy to achieve great results.

The quality of the relationship between the clinical supervisor and supervisee is critical to a positive learning alliance. Clinical supervisors exercise supervisory responsibilities in a culturally responsive, respectful, fair, and objective manner. They invest in a positive supervisory alliance and endorse the professional development process of supervisees through well-thought-out, documented, and actively supported learning plans. These more experienced and objective professionals also help to mitigate the potentially adverse effects of countertransference, compassion fatigue, and burnout.

Moving the field forward by integrating clinical supervision into all recovery-oriented systems of care requires increasing the value of clinical supervision amongst policy makers, administrators, supervisors, and direct-line staff; retooling staffing patterns to support the provision of clinical supervision as a primary responsibility; and including a clinical supervisor certification. Full integration across the State may require a mechanism to include clinical supervision as a reimbursable service, thereby endorsing the integrity of clinical supervision and staffing needs. Effective clinical supervisors have available specialized training in clinical supervision inclusive of formal education and direct supervision to supplement their clinical training. Clinical supervisors are recognized through an established credential that certifies their competency.

Individual and group clinical supervision is offered regularly through acceptable methods including direct observation. This can be through live face-to-face supervision, audio/video tapes, and/or other electronic resources. Supervisors use this information to target specific skill enhancement to improve performance.

The clinical supervision hour focuses on the clinical content of the work and how the worker performs as a professional helper. Clinical technique and theory are explored and integrated to empower the supervisee's conceptual understanding and application of practical skills.

Resources are available for supervisors to receive their own clinical supervision that coaches them in their own professional development and supports effective clinical care.

Adopting clinical supervision may require significant change in agency, local, and State operations. This system-wide investment will yield invaluable gains, including a quality improvement-oriented approach to monitoring and service delivery that is projected to lead to improved staff retention, enhanced counselor skills, and better clinical outcomes.

Appendix C: Advisory Meeting Panel

H. Westley Clark, M.D., J.D., M.P.H., CAS, FASAM
Director
Center for Substance Abuse Treatment
Substance Abuse and Mental Health Services
  Administration
Rockville, Maryland

Mady Chalk, Ph.D.
Director
Division of Services Improvement
Center for Substance Abuse Treatment
Substance Abuse and Mental Health Services
  Administration
Rockville, Maryland

Christina Currier
Public Health Analyst
Practice Improvement Branch
Division of Services Improvement
Center for Substance Abuse Treatment
Substance Abuse and Mental Health Services
  Administration
Rockville, Maryland

Michael T. Flaherty, Ph.D.
Northeast Addiction Technology Transfer
  Center
Institute for Research, Education and
Training in Addictions
Pittsburgh, Pennsylvania

Kevin Hennessy, Ph.D.
Science to Service Coordinator
Substance Abuse and Mental Health Services
  Administration/OPPB
Rockville, Maryland

Constance M. Pechura, Ph.D.
Senior Program Officer
Robert Wood Johnson Foundation
Princeton, New Jersey

Richard A. Rawson, Ph.D.
Pacific Southwest Addiction Technology
  Transfer Center
Los Angeles, California

Jack B. Stein, Ph.D.
Acting Deputy Director
Division of Epidemiology, Services, and
  Prevention Research
National Institute on Drug Abuse
National Institutes of Health
Bethesda, Maryland

Richard T. Suchinsky, M.D.
Associate Chief for Addictive Disorders
Mental Health and Behavioral Sciences
  Service
U.S. Department of Veteran Affairs
Washington, D.C.

Karl D. White, Ed.D.
Public Health Analyst
Practice Improvement Branch
Division of Services Improvement
Center for Substance Abuse Treatment
Substance Abuse and Mental Health
  Services Administration
Rockville, Maryland

Mark Willenbring, M.D.
Director
Division of Treatment and Recovery Research
National Institute on Alcohol Abuse and
  Alcoholism
National Institutes of Health
Bethesda, Maryland

Appendix D: Stakeholders Meeting Participants

H. Westley Clark, M.D., J.D., M.P.H., CAS, FASAM
Director
Center for Substance Abuse Treatment
Substance Abuse and Mental Health Services
 Administration
Rockville, Maryland

Mirean Coleman, M.S.W., LICSW, CT
Senior Policy Associate
National Association of Social Workers
 (NASW)
Washington, DC

Tom Durham, Ph.D.
Executive Director
The Danya Institute
Silver Spring, Maryland

Anne M. Herron, M.S.W.
Director, Division of State and Community
 Assistance
Center for Substance Abuse Treatment
Substance Abuse and Mental Health Services
 Administration
Rockville, Maryland

Ted Judson, M.Ed., ADC2, CCS
Certification and Contracts Officer
Navy Drug and Alcohol Counselor School
San Diego, California

Linda Kaplan
Special Expert
Division of Services Improvement
Center for Substance Abuse Treatment
Substance Abuse and Mental Health Services
 Administration
Rockville, Maryland

Peter J. Martieau
Public Health Analyst
Center for Substance Abuse Prevention
Substance Abuse and Mental Health Services
 Administration
Rockville, Maryland

Jack Stein, M.S.W., Ph.D.
Director, Division of Services Improvement
Center for Substance Abuse Treatment
Substance Abuse and Mental Health Services
 Administration
Rockville, Maryland

Bill Trefzger
Lead, Communication Services Team
Office of Communication
Substance Abuse and Mental Health Services
 Administration
Rockville, Maryland

Appendix E: Field Reviewers

L. DiAnne Borders, Ph.D.
Excellence Professor
University of North Carolina at Greensboro
Greensboro, NC

Donny Brock
Treatment Director, Outpatient Division Head
Charleston Center
Charleston, SC

Patricia A Burke, M.S.W., LCSW
Private Practice
West Baldwin, ME

Charlotte M. Chapman
Director of Training
Mid-Atlantic Addiction Technology Transfer
    Center
Richmond, VA

Thomas G. Durham, Ph.D.
Executive Director, The Danya Institute
Silver Spring, MD

Janet E. Falvey, Ph.D., NCC, ACS
Professor
University of New Hampshire
Durham, NH

Steven L. Gallon, Ph.D.
Northwest Frontier Addiction Technology
    Transfer Center
Salem, OR

John Hamilton LMFT, LADC
Regional Network of Programs, Inc.
Fairfield, CT

Ted Judson, M.Ed., ADC2, CCS
Assistant Department Head
Navy Drug and Alcohol Counselor School
San Diego, CA

Hunter McQuisition, M.D.
Director, Division of Integrated Psychiatric
    Services, Department of Psychiatry
The St. Luke's–Roosevelt Hospitals
New York, NY

Thomas A. Peltz, LMHC, CADAC I, CAS
Private Practice
Beverly Farms, MA

Annie Ramniceanu
Clinical Director
Spectrum Youth and Family Services
Burlington, VT

Sandra A. Rigazio-DiGilio, Ph.D.
Professor
Marriage and Family Therapy Program
University of Connecticut
Storrs, CT

**John (Jack) M. Schibik, Ph.D., LPC,
    LCADC, CCS, CPS**
Kairos Counseling, Consulting Coaching
    Services
Naples, Florida

Diane Shea, Ph.D.
Adjunct Professor
Holy Family University
Newtown, PA

Ernestine Winfrey
Executive Director
Good News Home for Women
Flemington, NJ

Appendix F— Acknowledgments

Numerous people contributed to the development of this TIP, including the TIP Consensus Panel (see page v), the Knowledge Application Program (KAP) Advisory Meeting Panel (see Appendix C), the SAMHSA Stakeholders Meeting attendees, (see Appendix D), and TIP Field Reviewers (see Appendix E).

This publication was produced under KAP, a Joint Venture of The CDM Group, Inc. (CDM), and JBS International, Inc. (JBS), for the Substance Abuse and Mental Health Services Administration, Center for Substance Abuse Treatment.

CDM KAP personnel included Rose M. Urban, M.S.W., J.D., LCSW, LCAS, KAP Executive Deputy Project Director; Susan Kimner, Managing Project Co-Director; Bruce Carruth, Ph.D., Expert Content Director; Janet Humphrey, M.A., former Editor; Virgie D. Paul, M.L.S., Librarian; Lee Ann Knapp, Quality Assurance Editor.

Index

A

AAMFT. See American Association for Marriage and Family Therapy
ACES. *See* Association for Counselor Education and Supervision
Addiction Counseling Competencies, 3
Addiction Technology Transfer Center
  The Change Book: A Blueprint for Technology Transfer, 101
  Leadership Institute, 77
Administrative tasks
  balancing with supervisory tasks, 5, 26, 33, 78, 88, 89–90
  documentation for administrative purposes, 33, 91, 94, 95–96
Administrators
  administrative supervision compared with clinical supervision, 89–90
  administrative support for clinical supervision, 81, 92–93
  assessing organizational readiness for clinical supervision, 88–89, 101–105
  assessing the competence of supervisors and counselors, 90, 92
  assessing the organization's receptivity to supervision, 97–98
  Change Teams and, 93
  competence of supervisors and counselors and, 90, 120–121
  confidentiality issues, 90–91
  developing a model for clinical supervision, 92
  direct and vicarious liability and, 90
  direct observation and, 93, 94
  diversity and cultural competence and, 91
  documentation and recordkeeping and, 33, 91, 94, 95–96
  dual relationships and, 90–91
  ethical issues for, 90–91
  feedback and, 94, 96, 97
  implementing a clinical supervision program, 92–99
  informed consent and, 90
  key issues for, 80, 88–89
  legal issues for, 90–91
  making the case for clinical supervision to (vignette), 78–84
  organizational structure considerations, 89, 97–98
  phasing in a clinical supervision system, 94–95
  pilot supervision systems and, 93
  professional development of supervisors and, 99
  recruiting personnel, 94
  scheduling supervisory sessions, 93
  substance abuse policy, 108–109
  supporting clinical supervisors in their jobs, 97–99
  understanding the differences between case management and clinical supervision, 81
Advisory Meeting Panel, members, 139
Al. *See* Walt vignette
Alicia. *See* Stan vignette
American Association for Marriage and Family Therapy
  ethical and legal guidelines, 106
American Psychological Association
  guidelines for retaining records of supervision, 113
Assessing organizational readiness
  administrator's role, 88–89
  elements of, 101
  identifying current barriers to implementing a supervision system (Tool 2), 104
  initial organizational assessment (Tool 1), 102
  organizational stage of readiness to change (Tool 2), 103–104
Association for Counselor Education and Supervision
  standards and ethical guidelines, 106
Association of State and Provincial Psychology Boards
  ethical and legal guidelines, 106
ATTC. *See* Addiction Technology Transfer Center
Audiotaped supervision
  confidentiality and (Tool 18), 126

description, advantages, and disadvantages of, 22, 31
instructions for (Tool 17), 124–125
recording consent (Tool 19), 126

B

Beauchamp, T.L.
  ethical and legal issue resource, 13
Behavioral contracting in supervision
  elements of, 17
Benefits of clinical supervision
  improvement of client outcome, 87
  professional development, 88, 99
  program evaluation and research, 88
  responsiveness to diversity, 87
  workplace development, 88
Bernard, J.M.
  examples of work samples and peer
    assessments, 18
  qualities of a good model of clinical super-
    vision, 9
Betty. *See* Margie vignette
Bibliography, 127–134
Bill vignette
  defining and building the supervisor-
    supervisee alliance, 44–51
Blended Model. *See* Integrated models of
  supervision
Boundary issues
  ethical and legal considerations, 14–15,
    51–58
Bradley, L.J.
  administrative supervision/clinical super-
    vision comparison, 89–90
  supervisor-focused personal development
    domain, 91
Brodsky, A.
  ethical and legal issue resource, 13
  examples of work samples and peer
    assessments, 18
  qualities of a good model of clinical super-
    vision, 9
Burnout
  helping counselors with, 19–20

C

Caldwell, C.F.
  Focused Risk Management Supervision
    System, 28, 98
Campbell, J.M.

examples of work samples and peer
  assessments, 18
supervision contract, 112
Carrie. *See* Walt vignette
Case consultation/case management
  description, advantages, and disadvan-
    tages, 31
  understanding the differences between
    case management and clinical supervi-
    sion, 81
Case presentations
  outline for, 123–124
  sample case consultation format (Tool 16),
    124
*The Change Book: A Blueprint for Technology
  Transfer,* 101
Childress, J.F.
  ethical and legal issue resource, 13
Clinical supervision. *See also* Supervision
  administrative benefits, 87
  administrative supervision comparison,
    89–90
  advocating for both administrators and
    workers and clients, 60
  benefits of, 87–88
  central principles of, 5–6
  definitions, 3, 87
  demonstrating the importance of adminis-
    trative support for, 81
  differences between supervision and coun-
    seling (figure), 24
  goals of, 17, 20, 24, 44, 51, 69, 87
  implementing a clinical supervision sys-
    tem, 82–83
  making the case for clinical supervision to
    administrators (vignette), 78–84
  presenting a proposal for, 79, 84
  qualities of effective supervisors, 62
  rationale for, 3–4, 37, 45, 78, 87
  time standard for, 14, 27, 28, 30, 50
Clinical supervisors
  competence of, 90, 92, 106
  functions of, 4
  gatekeeper role, 6, 13
  guidelines for new supervisors, 6–8
  identifying staff with high potential for
    advancement, 77
  roles of (figure), 4
  supervision of, 5

Coach role of clinical supervisors
    description, 4
    vignette illustrating, 35–44
Codes of ethics
    employees' signing of statements agreeing
        to abide by, 91
    resources, 34, 106
    reviewing, 91
Cofacilitation and modeling method of
    supervision
    description, advantages, and disadvan-
        tages of, 32
Cognitive-behavioral therapy. *See* Treatment-
    based supervision models
Cohen, C.R.
    Focused Risk Management Supervision
        System, 28, 98
Compassion fatigue
    communication and, 26
    helping counselors with, 19–20
Competence of clinical supervisors
    assessing, 90, 92, 106
    checklist for supervisor competencies
        (Tool 5), 107–108
*Competencies for Substance Abuse Treatment
    Clinical Supervisors,* 3, 87
Competency-based models of supervision
    description and key strategies, 8
Confidentiality
    audiotaping, 39, 126
    criteria for waiving, 15
    direct observation, 39
    duty-to-warn requirements and, 15, 90
    issues for administrators, 90–91, 106
    levels of, 15
    online counseling and supervision and,
        15, 17
    State legal and legislative standards for,
        15
    training counselors in, 15
    videotaping, 39, 126
Consensus Panel
    central principles of clinical supervision,
        5–6
    employee assistance program, 20
    peer supervision recommendation, 27
Constantine, M.G.
    Multicultural Model of supervision, 11
    questions supervisors can use with
        supervisees, 13

Consultant role of clinical supervisors, 4
Contextual factors. *See* Cultural and contextu-
    al factors
Counselors. *See also* Developmental stages of
    counselors; Evaluation of counselors and
    supervisors
    competency assessment (Tool 14),
        120–121
    counselor evaluation of the supervisor
        (Tool 13), 118–119
    outline for case presentations, 123–124
Countertransference
    between counselor and client, 25, 51–58,
        68
    signs of, 25
    between supervisors and supervisees, 25
Cross, T.L.
    stages of becoming culturally competent,
        12
Cultural and contextual factors. See also
    Diversity and cultural competence
    contextual issues in techniques and meth-
        ods of supervision, 30, 32, 101
Counselor Development domain and, 11
    example of, 54
    identifying, 11
    importance of culture in supervision, 11
    levels of cultural consideration, 12
    supervisor self-examination, 12–13, 34
    Supervisory Alliance domain, 11

D
Delworth, U.
    Integrated Developmental Model of super-
        vision, 8, 9
Developmental model of supervision
    description and key strategies, 8
Developmental stages of counselors
    cautions and principles, 9–10
    counselor developmental model
        (figure), 10
    defining and building the supervisory
        alliance (vignette), 44–51
    managing staff confrontations, 62
    mentoring and, 74
    working with counselors at different lev-
        els of proficiency, 60–61
Developmental stages of supervisors
    description, 10–11, 47–48, 94

supervisor developmental model (figure), 11

Direct liability
administrators and, 90
description, 13
vicarious liability and, 14, 90, 106

Direct observation
administrators and, 93, 94
advantages of, 21, 28, 31
confidentiality and, 39
disadvantages of, 31
effectiveness of, 6
encouraging acceptance of, 41
feedback and, 18, 21, 40
guidelines for, 21
implementing, 39
resistance to, 21, 39, 42
selecting cases for, 21
vignette on implementing, 35–44

Disciplinary actions
policies and procedures for dealing with unacceptable behavior by counselors, 20, 41

Discrimination Model. *See* Competency-based models of supervision

Diversity and cultural competence
addressing personal issues, 65
administrators' responsibilities, 91, 98
assessing, 89
communication issues, 91
continuum of cultural competence (figure), 12
description, 5, 11–12
importance of cultural competence, 5, 91
responsiveness to diversity, 87

Documentation and recordkeeping
for administrative purposes, 33, 91, 94, 95–96
duty-to-warn situations, 15
evaluations of counselors, 20, 28, 94, 96–97
Focused Risk Management Supervision System, 28, 98
formative and summative evaluations and, 29
importance of, 28
individual development plans, 17
initial supervision sessions, 113–117
purpose of, 95–96

records of supervisory sessions, 33
retention period for records of supervision, 113
systems to be documented, 28

Drug-Free Workplace Act
substance abuse policy requirement, 108

Dual relationships
between counselors and clients, 14, 51–58, 106
description and examples of, 14, 53, 106
ethical and legal considerations, 14–15, 51–58, 106
issues for administrators, 90–91, 106
between supervisors and supervisees, 14, 106

Due process
description, 106
documentation of, 28

Duty-to-warn requirements
confidentiality and, 15, 90

E

EAPs. *See* Employee assistance programs

EBPs. *See* Evidence-based practices

Ella vignette
making the case for clinical supervision to administrators, 78–84

Eloise. *See* Stan vignette

Employee assistance programs
informing supervisors and, 69
recommendation for, 20
videotaped supervision and, 22

Environmental variables in clinical supervision systems
description, 89

Ethical and legal issues
addressing ethical standards (vignette), 51–58
for administrators, 90–91
codes of ethics, 34, 91
competence of supervisors and counselors, 90, 92, 106, 120–121
confidentiality, 15, 17, 90–91, 106
deciding how to address potential legal or ethical violations (figure), 16
direct versus vicarious liability, 13–14, 90, 106
dual relationships and boundary issues, 14–15, 90–91, 106

due process and, 28, 106
how to ask questions in ethical decisionmaking, 57
informed consent, 15, 90, 106
orientation in for all employees, 91
policies and procedures for dealing with
   unacceptable behavior by counselors,
   20, 110–111
resources on, 13, 34
steps to ethical decisionmaking, 55
supervision note admissibility in court
   proceedings, 28–29
supervisor ethics, 17
underlying assumptions, 13
Evaluation of counselors and supervisors
client input, 18
counselor competency assessment (Tool
   14), 120–121
counselor evaluation of the supervisor
   (Tool 13), 118–119
documentation and, 28, 29, 96–97
feedback issues, 18, 96, 118
formal procedure for, 118
formative, 18, 96–97, 118
general areas of competence to assess, 118
goals of, 96
summative, 18, 97, 118
timely basis for, 99
Evidence-based practices
implementing an evidence-based practice
   (vignette), 58–64
integrated models of supervision and, 8
integration with clinical supervision, 5, 6,
   87, 88–89
staff resistance to incorporating, 58–64
treatment-based supervision models
   and, 8

F

Falvey, J.E.
   ethical and legal issue resource, 13
Focused Risk Management Supervision
   System, 28, 98, 113
   standardized format for documentation of
      supervision, 33
Feedback
   administrators and, 94, 96, 97
   direct observation and, 18, 21, 40
importance of, 118
   live observation and, 24, 40
Field reviewers, 143
Focused Risk Management Supervision
   System
   description, 28, 98, 113
Fong, M.L.
   diversity and cultural competence issues,
      91
Formative evaluation of counselors
   description, 18, 118
   documentation of, 29
   focus of, 18, 96–97
FoRMSS. *See* Focused Risk Management
   Supervision System

G

Gatekeeper role of clinical supervisors
   ethical and legal issues and, 13
   importance of, 6
   managing problem staff, 20
   policies and procedures for dealing with
      unacceptable behavior by counselors,
      20, 41
Glenn, E.
   standardized format for documentation of
      supervision, 33
Gloria vignette
   implementing an evidence-based practice,
      58–64
Goals of clinical supervision
   description, 17, 20, 24, 44, 51, 69, 87
   form for identifying (Tool 3), 105
Goodyear, R.K.
   examples of work samples and peer
      assessments, 18
   qualities of a good model of clinical super-
      vision, 9
Greene, B.
   ethical and legal issue resource, 13
Group clinical supervision
   description, 27
   as a means of engaging all staff in dialog,
      sharing ideas, and promoting team
      cohesion, 28
Gutheil, T.G.
   ethical and legal issue resource, 13

H

Health Insurance Portability and
    Accountability Act
      confidentiality and, 15, 90–91
HIPAA. *See* Health Insurance Portability and
    Accountability Act
Holloway, E.
    cultural issues in supervision, 12
    Systems Model, 11

I

IC&RC. *See* International Certification and
    Reciprocity Consortium
IDM. *See* Integrated Developmental Model of
    supervision
IDPs. *See* Individual development plans
Implementing a clinical supervision system
    administrators and, 92–99
    barriers to (Tool 2), 104
    supervisors and, 82–83
Indirect observation
    drawbacks to, 21
Individual development plans
    as a basis for evaluation, 96
    beginning discussion of, 44–51
    elements of, 17, 122
    implementing for each supervisee, 48
    initial supervision sessions and, 29
    for potential successors, 73
    professional development plan (Tool 15),
      122–123
    for supervisors, 17–18, 99
Individual supervision
    description, 27
Informed consent
    description, 15, 106
    importance of, 106
    issues for administrators, 90
    levels of, 15
    live observation and, 22, 39
    observation and/or taping of
      sessions, 21, 39
    supervision contract and, 15
    template for, 106–107
Initial supervision sessions
    checklist (Tool 9), 114–115
    current risk management review (Tool
      11), 116
    documentation and recordkeeping,
      113–117

goal of, 113
    helpful practices, 29
    individual development plans and, 29
    learning environment of supervision and,
      29
    supervision content (Tool 10), 115
    supervision note sample (Tool 10), 115
    supervisory interview observations (Tool
      12), 117
Integrated Developmental Model of supervi-
    sion
    description and key strategies, 8, 9
Integrated models of supervision
    description and key strategies, 8
Intensive supervision
    description, 27
International Certification and Reciprocity
    Consortium
    Role Delineation Study for Clinical
      Supervisors, 107

J

Jaime. *See* Gloria vignette
Jan. *See* Bill vignette
Juanita vignette
    maintaining focus on job performance,
      64–69

K

Kadushin, A.
    administrative tasks for clinical supervi-
      sors, 88
Kate vignette
    promoting a counselor from within, 69–73
Kevin. *See* Kate vignette

L

Ladany, N.
    administrative supervision/clinical super-
      vision comparison, 89–90
    supervisor-focused personal development
      domain, 91
Larry. *See* Gloria vignette
Lease, S.H.
    diversity and cultural competence
      issues, 91
Legal issues. *See* Ethical and legal issues
Liability
    direct versus vicarious liability, 13–14, 90
    issues for administrators, 90

issues in supervisory vulnerability, 14

"reasonable effort to supervise" and, 14

Live observation

    description, 22

    disadvantages of, 23

    effectiveness of, 23

    feedback and, 24, 40

    guidelines for conducting, 23–24

    helping counselors and clients become comfortable with, 38

    intervening during the session, 23–24, 40

    one-way mirrors and, 22–23

    videotaping and, 22–23

    vignette on implementing, 35–44

M

Maggie. *See* Kate vignette

Margie vignette

    mentoring a successor, 73–77

McNeill, B.

    Integrated Developmental Model of supervision, 8, 9

Melissa. *See* Juanita vignette

Mentor/role model role of clinical supervisors

    description, 4, 43, 75

    mentoring a successor (vignette), 73–77

    resources on mentorship, 77

    vignette illustrating, 35–44

Methods and techniques of clinical supervision

    assessing, 89

    contextual issues, 30, 32, 101

    description, advantages, and disadvantages (figure), 30–32

    implementing a new method of supervision (vignette), 35–44

    introducing changes in clinical practices, 59–60

Methods of observation

    choice of method, 22

    direct, 6, 20–21, 28, 31, 35–44, 93, 94

    indirect, 21

    live, 22–24, 35–44

    recorded, 22, 35–44, 124–125, 126

MI. *See* Motivational interviewing

Michael E. Townsend Leadership Academy

    description and contact information, 77

Microtraining. *See* Competency-based models of supervision

Modalities of supervision

group clinical supervision, 27

individual supervision, 27

intensive supervision, 27

peer supervision, 27, 42–43, 94

sample clinical supervision schedule (figure), 28

triadic supervision, 27

Models of clinical supervision. *See also* Evidence-based practices

    competency-based, 8

    cultural and diversity factors and, 8–9

    development of, 92

    developmental, 8

    identifying and selecting your model, 9

    integrated, 8

    introducing changes in clinical practices, 59–60

    qualities of a good model, 9

    time management and, 26

    treatment-based, 8

Monitoring performance

    addressing personal issues that affect job performance, 65–66

    behavioral contracting, 17

    burnout and compassion fatigue and, 19–20, 26

    evaluation of counselors, 18, 96–97

    gatekeeping role and, 20

    individual development plan, 17–18

    maintaining focus on job performance (vignette), 64–69

Motivational interviewing. *See also* Treatment-based supervision models

    implementing (vignette), 58–64

    staff resistance and, 42

    Multicultural Model of supervision description, 11

Munson, C.E.

    administrative tasks for clinical supervisors, 88

N

NASW. *See* National Association of Social Workers

National Association of Social Workers

    ethical and legal guidelines, 106

National Board for Certified Counselors, Inc.

    Code of Ethics, 106

New supervisors

    building a leadership position, 69–73

guidelines for, 6–8

implementing a new method of supervision and, 37

promoting a counselor from within (vignette), 69–73

qualities of an effective leadership style, 71

things a new supervisor should know, 7–8

New York State Office of Alcoholism and Substance Abuse Services

    Clinical Supervision Vision Statement, 135–137

North Carolina Addiction Fellows Program

    description and contact information, 77

O

Online classroom training programs

    list, 34

Online counseling and supervision

    confidentiality issues, 15, 17

P

Peer supervision

    advantages and disadvantages, 42–43

    description, 27

    developing a system for, 94

Personal problems. *See* Stress

Pope, K.S.

    ethical and legal issue resource, 13

Powell, D.J.

    examples of work samples and peer assessments, 18

    qualities of a good model of clinical supervision, 9

Practical issues

    balancing clinical and administrative functions, 26

    countertransference and, 25–26, 51–58, 68

    distinguishing between supervision and therapy, 24–26, 65, 66

    documenting and recordkeeping issues, 28–29

    finding the time to do clinical supervision, 26–28

    selecting a modality of supervision, 26–27

    structuring the initial supervision sessions, 29

    transference and, 25, 51–58

Prison settings

    videotaped supervision and, 22

Professional development benefits of clinical supervision, 88, 99

Professional development plan (Tool 15), 122–123

Program evaluation and research benefits of clinical supervision

    description, 88

Psychodynamic psychotherapy. *See* Treatment-based supervision models

R

Racism. *See* Diversity and cultural competence

Rationale for clinical supervision

    description, 3–4, 45, 78, 87

    providing, 37

Reamer, F.G.

    ethical and legal issue resource, 13

Reasonable effort to supervise

    importance of, 78

    liability issues, 14

Recorded observation

    audiotaped, 22, 124–126

    videotaped, 22, 35–44, 124–126

Recordkeeping. *See* Documentation and recordkeeping

Resources

    bibliography, 127–134

    competencies of clinical supervisors, 108

    counselor competency assessment, 122

    ethical and legal issues, 13, 34, 106

    for supervision, 34

Risk management issues

    current risk management review (Tool 11), 116

    documentation, 28, 33

    videotaped supervision and, 22

Role playing method of supervision

    description, advantages, and disadvantages of, 32

S

Serovick, J.M.

    standardized format for documentation of supervision, 33

Sexual relationships. *See* Boundary issues; Dual relationships

SMART. *See* Specific, measurable, attainable, realistic, and timely
Sonne, J.L.
    ethical and legal issue resource, 13
South Carolina Addiction Fellows Program
    description and contact information, 77
Specific, measurable, attainable, realistic, and timely competency-based models of supervision and, 8
    feedback and, 18
Spice, C. G., Jr.
    triadic supervision, 27
Spice, W.H.
    triadic supervision, 27
Staff resistant to supervision
    working with, 7
Stakeholders meeting participants, 141
Stan vignette
    addressing ethical standards, 51–58
Stoltenberg, C.D.
    Integrated Developmental Model of supervision, 8, 9
Stress
    addressing personal issues that affect job performance, 65–66
    helping counselors with, 19–20, 64–69
Substance abuse policy
    sample policy (Tool 6), 108
Summative evaluation of counselors
    description, 18, 97, 118
    documentation of, 29
Supervision. *See also* Clinical supervision
    definitions of, 3, 87
Supervision contracts
    elements of, 50
    informed consent and, 15
    template (Tool 8), 111–112
    uses for, 111
Supervision guidelines
    clinical supervision policy and procedure (Tool 7), 110–111
Supervisor ethics
    standards for, 17
Supervisor self-examination
    feelings toward counselors, 47, 50
    questions for, 12–13, 47
    resources, 34
Supervisor-supervisee alliance
    countertransference issues, 25

cultural issues, 11, 13
    defining and building the alliance (vignette), 44–51
    developing and maintaining a strong and professional relationship, 73–77
    dual relationships and boundary issues, 14–15, 51–58
    importance of, 4
    mentorship and, 74
    power issues, 13, 14, 18, 57, 91
Systems Model of supervision
    description, 11

T

Task-Oriented Model. *See* Competency-based models of supervision
Teacher role of clinical supervisors, 4
Techniques of clinical supervision. *See* Methods and techniques of clinical supervision
Time management
    adding components of a supervision model one at a time, 26–27
    administrative tasks and, 33–34
    plan for scheduling supervision, 27–28
    questions about one's priorities, 33–34
    Time standard for clinical supervision 20:1 rule of client hours, 14, 27, 28, 30
Training programs
    choosing a course on clinical supervision, 43
    establishing a training plan and learning goals, 95
    online, 34, 43
Transference
    examples of, 25
    vignette, 51–58
Treatment-based supervision models
    description and key strategies, 8
Triadic supervision
    description, 27

V

Verbal reports
    description, advantages, and disadvantages, 30
Verbatim reports
    description, advantages, and disadvantages, 30

Vicarious liability
    administrators and, 90
    confidentiality and, 15
    description, 14
    direct liability and, 13–14, 106
    examples of negligence, 14
Videotaped supervision
    confidentiality and, 39, 126
    description, advantages, and disadvan-
        tages of, 22, 31
    guidelines for, 22
    implementing, 39
    instructions for (Tool 17), 124–125
    live observation and, 22–23
    recording consent (Tool 19), 126
    resistance to, 22, 42
    risk-management issues, 22
    vignette on implementing, 35–44
Vignettes
    addressing ethical standards, 51–58
    defining and building the supervisory
        alliance, 44–51
    establishing a new approach for clinical
        supervision, 35–44
    implementing an evidence-based practice,
        58–64
    maintaining focus on job performance,
        64–69
    making the case for clinical supervision to
        administrators, 78–84
    mentoring a successor, 73–77
    promoting a counselor from within, 69–73
VTS. *See* Videotaped supervision

W

Walt vignette
    implementing a new method of supervi-
        sion, 35–44
Webcam method of supervision
    description, advantages, and disadvan-
        tages of, 32
Williams, L.
    standardized format for documentation of
        supervision, 33
Work setting
    benefits of clinical supervision, 88
    problems and resources, 7
Written/file reviews
    description, advantages, and disadvan-
        tages, 30

CSAT TIPs and Publications Based on TIPs

What Is a TIP?

Treatment Improvement Protocols (TIPs) are the products of a systematic and innovative process that brings together clinicians, researchers, program managers, policymakers, and other Federal and non-Federal experts to reach consensus on state-of-the-art treatment practices. TIPs are developed under CSAT's Knowledge Application Program to improve the treatment capabilities of the Nation's alcohol and drug abuse treatment service system.

What Is a Quick Guide?

A Quick Guide clearly and concisely presents the primary information from a TIP in a pocket-sized booklet. Each Quick Guide is divided into sections to help readers quickly locate relevant material. Some contain glossaries of terms or lists of resources. Page numbers from the original TIP are referenced so providers can refer back to the source document for more information.

What Are KAP Keys?

Also based on TIPs, KAP Keys are handy, durable tools. Keys may include assessment or screening instruments, checklists, and summaries of treatment phases. Printed on coated paper, each KAP Keys set is fastened together with a key ring and can be kept within a treatment provider's reach and consulted frequently. The Keys allow you—the busy clinician or program administrator—to locate information easily and to use this information to enhance treatment services.

TIP 1   State Methadone Treatment Guidelines—Replaced by TIP 43

TIP 2*   Pregnant, Substance-Using Women— *BKD107*

    Quick Guide for Clinicians *QGCT02*

    KAP Keys for Clinicians *KAPT02*

TIP 3   Screening and Assessment of Alcohol- and Other Drug-Abusing Adolescents—Replaced by TIP 31

TIP 4   Guidelines for the Treatment of Alcohol- and Other Drug-Abusing Adolescents—Replaced by TIP 32

TIP 5   Improving Treatment for Drug-Exposed Infants— *BKD110*

TIP 6*   Screening for Infectious Diseases Among Substance Abusers—*BKD131*

    Quick Guide for Clinicians *QGCT06*

    KAP Keys for Clinicians *KAPT06*

TIP 7   Screening and Assessment for Alcohol and Other Drug Abuse Among Adults in the Criminal Justice System—Replaced by TIP 44

TIP 8   Intensive Outpatient Treatment for Alcohol and Other Drug Abuse—Replaced by TIPs 46 and 47

TIP 9   Assessment and Treatment of Patients With Coexisting Mental Illness and Alcohol and Other Drug Abuse— Replaced by TIP 42

TIP 10   Assessment and Treatment of Cocaine-Abusing Methadone-Maintained Patients—Replaced by TIP 43

TIP 11*   Simple Screening Instruments for Outreach for Alcohol and Other Drug Abuse and Infectious Diseases— *BKD143*

    Quick Guide for Clinicians *QGCT11*

    KAP Keys for Clinicians *KAPT11*

TIP 12   Combining Substance Abuse Treatment With Intermediate Sanctions for Adults in the Criminal Justice System—Replaced by TIP 44

TIP 13   Role and Current Status of Patient Placement Criteria in the Treatment of Substance Use Disorders—*BKD161*

    Quick Guide for Clinicians *QGCT13*

    Quick Guide for Administrators *QGAT13*

    KAP Keys for Clinicians *KAPT13*

TIP 14   Developing State Outcomes Monitoring Systems for Alcohol and Other Drug Abuse Treatment—*BKD162*

TIP 15   Treatment for HIV-Infected Alcohol and Other Drug Abusers—Replaced by TIP 37

TIP 16   Alcohol and Other Drug Screening of Hospitalized Trauma Patients—*BKD164*

    Quick Guide for Clinicians *QGCT16*

    KAP Keys for Clinicians *KAPT16*

TIP 17   Planning for Alcohol and Other Drug Abuse Treatment for Adults in the Criminal Justice System— Replaced by TIP 44

TIP 18   The Tuberculosis Epidemic: Legal and Ethical Issues for Alcohol and Other Drug Abuse Treatment Providers—*BKD173*

    Quick Guide for Clinicians *QGCT18*

    KAP Keys for Clinicians *KAPT18*

TIP 19   Detoxification From Alcohol and Other Drugs— Replaced by TIP 45

TIP 20   Matching Treatment to Patient Needs in Opioid Substitution Therapy—Replaced by TIP 43

*Under revision

TIP 21 Combining Alcohol and Other Drug Abuse Treatment With Diversion for Juveniles in the Justice System—(SMA) 08-4073

Quick Guide for Clinicians and Administrators QGCA21

TIP 22 LAAM in the Treatment of Opiate Addiction—Replaced by TIP 43

TIP 23 Treatment Drug Courts: Integrating Substance Abuse Treatment With Legal Case Processing—(SMA) 08-3917

Quick Guide for Administrators QGAT23

TIP 24 A Guide to Substance Abuse Services for Primary Care Clinicians—(SMA) 08-4075

Concise Desk Reference Guide BKD123

Quick Guide for Clinicians QGCT24

KAP Keys for Clinicians KAPT24

TIP 25 Substance Abuse Treatment and Domestic Violence—(SMA) 08-4076

Linking Substance Abuse Treatment and Domestic Violence Services: A Guide for Treatment Providers MS668

Linking Substance Abuse Treatment and Domestic Violence Services: A Guide for Administrators MS667

Quick Guide for Clinicians QGCT25

KAP Keys for Clinicians KAPT25

TIP 26 Substance Abuse Among Older Adults—(SMA) 08-3918

Substance Abuse Among Older Adults: A Guide for Treatment Providers MS669

Substance Abuse Among Older Adults: A Guide for Social Service Providers MS670

Substance Abuse Among Older Adults: Physician's Guide MS671

Quick Guide for Clinicians QGCT26

KAP Keys for Clinicians KAPT26

TIP 27 Comprehensive Case Management for Substance Abuse Treatment—(SMA) 08-4215

Case Management for Substance Abuse Treatment: A Guide for Treatment Providers MS673

Case Management for Substance Abuse Treatment: A Guide for Administrators MS672

Quick Guide for Clinicians QGCT27

Quick Guide for Administrators QGAT27

TIP 28* Naltrexone and Alcoholism Treatment—(SMA) 05-4077

Naltrexone and Alcoholism Treatment: Physician's Guide MS674

Quick Guide for Clinicians QGCT28

KAP Keys for Clinicians KAPT28

TIP 29 Substance Use Disorder Treatment for People With Physical and Cognitive Disabilities—(SMA) 08-4078

Quick Guide for Clinicians QGCT29

Quick Guide for Administrators (SMA) 08-3592

KAP Keys for Clinicians KAPT29

TIP 30 Continuity of Offender Treatment for Substance Use Disorders From Institution to Community—(SMA) 08-3920

Quick Guide for Clinicians QGCT30

KAP Keys for Clinicians KAPT30

TIP 31 Screening and Assessing Adolescents for Substance Use Disorders—(SMA) 08-4079

See companion products for TIP 32.

TIP 32 Treatment of Adolescents With Substance Use Disorders—(SMA) 08-4080

Quick Guide for Clinicians QGC312

KAP Keys for Clinicians KAP312

TIP 33 Treatment for Stimulant Use Disorders—(SMA) 06-4209

Quick Guide for Clinicians QGCT33

KAP Keys for Clinicians KAPT33

TIP 34 Brief Interventions and Brief Therapies for Substance Abuse—(SMA) 07-3952

Quick Guide for Clinicians QGCT34

KAP Keys for Clinicians KAPT34

TIP 35 Enhancing Motivation for Change in Substance Abuse Treatment—(SMA) 08-4212

Quick Guide for Clinicians QGCT35

KAP Keys for Clinicians KAPT35

TIP 36 Substance Abuse Treatment for Persons With Child Abuse and Neglect Issues—(SMA) 08-3923

Quick Guide for Clinicians QGCT36

KAP Keys for Clinicians KAPT36

Helping Yourself Heal: A Recovering Woman's Guide to Coping With Childhood Abuse Issues—(SMA) 08-4132

Available in Spanish: PHD981S

Helping Yourself Heal: A Recovering Man's Guide to Coping With the Effects of Childhood Abuse—(SMA) 08-4134

Available in Spanish: PHD1059S

TIP 37 Substance Abuse Treatment for Persons With HIV/AIDS—(SMA) 08-4137

Quick Guide for Clinicians MS678

KAP Keys for Clinicians KAPT37

Drugs, Alcohol, and HIV/AIDS: A Consumer Guide—(SMA) 08-4127

Drugs, Alcohol, and HIV/AIDS: A Consumer Guide for African Americans—(SMA) 07-4248

*Under revision

TIP 38   Integrating Substance Abuse Treatment and
          Vocational Services—*(SMA) 06-4216*

          Quick Guide for Clinicians *QGCT38*

          Quick Guide for Administrators *QGAT38*

          KAP Keys for Clinicians *KAPT38*

TIP 39   Substance Abuse Treatment and Family Therapy—
          (SMA) 08-4219

          Quick Guide for Clinicians *QGCT39*

          Quick Guide for Administrators *QGAT39*

TIP 40   Clinical Guidelines for the Use of Buprenorphine in
          the Treatment of Opioid Addiction—*(SMA) 07-3939*

          Quick Guide for Physicians *QGPT40*

          KAP Keys for Physicians *KAPT40*

TIP 41   Substance Abuse Treatment: Group Therapy—
          (SMA) 05-3991

          Quick Guide for Clinicians *QGCT41*

TIP 42   Substance Abuse Treatment for Persons With Co-
          Occurring Disorders—*(SMA) 08-3992*

          Quick Guide for Clinicians *(SMA) 07-4034*

          Quick Guide for Administrators *QGAT42*

          KAP Keys for Clinicians *(SMA) 08-4036*

TIP 43   Medication-Assisted Treatment for Opioid Addiction
          in Opioid Treatment Programs—*(SMA) 08-4214*

          Quick Guide for Clinicians *QGCT43*

          KAP Keys for Clinicians *(SMA) 07-4108*

TIP 44   Substance Abuse Treatment for Adults in the Criminal
          Justice System—*(SMA) 05-4056*

          Quick Guide for Clinicians *QGCT44*

          KAP Keys for Clinicians *(SMA) 07-4150*

TIP 45   Detoxification and Substance Abuse Treatment—
          (SMA) 08-4131

          Quick Guide for Clinicians *(SMA) 06-4225*

          KAP Keys for Clinicians *(SMA) 06-4224*

          Quick Guide for Administrators *(SMA) 06-4226*

TIP 46   Substance Abuse: Administrative Issues in Outpatient
          Treatment—*(SMA) 06-4157*

          Quick Guide for Administrators—*(SMA) 07-4232*

TIP 47   Substance Abuse: Clinical Issues in Outpatient
          Treatment—*(SMA) 06-4182*

          Quick Guide for Clinicians—*(SMA) 07-4233*

          KAP Keys for Clinicians—*(SMA) 07-4251*

TIP 48   Managing Depressive Symptoms in Substance Abuse
          Clients During Early Recovery—*(SMA) 08-4353*

TIP 49   Incorporating Alcohol Pharmacotherapies Into
          Medical Practice—*(SMA) 09-4380*

TIP 50   Addressing Suicidal Thoughts and Behaviors in
          Substance Abuse Treatment—*(SMA) 09-4381*

TIP 52   Clinical Supervision and Professional Development of
          the Substance Abuse Counselor—*(SMA) 09-4435*

Treatment Improvement Protocols (TIPs) from the Substance Abuse and Mental Health Services Administration's (SAMHSA's) Center for Substance Abuse Treatment (CSAT)

Place the quantity (up to 5) next to the publications you would like to receive and print your mailing address below.

___**TIP 2*** BKD107
___QG+ for Clinicians QGCT02
___KK+ for Clinicians KAPT02

___**TIP 5** BKD110

___**TIP 6*** BKD131
___QG for Clinicians QGCT06
___KK for Clinicians KAPT06

___**TIP 11*** BKD143
___QG for Clinicians QGCT11
___KK for Clinicians KAPT11

___**TIP 13** BKD161
___QG for Clinicians QGCT13
___QG for Administrators QGAT13
___KK for Clinicians KAPT13

___**TIP 14** BKD162

___**TIP 16** BKD164
___QG for Clinicians QGCT16
___KK for Clinicians KAPT16

___**TIP 18** BKD173
___QG for Clinicians QGCT18
___KK for Clinicians KAPT18

___**TIP 21** (SMA) 08-4076
___QG for Clinicians & Administrators QGCA21

___**TIP 23** (SMA) 08-3917
___QG for Administrators QGAT23

___**TIP 24** (SMA) 08-4075
___Desk Reference BKD123
___QG for Clinicians QGCT24
___KK for Clinicians KAPT24

___**TIP 25** (SMA) 08-4076
___Guide for Treatment Providers MS668
___Guide for Administrators MS667
___QG for Clinicians QGCT25
___KK for Clinicians KAPT25

___**TIP 26** (SMA) 08-3918
___Guide for Treatment Providers MS669
___Guide for Social Service Providers MS670
___Physician's Guide MS671
___QG for Clinicians QGCT26
___KK for Clinicians KAPT26

___**TIP 27** (SMA) 08-4215
___Guide for Treatment Providers MS673
___Guide for Administrators MS672
___QG for Clinicians QGCT27
___QG for Administrators QGAT27

___**TIP 29** (SMA) 08-4078
___QG for Clinicians QGCT29
___QG for Administrators (SMA) 08-3592
___KK for Clinicians KAPT29

___**TIP 30** (SMA) 08-3920
___QG for Clinicians QGCT30
___KK for Clinicians KAPT30

___**TIP 31** (SMA) 08-4079
(see products under TIP 32)

___**TIP 32** (SMA) 08-4080
___QG for Clinicians QGC312
___KK for Clinicians KAP312

___**TIP 33** (SMA) 06-4209
___QG for Clinicians QGCT33
___KK for Clinicians KAPT33

___**TIP 34** (SMA) 07-3952
___QG for Clinicians QGCT34
___KK for Clinicians KAPT34

___**TIP 35** (SMA) 08-4212
___QG for Clinicians QGCT35
___KK for Clinicians KAPT35

___**TIP 36** (SMA) 08-3923
___QG for Clinicians QGCT36
___KK for Clinicians KAPT36
___Brochure for Women (English) (SMA) 08-4132
___Brochure for Women (Spanish) PHD981S
___Brochure for Men (English) (SMA) 08-4134
___Brochure for Men (Spanish) PHD1059S

___**TIP 37** (SMA) 08-4137
___QG for Clinicians MS678
___KK for Clinicians KAPT37
___**Consumer Guide** (SMA) 08-4127
___**Consumer Guide for African Americans** (SMA) 07-4248

___**TIP 38** (SMA) 06-4216
___QG for Clinicians QGCT38
___QG for Administrators QGAT38
___KK for Clinicians KAPT38

___**TIP 39** (SMA) 08-4219
___QG for Clinicians QGCT39
___QG for Administrators QGAT39

___**TIP 40** (SMA) 07-3939
___QG for Physicians QGPT40
___KK for Physicians KAPT40

___**TIP 41** (SMA) 05-3991
___QG for Clinicians QGCT41

___**TIP 42** (SMA) 08-3992
___QG for Clinicians (SMA) 07-4034
___QG for Administrators QGAT42
___KK for Clinicians (SMA) 08-4036

___**TIP 43** (SMA) 08-4214
___QG for Clinicians QGCT43
___KK for Physicians (SMA) 07-4108

___**TIP 44** (SMA) 05-4056
___QG for Clinicians QGCT44
___KK for Clinicians (SMA) 07-4150

___**TIP 45** (SMA) 08-4131
___QG for Clinicians (SMA) 06-4225
___QG for Administrators (SMA) 06-4226
___KK for Clinicians (SMA) 06-4224

___**TIP 46** (SMA) 06-4151
___QG for Administrators (SMA) 07-4232

___**TIP 47** (SMA) 06-4182
___QG for Clinicians (SMA) 07-4233
___KK for Clinicians (SMA) 07-4251

___**TIP 48** (SMA) 08-4353

___**TIP 49** (SMA) 09-4380

___**TIP 50** (SMA) 09-4381

___**TIP 52** (SMA) 09-4435

*Under revision
+*QG = Quick Guide; KK = KAP Keys*

Name: _____

Address: _____

City, State, Zip: _____

Phone and e-mail: _____

You can either mail this form or fax it to (240) 221-4292. Publications also can be ordered by calling SAMHSA's NCADI at 1-877-SAMHSA-7 (1-877-726-4727) (English and Español).

TIPs can also be accessed online at http://www.kap.samhsa.gov.

‑‑‑‑‑‑‑‑‑‑‑‑‑‑‑‑‑‑‑‑‑‑‑‑‑‑‑‑‑‑‑‑‑ FOLD ‑‑‑‑‑‑‑‑‑‑‑‑‑‑‑‑‑‑‑‑‑‑‑‑‑‑‑‑‑‑‑‑‑

STAMP

SAMHSA's National Clearinghouse for Alcohol and Drug Information
P.O. Box 2345
Rockville, MD 20847-2345

‑‑‑‑‑‑‑‑‑‑‑‑‑‑‑‑‑‑‑‑‑‑‑‑‑‑‑‑‑‑‑‑‑ FOLD ‑‑‑‑‑‑‑‑‑‑‑‑‑‑‑‑‑‑‑‑‑‑‑‑‑‑‑‑‑‑‑‑‑